Higher Education in a Learning Society

Jerold W. Apps

Higher Education in a Learning Society

Meeting New Demands for Education and Training

Jossey-Bass Publishers

San Francisco • London • 1988

HIGHER EDUCATION IN A LEARNING SOCIETY
Meeting New Demands for Education and Training
by Jerold W. Apps

Copyright © 1988 by: Jossey-Bass Inc., Publishers
350 Sansome Street
San Francisco, California 94104
&
Jossey-Bass Limited
28 Banner Street
London EC1Y 8QE

Library of Congress Cataloging-in-Publication Data

Apps, Jerold W., date.
    Higher education in a learning society.

    (The Jossey-Bass higher education series)
    Bibliography: p.
    Includes index.
    1. Universities and colleges—United States—
Planning. 2. Continuing education—United States.
3. Adult education—United States. I. Title.
II. Series.
LB2341.A68   1988   378'.107   88-42775
ISBN 1-55542-115-6 (alk. paper)

Manufactured in the United States of America

The paper in this book meets the guidelines for
permanence and durability of the Committee on
Production Guidelines for Book Longevity of the
Council on Library Resources.

JACKET DESIGN BY WILLI BAUM

FIRST EDITION

Code 8828

The Jossey-Bass
Higher Education Series

Consulting Editor
Adult and Continuing Education

Alan B. Knox
University of Wisconsin, Madison

Contents

Preface

Facing the future has never been easy for colleges and universities. There are many well-known cases of institutions that have resisted change or missed important opportunities. Thus progressive officials in higher education—whether presidents, deans, department chairs, or faculty committee chairs—face tough decisions about how their institutions will respond to a changing society.

This change is taking many forms. In particular, we are increasingly becoming a learning society. People of all ages are learning, and more than ever before these learners are adults. Some members of society are forced to learn new skills because of lost jobs; many, particularly women, are returning to the job market after years away and require new skills; and a growing number want to learn for the sake of learning. New institutions and services are cropping up to meet this new demand for education, particularly for adults. The proportion of adults in the population is increasing rapidly, and the pool of traditional college age students is declining.

The questions facing higher education decision makers include: Where do colleges and universities fit into a learning society? What unique contributions can colleges and universities make that other agencies and institutions in the education business cannot make? What planning approaches can institutions of higher education follow that will help them implement their contributions to a learning society?

Higher Education in a Learning Society: Meeting New Demands for Education and Training includes a careful analysis of these questions as well as numerous recommendations for answering them. The unique contribution of this book lies in three areas: (1) its theoretical formulation of the problems higher education faces; (2) the practical analysis and planning strategies it offers as a means of helping colleges and universities meet the challenges from a learning society; and (3) the extensive examples it provides of how institutions are successfully dealing with these questions now.

This book is written for higher education officials responsible for planning, including chancellors, provosts and presidents, deans, department chairpersons, and faculty planning committee members, as well as continuing education deans and directors. Individuals at state and national levels who are concerned with higher education and its future will also be interested in this book; these include state higher education executive officers and their staffs who have responsibility for statewide planning and program review. Additionally, those persons who have responsibility for higher education accrediting will find the book useful.

Overview of Contents

Chapter One addresses the demands placed on higher education by older students for both degree and nondegree opportunities as well as the increasing requests from communities, businesses, and government units for assistance. As a result of contacting colleges and universities known for their special responses to changing conditions, I have identified several important themes, such as structural changes, new images of teaching and learning, and creative approaches to financing and development of special programs for specific populations.

In Chapter Two I explore forces influencing a learning society, including population trends, economic conditions, international situations, new technology, illiteracy, and changing assumptions about society.

Where higher education might fit into the learning society

is the topic of Chapter Three. For higher education to make the most positive contributions, it must confront many problem areas: student enrollments, curriculum shifts, competition within higher education as well as between higher education and many other providers of education, approaches to cooperation among educational providers, teaching-learning strategies particularly in light of new educational technology, and financial concerns.

In Chapter Four, I discuss planning approaches for contributing to a learning society. They include attention to curriculum, teaching approaches, administrative and student service needs of older students, and on- versus off-campus and credit versus noncredit courses; meeting public service demands from the community, state, region, and often beyond; and for research institutions, meeting the demand that research findings be related to the practical needs of communities, business and industry, and government. In this chapter I also compare various planning approaches that higher education has followed, and discuss in some depth how strategic planning can be applied to making a long-term response to the learning society. Moreover, I introduce a transformation process that can assist planners in identifying and examining the assumptions that undergird their planning approaches and the decisions that result.

Chapter Five is about aims. How does a college or university set priorities? As case examples, I show how two institutions, one small and one large, have systematically examined their aims.

In Chapter Six I explore the audiences who are knocking on the doors of colleges and universities for service: professionals who need to keep up to date, the elderly, displaced workers, minorities seeking job skills, and women. These groups present higher education with many challenges. Many of these "new" audiences want a career-related curriculum, and they want to see how their educational participation helps in obtaining employment or advancing on a job.

Deciding on instructional approaches is the topic of Chapter Seven. I begin with summary material about adults as learners. Then I examine how educational technology and the information society are affecting teaching approaches. Finally I offer suggestions and examples of how to adjust instructional approaches in light of increasing numbers of older students.

Chapter Eight is about alternative degree formats for older students. These options range from adjusting current degrees to developing entirely new ones with older students in mind. I also present examples of new institutions that have sprung up solely for the purpose of offering degree programs to adult students.

The public service role is the subject of Chapter Nine. I talk about public service broadly, ranging from faculty consulting, technology transfer, and staff and employee development programs, to community problem solving, social criticism, social action, and international service. Public service has often been a problem for colleges and universities, yet if higher education truly wants to become an active force in a learning society, public service activities will play extremely important roles.

Chapter Ten is about student services, particularly in relation to older students. I discuss orientation and counseling services, academic support, and administrative services.

How faculty roles will change is what Chapter Eleven is about. The learning society demands instructors who understand older students, who are aware of adult learning needs, and who are willing to adjust teaching approaches to accommodate older student life situations.

And finally, in Chapter Twelve, I examine the external and internal challenges higher education faces as it moves toward active involvement in a learning society. External challenges include a sometimes negative public attitude toward higher education, resulting among other things in budget decline; competition among disadvantaged social groups for scarce resources; competition with other providers of educational services for adults; widespread doubts about the quality of continuing education programs; and information technology that has revolutionized the way information is stored and communicated. Internal challenges include the need to overcome higher education's reluctance to change; the task of transcending internal organizational structures that often prevent change; the problem of deciding which programs should or should not be offered in response to the requests and demands from a learning society; the task of meeting the needs of older learners; the need to develop strategies for cooperating with other educational providers, with business and industry, and with government agencies; and the difficulty of moving ahead during periods of budget decline.

Acknowledgments

Many people helped with the preparation of this book. I particularly want to thank those higher education administrators and faculty who generously provided me with information about their programs, problems, and approaches. This information provides the "for instances" that appear throughout this book.

Timothy Turner and Betty Hasselkus worked with me as research assistants, and helped me with both library and survey research for this project. Robert Domaingue provided invaluable assistance by searching out writing errors and doublechecking everything. Finally, I wish to thank the following reviewers for their exceedingly helpful comments: Philip C. Chamberlain, chair, Higher Education Program, Indiana University; Richard M. Millard, Bethesda, Md.; James C. Votruba, dean, School of Education and Human Development, State University of New York, Binghamton; and Joan Wadlow, provost, University of Oklahoma.

Madison, Wisconsin   Jerold W. Apps
July 1988

The Author

Jerold W. Apps is professor of adult/continuing education and former chairperson of the Department of Continuing and Vocational Education at the University of Wisconsin–Madison. He received his B.S. degree (1955), his M.S. degree (1957), and his Ph.D. (1967) all from the University of Wisconsin. His doctorate is in adult education.

Apps's research has focused on analyzing continuing education policy and future direction. In 1982 he won the Research to Practice Award presented by the Adult Education Association of the United States for his research and writings in adult/continuing education. In 1987 he received the Outstanding Leadership award presented by the Wisconsin Association for Adult and Continuing Education for his research and writings. Apps's books include *Toward a Working Philosophy of Adult Education* (1973), *Problems in Continuing Education* (1979), *Redefining the Discipline of Adult Education* (1980, with Robert D. Boyd), *The Adult Learner on Campus* (1981), *Improving Your Writing Skills* (1982), *Study Skills for Adults Returning to School* (2nd ed.) (1982), and *Improving Practice in Continuing Education: Modern Approaches for Understanding the Field and Determining Priorities* (1985).

Higher Education
in a Learning Society

1

The Increasing Demand for Learning Opportunities

The last decade has been troublesome for higher education. Many colleges and universities faced budget problems as the economy weathered a recession. Critics snapped at the heels of educational leaders, attacking everything from the curriculum to ethics, from college athletics to spending approaches. Tax-supported higher education, in the eyes of some lawmakers, had become just another big spender shouldering up to the public dollar trough. Emerging from all this was a cry for higher education to look ahead and carefully consider its contributions to society.

As all of this has been happening, we have rapidly become a learning society. This learning society beckons higher education to become a more integral part of it. Indeed, more than ever before, colleges and universities are being asked to become lifelong learning institutions. It is not enough for them to provide educational opportunities for young people immediately out of high school, nor is it enough for higher education to conduct research and produce scholarship. Today, society expects colleges and universities to serve older and part-time students with both credit and noncredit offerings. Society expects colleges and universities to serve business and industry. And communities often turn to colleges and universities for help with local problems, ranging from economic development to training courses for local officials.

Society's pressures on higher education are resulting in debates, institutional examination, and change. These pressures

1

can be translated into questions that colleges and universities need to address:

1. *What adjustments must higher education make to accommodate older students seeking degrees?* What changes are necessary in administrative structures, faculty and staff development approaches, facilities and student services, academic support services, curriculum and teaching approaches, admissions, orientation, and advising procedures? Many authors have written about how higher education must respond to the increasing numbers of older students returning to colleges and universities (Apps, 1981, 1982b; Astin, 1976b; Cross, 1971, 1976; Cross and Valley, 1974; Harrington, 1977; Houle, 1973; Keller, 1983). These authors mostly focus on the adult returning to school for a degree program. They assume adults are returning to college campuses—they are. But adult learners are also increasingly demanding college degree opportunities in off-campus settings; they are asking for courses taught in their communities and in their workplaces. Many are requesting courses offered via computers or videotape so that they can learn in their homes or workplaces, on their own time and at their own pace.

2. *How can higher education best provide noncredit opportunities for adults who do not wish to study for a degree?* (A specific issue is how noncredit programs can be meshed with credit programs.)

3. *How can colleges and universities meet public service requests from the community or region, including being of assistance to government and business and industry in a variety of ways?* An example might be to develop a product innovation center where new-product ideas can be developed and tested and then given to a business or industry to expand and make commercially feasible.

4. *How can institutions with research as a high priority best respond to requests from the community for applied research to solve specific problems?* This could range from supplying a milk producer organization with research on alternative uses of milk products to surveying people in an area on whether a new bridge should replace a ferry across a river.

5. *How can colleges and universities maintain a high level of quality and rigor in all their programs?*

6. *How can higher education institutions gain acceptance by faculty, staff, and administration for a broadened mission?*

These are the questions I will explore in this book. I do not intend to examine research programs, nor do I plan to discuss needed changes in undergraduate programs and curricula for traditional-age students (those attending a college or university immediately after high school). But many of the changes I will discuss do, of necessity, involve all students no matter what their age.

Institutional Transformation

As colleges and universities consider their contributions to a learning society, many face the need for profound change. The higher education institutions cited in this book have gone through such change as they have developed new programs and new directions. Such change, particularly when it involves an examination of basic questions such as who a college or university should serve and how it should serve them, often implies an institutional transformation. (Throughout this book, the term *institution* is used synonymously with *college* and *university*.) Institutional transformation means that a college or university looks at itself in reference to the forces and pressures around it and within it, decides how it wants to change, and then changes. As Lynton and Elman (1987) argue, American universities "must establish new priorities for their functions because the nature and importance of knowledge in modern society are changing quantitatively and qualitatively" (p. 1).

To make such fundamental change requires more than a fine tuning of existing programs. It often means a conscious giving up of previous positions in favor of something new. It may mean that an institution experiencing increased pressure from adult students for curricular changes and mounting interest in off-campus programs may need to examine its commitment to older students. Or the institution may consider making cosmetic changes to accommodate older students, with continued emphasis on recent high school graduates as the prime audience.

Niebuhr (1984) discusses the difficulties that arise when a

transformation or a paradigm shift is attempted: "Paradigm shifts, discontinuities, or watersheds generate much heat before there is light. Whether one is trying to give up smoking, transform an economy, or re-create a community, change is hard. Conflict arises as diehards refuse to seek the new truth and evangelists of the new truth grow impatient with the diehards" (p. 29). A transformation process for higher education is discussed in depth in Chapter Four.

Themes for Change

In preparing this book, I formed an advisory panel of leaders in continuing and higher education. I asked the panel members to give me names of colleges and universities that were, in one way or another, responding to the learning society. I contacted more than fifty colleges and universities for information about their programs. Not only was I interested in the examples, but I was also interested in the process these institutions followed in developing these new approaches. I focused particularly on colleges and universities that had made special efforts to provide opportunities for adults, both on and off campus and in degree as well as noncredit programs. I also looked for colleges and universities that were conducting innovative public service programs. And I was particularly interested in institutions using information technology in innovative ways in making their programs available to students. In addition to collecting detailed information from more than fifty institutions, we interviewed twenty-eight leaders in higher education. Information from interviews with college and university officials and from the supporting materials is found throughout this book. Reflecting on the interviews and the other materials reveals some interesting themes. These themes represent many of the changes taking place in higher education. Nine themes in particular emerged:

- the occurrence of structural changes
- the appearance of alternative educational providers
- a blurring of boundaries between what is academic and what is business

- a blurring of traditional distinctions between teaching, research, and outreach/extension
- the adoption of a variety of change strategies
- the development of new approaches to teaching and learning
- the use of creative financing
- the development of special programs for specific populations
- the growth of a new language

The Occurrence of Structural Changes: Structural changes may take various forms. New institutions are developing to provide educational opportunities for adults (the Electronic University Network in San Francisco and the National Technological University in Fort Collins, Colorado, are examples—more about each of these later). Colleges and universities are also making internal structural changes—some rather dramatic and others less so—in response to demands for change. These institutions include Michigan State University, Alverno College in Milwaukee, and Metropolitan College in New Orleans; I will elaborate on the changes they are making later.

In addition, new connections are forming among existing institutions to provide educational opportunities in innovative ways. With 205 member institutions, the National University Teleconference Network—located at Oklahoma State University—is an example. Some 40 of these institutions are able to broadcast programs to a satellite and then have them distributed around the country and around the world.

Another development is that both formal and informal connections are increasingly being made between higher education and industry, in providing formal course offerings as well as in the traditional areas of research and public service. As an example, the University of Kentucky has made special efforts to provide course work for 3M employees who work on swing shifts at the plant in that area. Instructors make both videotapes and audiotapes of classes available to students who have to be absent because of swing shift changes. Some swing shifters come to class before their shift starts; others attend after their shift ends. All have the opportunity to take videotapes of class sessions home with them.

The Appearance of Alternative Educational Providers: Business, industry, government, and many community organizations have moved into educational activity in a big way. Business and industry have long been associated with providing employee training programs. Estimates of costs for these educational programs range from $40 billion upward (Boyer, 1985, p. ix). Eurich (1985) reports that eighteen firms are offering accredited degree programs, or have applied for accreditation, and more are planning to do so.

A Blurring of Boundaries Between What Is Academic and What Is Business: Academia and business are taking on the characteristics of the other more and more. Higher education is increasingly concerned about budget, about income and expenses, and about profits from certain types of educational offerings. (The word *profit* is not used, however. People in higher education talk about surplus income over expenses or about positive income, or they employ other language that usually means profit.)

As we have just noted, business and industry are heavily involved in pursuits traditionally associated with higher education, including the offering of degrees. Higher education is also increasingly working out joint research projects with business and industry, including the sharing of budgets and researchers. And, as has been true for many large companies, institutions of higher education have established their own foundations to deal with nonappropriated funds and other funds such as gifts.

A Blurring of Traditional Distinctions Between Teaching, Research, and Outreach/Extension: Many colleges and universities make a clear distinction among the teaching, research, and outreach functions. The distinction is especially sharp between degree-credit teaching and noncredit teaching, and between courses taught on and off campus. Increasingly, degree-credit teaching is done away from campus, at work sites, and is often provided via educational technology. And the same instructors are teaching credit and noncredit courses both on and off campus. There seems to be some movement away from having an "extension faculty" who teach both the noncredit and off-campus credit courses and organize the conferences and workshops, but are not involved in on-campus degree-credit teaching.

Thus there are some small steps toward eliminating the two-tier system among college and university instructors with the associated pecking order and stereotypes. Disappearing is the old myth that said that those who cannot meet the rigorous selection procedures for traditional degree-credit teaching take second best and teach in the outreach/extension programs.

At the University of Wisconsin–Madison (organized differently from many institutions) there has been an attempt to integrate the outreach/extension faculty into mainline campus departments. Many departments with integrated faculty have assumed responsibility for both credit and noncredit teaching. In these departments the faculty members who formerly only taught degree-credit courses now teach noncredit courses together with the integrated extension faculty. And, in turn, in many instances, the former extension faculty are involved in teaching on-campus degree-credit courses.

There is also a movement to tie research activity to outreach/extension activity, and thus a blurring of research and outreach has occurred. This blurring is not particularly new for many institutions, since there has long been a close connection between an instructor's research activity and his or her teaching. Increasingly, though, the research activity is now becoming a part of special relationships between universities and corporations in such areas as product development.

These relationships, as one might guess, are fraught with problems and controversy. Public colleges and universities are criticized for assisting some firms and not others. Some taxpayers argue that close relationships with firms will tarnish the reputation of academic institutions. Moreover, some say these new relationships will challenge the objective, nonbiased stance of these institutions and may damage their ability to speak out on environmental problems, consumer protection questions, and other controversial issues—issues sometimes viewed differently by higher education and business and industry.

The Adoption of a Variety of Change Strategies: How did the various changes occur? What was it that influenced a college or university to open a center city campus or start a returning student center? How did a new institution begin?

These questions often have complicated answers, with a

number of forces intertwined, each influencing the change in some unique way and often influencing other forces as well. But some primary change patterns do emerge from the examples we have examined.

For example, a number of the changes occurred because of strong individuals who had a vision. Johns Hopkins University opened a downtown center in Baltimore. This center and its programs were designed to focus on older, part-time students interested in business topics. The downtown center, located in the heart of the business district, is far more accessible to students than the main campus. The idea for this center developed because of a close relationship between the president of Johns Hopkins and the mayor of Baltimore. Both officials concluded that there was need for such a downtown educational center.

The Electronic University Network, a new institution in San Francisco, provides another example. Ron Gordon, former head of this innovative institution, says, "I got the idea basically from a product I developed called the handheld computer. When I tried to teach people how to use this computer, someone suggested I hook them to a modem and teach people wherever they happened to live, via telephone. To make a long story short, that night I woke up with an idea that if we could teach people how to use the handheld computer from anywhere in the country, we could teach anybody anything from anywhere" (personal communication, Feb. 4, 1987). Gordon owned the company that made the handheld computers. With his new idea, he organized a new company and called it the Electronic University Network.

To turn to a third example, Margaret Giesler, a returning adult student, enrolled at the University of Wisconsin for graduate study. For her research she surveyed older returning students to assess the problems they experienced on returning to school. In her master's thesis she reported on the need for counseling before these students ever arrived in a classroom. She shared her study results with Dr. Joy Rice, from the University Counseling Center, and a segment of this center began focusing on older students. Eventually the adult counseling portion broke away and became known as Continuing Education Services (on the University of Wisconsin–Madison campus). But the initial idea essentially came from one person, in this case with research results to back up a need for something new.

In each of these cases, one could argue that the situation was more complicated than it seems; it was not just that one person made a difference. Of course there were situational forces at work. In the Johns Hopkins example, the city of Baltimore was anxious to develop its downtown area, and a downtown center was viewed as helping that effort. Ron Gordon could not have done what he did without the technology that was becoming rapidly available and dropping in price, and without the interest of educational consumers who were searching for alternatives to attending classes on college and university campuses. And Dr. Giesler, now an administrator in the University of Wisconsin–Madison's Division of University Outreach, would not have been successful had there not already been a large number of older returning students on campus who had problems and were looking for assistance.

Many of the changes that occurred were clearly aided by outside financing. Oklahoma State University's Teleconference Network has been assisted by funding from the Kellogg Foundation. The National Technological University has been assisted by grants from the National Science Foundation, the Sloan Foundation, Hewlett-Packard, IBM, and the U.S. Department of Commerce. WHA Radio's (University of Wisconsin–Extension) work with audiotape course development was financed by an Annenberg Foundation grant, and so on. Which came first—the idea, and then a request for money, or the foundation, firm, or other money provider looking for ideas? I suspect some of both. But nonetheless, outside money has had and continues to have a great influence on the development of new ideas in higher education.

Many of the changes also grew out of deliberate planning efforts developed by an institution. Many examples of this could be mentioned. The University of Georgia Cooperative Extension Service carried out an extensive planning effort called *Georgia: 2000*, resulting in new directions for programming. At the College of St. Catherine, a women's Catholic college in St. Paul,

Minnesota, a carefully constructed, long-range planning effort resulted in many suggestions for change so that the college could be more responsive to changing student needs.

A number of colleges and universities—those that were campus-based serving adults only, those campus-based serving adult and traditional students, and those non-campus-based serving adults—made changes as a result of conducting a self-study program developed by the Commission on Higher Education and the Adult Learner (Warren, 1986b). This commission is a joint project of the American Council on Education, the Council for Adult and Experiential Learning, National University Continuing Education Association, and the University of Maryland's University College. Colleges and universities that sign up for this program carry out a comprehensive self-assessment process to determine the institution's current effectiveness in serving adult learners. The self-assessment is designed to provide basic information for institutional planning to enhance instruction and services for adult learners.

The Development of New Approaches to Teaching and Learning: A theme that emerged throughout our study of colleges and universities is a redefinition of teaching and learning for adults. Institutions we studied use a variety of instructional approaches compared to the traditional one of an instructor leaning on a podium lecturing to a hall filled with students frantically scribbling notes.

At Iowa State University, for example, a course in agricultural economics is taught via satellite to students who are often more than sixty miles from the classroom. As H. R. Crawford explains, "Students need only find a place where there is a downlink system, which could be a community college, a Cooperative Extension office, or even their own home if they have a satellite dish" (personal communication, Dec. 15, 1986).

Cardinal Stritch College in Milwaukee holds off-campus courses for its management education programs at hospitals, businesses, vocational schools, and conference rooms in hotels and motels.

Nova University in Florida is an example of those institutions that are now offering computer courses. In fact, Nova offers a doctor of arts degree in training and learning, via computer and telecommunications technology. An electronic library provides students access to national on-line databases. Wherever they are, students communicate with instructors using electronic bulletin boards.

Some institutions are developing their programs with an emphasis on outcomes, competencies that students have developed as a result of participation. Alverno College in Milwaukee is one such institution. The School for New Learning at DePaul University in Chicago is another. The School for New Learning is organized around a competency framework, which includes some fifty statements spread across five domains. These, taken as a whole, constitute the institution's definition of an educated adult in contemporary society. Adults entering the school begin with an assessment of their prior learning that is compared to the competency statements. When this step is completed, the student begins to chart his or her "new learning"—hence the name for the school.

The Use of Creative Financing: As mentioned previously, many programs with new ideas actively seek outside financial support from the federal government, foundations, and business and industry. Some of the more elaborate arrangements are those established by the National Technological University with its consortium of universities and firms and Oklahoma State University's National University Teleconference Network. For example, everyone involved with the National Technological University network pays an access fee, which varies from $200,000 for large corporations like AT&T, General Electric, and IBM to $160,000 for mid-size firms and $50,000 for smaller firms.

User fees continue to provide much of the required income for adult/continuing education courses, both credit and noncredit. This of course raises the continuing question about how those who cannot afford the fees can participate. Loan programs for part-time students are one way of helping solve this problem, but more creativity is necessary if higher education's contribution to the learning society is not to be only for those who can afford to participate. Considerable financial creativity has been taking place, as evidenced by the examples just given.

But most of this creativity has been in organizing new structures, and in offering adult/continuing education progeams with various types of educational technology.

The Development of Special Programs for Specific Populations: Several institutions we studied attempt to reach specific audiences. At Seward County Community College in Kansas, for example, special attempts are made to provide counseling services to part-time students attending off-campus courses. As Theodore Wischropp, the college's president, explains, "We take a counselor along to those outreach locations. We set up a special night once or twice a semester and invite part-time students to come and discuss the progress they're making toward their degree—what the degree requirements are, how they can best meet these requirements, and so on" (personal communication, Jan. 21, 1987).

Programs of the National Technological University are designed especially for practicing engineers in firms at widely separated locations—reached via satellite.

Johns Hopkins University's downtown center is designed for businesspeople working in the downtown area of Baltimore. The courses are offered in the early morning, over the lunch hour, and in the late afternoon, to accommodate businesspeople who are working full time.

The Elders Institute at Florida International University focuses its programs on retired people living in the area. It has been careful to offer programs that are consistent with the overall mission of the university—currently its most popular courses are in foreign policy and world events. It has steered away from leisure-time courses that are available through the community schools and the community college.

The Growth of New Language: Changes in language are often subtle but powerful. The traditional language of higher education, which includes words such as *curriculum, lecture, examination, semester* or *quarter, extracurricular activity, campus, library,* and even *student,* is changing. Some of the words continue to be used with different or expanded meanings. The term *student* is a good example. It is still common to talk about nontraditional and traditional students, with nontraditional applied to those who are older. But changes are occurring. The word *student* is coming to mean all those who attend higher educational offerings. Some are younger and some older, some part-time and some full-time, some are working and some are not. Thus *student* describes a greater variety of people than it used to.

The language pertaining to information storage is also going through a revolutionary change. Although *library* is not being replaced, new words are entering our vocabulary; these include *computer database* and *compact disk*, to mention two relatively new storage technologies.

Even *campus* shows signs of developing new meanings or of being replaced. Students who do all of their degree work at home or at their place of business are enrolled in the college or university, but their "campus" is where they study. We then talk about *main campuses* as a base of operations for an institution. Yet some of the new institutions, like the Electronic University Network and the National Technological University, have a headquarters but do not have a campus. There is still no good word to describe an alternative to campuses, at least not yet. Traditional terms such as *off-campus, outreach,* and *extension programs* are still common. The phrase *learning at a distance* is gaining some prominence these days to describe people who never set foot on a campus yet are actively enrolled in course taking, though.

Competency and *assessment* are also words that college and university faculty and administrators are adding to their vocabularies. Increasingly, administrators and faculty members are assessing their institution's ability to provide adequate opportunities for older learners. And they are also assessing the experiences and prior learning of entering students. For instance, when a student enrolls in the New York Institute of Technology's American Open University, he or she first works with a special adviser to build a background portfolio of previous college credit, corporate training, and life experience. The student's course of study is then planned, using the assessment recorded in the portfolio as a basis for the planning process. Some institutions, such as the School for New Learning at DePaul University and Alverno College, also focus on competencies of students as a measure of outcomes.

Integrated programming is another term often heard these days, to mean some integration of continuing education activity with graduate and undergraduate education. For example, at Michigan State University an attempt has been made to integrate continuing activities into all units of the university. That is, each unit is responsible for continuing education (they call it *lifelong learning)* programs, just as it is responsible for graduate and undergraduate education.

Summary

Colleges and universities are feeling increasing pressure from adult students returning to college classrooms for both degree and noncredit work. In addition, the demands for off-campus offerings are on the rise, particularly those utilizing new educational technology. Adding to these demands is the assumption that colleges and universities ought to be of service to their communities in ways that range from assisting with economic development to providing educational programs to better preparing local elected officials for their jobs. Along with pressure to broaden their mission, many colleges and universities are also faced with the challenge of maintaining quality and rigor and with the need to gain acceptance from faculty, staff, and administrators, all of this within an often precarious budget situation.

To be able to make major contributions to a learning society, many colleges and universities need to undergo an institutional transformation. This transformation involves an examination of basic premises about the clientele, aims, teaching-learning approaches, and curriculum for the institution. To recapitulate, nine trends are emerging as higher education attempts to make the necessary changes: (1) the occurrence of structural changes; (2) the appearance of alternative educational providers; (3) a blurring of boundaries between what is academic and what is business; (4) a blurring of traditional distinctions between teaching, research, and outreach/extension; (5) the adoption of a variety of change strategies; (6) the development of new approaches to teaching and learning; (7) the use of creative financing; (8) the development of special programs for specific populations; and (9) the growth of a new language.

2

How Societal Forces
Affect Learning Needs

Twenty years ago Robert Hutchins (1968), former president of the University of Chicago, had a vision about a learning society. He said a learning society is "one that, in addition to offering part-time adult education to every man and woman at every stage of grown-up life, had succeeded in transforming its values in such a way that learning, fulfillment, becoming human, had become its aims and all its institutions were directed to this end" (pp. 164–165). Hutchins said two forces would propel society toward becoming a learning society—the rapidity of change and an increase in leisure time. Today, we see an occasional reference to a learning society, but with little agreement on its meaning. We have also seen rapid change, but some might question whether or not we have additional leisure time.

Eduard Lindeman ([1926] 1961) did not use the expression *learning society,* as far as I can determine. Yet Lindeman's emphasis on adult education and on the need for a lifetime of learning was evident. He wrote, "A fresh hope is astir. From many quarters comes the call to a new kind of education with its initial assumption affirming that *education is life*—not a mere preparation for an unknown kind of future living. . . . The whole of life is learning, there education can have no ending" (pp. 4–5).

Although these two educators expressed similar opinions, their views also differed in certain respects. In a biography of Lindeman, Stewart (1987) notes that "Robert Hutchins and

16

Eduard Lindeman might agree on outcomes as represented by Hutchins' 'learning society,' but their methods for getting there would be quite different" (p. 160).

In recent years we have all heard much about lifelong learning, lifelong education, lifelong learners, and so on. It is important that the concepts of learning society and lifelong learning do not become tangled. The two ideas are of course related. A learning society requires lifelong learning. But there is more to the metaphor of a learning society than lifelong learning.

Donald Smith (1985), former executive vice president of the University of Wisconsin–System, observes that "in America, the concept of Lifelong Learning is expanding. This growth is an essential educational response to the escalating complexity of our society, the rapid obsolescence of both professional knowledge and some forms of scientific knowledge, and the multiplicity of our individual goals: the searches for health, companionship, and intellectual and cultural stimulation" (p. 7). Smith asserts that the metaphor of a learning society could provide a unifying vision for human beings. He continues that "humankind, we may observe, is most distinctively a learning species, and people are never more human or more themselves than when engaged in learning. . . . Here is pleasure, a sense of growth, and an increased capacity for wisdom potentially available in ways that require no necessary differences of power, wealth, status, or fame among us. This is a healing vision that need not challenge the plurality of other goals" (pp. 10–11). Smith feels that a learning society could unify a society of special interest groups, ethnic groups intent on maintaining their unique cultural characteristics, and people celebrating their individualism and other forms of diversity. He says that "the learning society is a vision responding to the reconciliation of unity within diversity, of free people joined in common cause; a vision of creating a universalizing culture which joins together the variety of old memories; a vision in which equalities of opportunity and differences in results may be freely chosen; a vision of a fulfilling life disentangled from the old passion of power, wealth, status, or fame" (p. 18).

A recent study of U.S. education ("A Nation at Risk: The

Imperative for Educational Reform," 1983) includes these words: "In a world of ever-accelerating competition and change in the conditions of the workplace, of ever-greater danger, and of ever-larger opportunities for those prepared to meet them, educational reform should focus on the goal of creating a learning society. At the heart of such a society is the commitment to a set of values and to a system of education that affords all members the opportunity to stretch their minds to full capacity, from early childhood through adulthood, learning more as the world changes. Such a society has as a basic foundation the idea that education is important not only because of what it contributes to one's career goals but also because of the value it adds to the general quality of one's life" (p. 12).

One can view the need for a learning society narrowly. Much evidence suggests that all of us, to find jobs and remain employed, must embark on a lifetime of learning. To survive we must continue to learn. But the excitement of a learning society goes beyond survival. A learning society can help all of us to examine larger questions about human nature and our place in the world.

To understand the metaphor of learning society, we must also realize the diversity of educational opportunities available. Coombs (1979) provides a useful framework. He says that we can think of *formal, informal,* and *nonformal education.* Formal education refers to education provided by institutions ranging from preschools through colleges and universities. It generally results in credits, diplomas, and degrees. Informal education is that truly lifelong process that recognizes that we all learn from our daily experiences at work, with our families, from the persons and situations we come in contact with each day, from watching television and reading newspapers, from carrying out the garbage and walking through the woods. This form of education is neither organized nor planned, yet it contributes greatly to our lifelong learning. Nonformal education includes any organized educational activity outside the established formal system. Nonformal education is usually short-term and specific, although such opportunities tend to be organized with specific learning results identified. Examples include conferences, workshops, and short courses (pp. 210–233).

In summary, one can view the learning society as (1) a practical idea for human beings living in a rapidly changing world where a lifetime of learning is a requirement for survival; (2) an attitude that learning need not only occur for practical reasons but can happen for its own sake; (3) a unifying attitude, and an approach for bringing together an ever more diverse society; and (4) a metaphor for a new age of defining the relation of education to learning, and a recognition that educational opportunities and thus learning potential go well beyond what is provided by those institutions we ordinarily associate with education.

Influences on a Learning Society

In this book I focus on higher education's contributions to a learning society. To discuss such contributions, we must be aware of the societal forces that have an impact on the learning process. These forces influence what is learned, when certain things should be learned, who should learn what, what or who should provide opportunities for learning, and even the methods by which something should be taught.

Population Trends The U.S. population is rapidly becoming older. In 1970, when the population of this country was 203.7 million people, 14 percent or 28.7 million were 60 and older. By 1980 that percentage had increased to 16 percent, and by 1990 demographers predict those 60 and older will make up nearly 17 percent of the population. In 1983, for the first time in the history of the country, more people were older than 65 than were teenagers (Hodgkinson, 1986a, p. 5).

We often talk about "baby boomers," those 70 million people born between 1946 and 1964. The oldest members of that group are now in their forties. After 1964 we began to see a dramatic drop in birthrates. For example, in 1960 there were 23.7 births per 1,000 population. In 1975 the birthrate had dropped to 14.6 births per 1,000. By 1981 we began to see a slight increase in birthrates, 15.8 per 1,000 population.

This rather dramatic shift in birthrates has meant a decrease in eighteen- to twenty-six-year-olds for the next decade or so. Looking at birthrates more closely, we see diversity among societal groups. The birthrates among blacks and Hispanics remain at higher levels than for whites, and we will thus see increasingly larger numbers of minorities in our society.

We are currently experiencing a "baby boomlet," though, because of the huge number of fertile white women in the child-bearing years. For a few years at least this will result in larger actual numbers of white births. As Hodgkinson (1986a) points out, "If [the baby boom mothers] were having 2.7 children as their mothers did, we would be in the middle of another white Baby Boom. In the next decade, large numbers of white women will be moving out of the child rearing years producing a sharp decline after the current 'Baby Boomlet' ends. The current Baby Boom age stretches from 22 to 40; by 1995 they will span 31 to 49, meaning that the 'boomlet' for whites will last not more than five more years" (p. 9).

In examining population trends, one must also consider immigration patterns. For example, in 1981 Asia and Latin America contributed 81 percent of the 600,000 legal immigrants who came to this country. The largest number of these immigrants came from Vietnam, Korea, and the Philippines. Hodgkinson (1986a) predicts that by about 2010, one in three in the U.S. population will be black, Hispanic, or Asian American (p. 9). As noted later, these demographic changes will have a dramatic effect on most of society's institutions, none more so than educational institutions, particularly in higher education.

Economic Conditions   In the past twenty-five years the United States has seen a dramatic shift in the nature of the economy, from an emphasis on producing goods to providing services. For instance, in 1970 21.8 percent of the labor force was classed as operators, fabricators, and laborers. By 1980 this had decreased to 19.2 percent. In 1970, 3.8 percent of the labor force were farmers; in 1980 the percentage of farmers had decreased to 2.9 percent. Meanwhile, white collar jobs (managerial and professional) had increased from 18.5 percent of the labor force in 1970 to 21.8 percent in 1980. (U.S. Bureau of the Census, 1985). The trend has continued from 1980 to the present.

With these shifts, large numbers of workers have lost jobs as the economy struggles with one of the most dramatic structural changes in the history of the country. One example is agriculture. During the past decade, thousands of farmers have sold their farms or lost them to mortgage foreclosures and have left the land, victims of changing conditions. Many of these displaced farmers are in their prime working years but are ill-suited for many jobs. Yet they must work in order to maintain some semblance of the living standard that they have become accustomed to. We can also look at steel workers, auto workers, heavy equipment laborers, foundry workers, oil drillers, and a host of other workers in our society to see similar evidence of lost jobs and disrupted lives.

These structural changes influence a learning society in ways not yet realized. The most visible is the critical need for displaced workers to gain additional knowledge and skills to find new employment. Who should provide these educational opportunities, and who should pay for them? How much responsibility does a society have for retraining the workers who have been displaced? How is it decided which educational institutions and other providers should be involved in making these educational opportunities available? These are some of the educational policy questions that emerge from the most cursory examination of the structural changes occurring in our society.

International Forces The United States belongs to a global community in hundreds of ways. We were abruptly reminded of this in 1973, when OPEC decided to increase prices of crude oil severalfold, resulting in an inflation shock in our country, to say nothing of the inconvenience of gasoline shortages.

We need only visit an appliance store and note the "made in Japan" labels on VCRs, radios, and television sets to see an everyday reminder of our dependence on that country for much of our electronic equipment, automobiles, motorcycles, cameras, and telescopes. An inspection of the United States' current trade deficit helps us realize how much we import from other countries. For example, the U.S. trade deficit in 1980 was $25.5 bil-

lion, in 1982 $36.4 billion, in 1984 $112.5 billion, and in 1986
$146.4 billion (*Economic Report of the President,* 1987, p. 361).

As analyst George Keller (1986) points out, "every year
since 1979 we have traded more with Asia and less proportion-
ately with Europe" (p. 13). So not only have we increased the
amount of trading we do with other countries, but our trading
partners have changed as well. And the United States has become increasingly concerned about competitiveness in a world
market. In agriculture, for example, several countries sell wheat,
corn, and soybeans on the world market. And we are all quite
aware of foreign competition in the auto industry. Because of
this country's involvement in world markets, we are influenced
by what happens in other countries.

The global community's influence on a learning society is
profound. We are beginning to see Asian languages taught in our
public schools. We see short courses for American businesspeople
who must learn something of the cultural characteristics of their
Japanese counterparts. Increasing numbers of citizens want to
learn about people and events beyond the borders of their cities
and states. And more subtly perhaps, we may see the beginnings
of changes in fundamental assumptions Americans hold about
other peoples and cultures.

Technology   Technology increasingly influences society.
Robotics and computer-controlled machines have become com-
monplace in factories across the country. Microelectronics has
given us radios and calculators the size of credit cards, and allows
surgeons to see within our bodies with tiny exploratory cameras.

Biotechnology and recombinant DNA technology lead to
improved crop varieties and even new crop types. It is technically possible to develop a wheat variety with the ability to fix
nitrogen as legumes do. A special genetically engineered bac-
terium can be sprayed on potato plants and lower the tempera-
ture at which the plants will freeze.

High-performance computing provides for artificial intelligence, allowing machines to distinguish between fragrances
and read, hear, and even speak using natural language. In many
other ways, too, technology has had a dramatic effect on information and communications.

Naisbitt (1982) argues that we are moving from an industrial society to an information society. Technology is revolutionizing how we store, transmit, and manipulate information. The compact disk, using laser technology, allows us to store thousands of pages of information on one disk. One 4¾" compact disk–read-only memory (CD-ROM) holds up to 250,000 printed pages, or 250 large books. All the pages in the bible take up only a fraction of the space of one disk. A laser beam encodes the information on each disk, and the same technique retrieves the information. Nothing ever touches the disk directly, eliminating the possibility of wear. The optical digital disk stores up to a million pages of information, including illustrative material, on one disk. Also, satellites can transmit vast amounts of information anywhere in the world. Never before have people had access to information so readily. And never has there been so much information. In fact, it is sometimes said that the amount of information in the world doubles every seven years.

These developments are extremely relevant for our purposes, because technology influences the learning society in many ways. On a practical level, it often creates job layoffs and requires job retraining. Think of the newspaper business. We no longer find linotype operators setting type for the daily editions. Computers perform this function. Not only are far fewer workers needed, but their skills are different as well.

Information technology (laser disks, computers, fiber optics, satellites) provides an especially good example of how technology profoundly influences the learning society. Think only of the amount of up-to-date information that most of us have readily available. Also think about low-income people without the financial resources to obtain information from computer databases on their home computers or from other modern information sources. Will we see an even greater gap between the haves and have-nots because of who can afford to purchase information? We can raise many moral and ethical questions. How do we decide the accuracy of the information available? Who decides what information should be available to the public? Who decides what should be included in a computer database, for example? And how are this person's decisions monitored, and by whom? These become important questions when we discuss national policy, and particularly when questions of national security are involved. More general philosophical questions emerge, too. What is the meaning of humanness in a highly technological world where many day-to-day activities are performed by machines? What is the place for the arts and the humanities in the lives of people who are often driven by economic and technological concerns?

What is the role of educational institutions in storing and dispersing information versus the role of, say, libraries and national computer databases? How are such questions as copyright issues resolved when one can so easily reproduce information?

What does "curriculum" mean when new information is available at ever-increasing rates, and old information becomes obsolete nearly as quickly? Roszak (1986) admonishes us to keep clear the difference between ideas and information and the relationship between the two. According to him, "Information, even when it moves at the speed of light, is no more than it has ever been: discrete little bundles of facts, sometimes useful, sometimes trivial, and never the substance of thought . . . . Ideas are integrating patterns which satisfy the mind when it asks the question, What does this mean? What is this all about?" (pp. 87, 90).

We must not be tempted to believe that the more information we have, the higher the quality of our thinking and problem solving will be. We must not be deceived into thinking that the more information we have, the more ideas will emerge. In fact the opposite may happen. Again, as Roszak (1986) underlines, "The mind thinks with ideas, not with information. Information may helpfully illustrate or decorate an idea; it may, where it works under the guidance of a contrasting idea, help to call other ideas into question. But information does not create ideas; by itself, it does not validate or invalidate them. An idea can only be generated, revised, or unseated by another idea" (p. 88). Computers and other information technology allow us access to great amounts of information through computer databases and other storage devices. But we must constantly remind ourselves that information by itself does not replace critical and creative thinking. Information is an often necessary adjunct to an active, exploring mind. But information, no matter how sophisticated, cannot replace ideas the human mind generates, ideas that often go well beyond the related information.

In a recent book (Apps, 1985), I discuss the difference between information and knowledge. I point out that information transmitted and accumulated by human beings remains information—discrete bits of data—until the individual human mind wrestles with this information, tries to make sense out of it, and tries to see particular and specific personal applications (pp. 164–170). Information is of course extremely useful to the enhancement of ideas, as Roszak points out, and to the creation of knowledge, as I have argued, but it must be kept in perspective. As we move into Naisbitt's "information society," we must be prepared to address the question of how this store of readily available information will influence the learning society. I will explore these and other issues later, when I examine how societal trends influence higher education.

Illiteracy This country has not yet solved its illiteracy problem. With increasing amounts of information available, and with extensive, compulsory schooling, we would think illiteracy would have disappeared. But, as Kozol (1985) notes, up to twenty-five million adults in this country cannot read the label on a bottle of poison, and another thirty-five million cannot read well enough to function in society (p. 4). Stedman and Kaestle (1987) summarize literacy and reading achievement trends over the past century. They concluded that from 20 to 30 percent of the population has difficulty coping with common reading tasks and materials. They do not believe that illiteracy is rapidly increasing in this country, but they argue that the demand for more literacy is on the increase. "The solution to rising literacy demands is now more difficult. . . . Even if the workplace is not truly demanding more reading ability, we shall nonetheless need much better reading skills across the entire population if we are to survive and improve as a democratic society in an increasingly complex age. Seen in this light, there is much to galvanize renewed efforts at literacy training, at all levels" (p. 42). Not only is the inability to read, write, and do numerical manipulation a problem, but there is also political illiteracy. We have only to examine the poor voting records and the lack of involvement by people in discussing issues that affect them. There is also economic illiteracy—people failing to understand how economic phenomena (their jobs, for example) are affected by international markets.

In short, a learning society presupposes literacy. Members of a learning society must be able to read and write and understand the workings of the country. Literacy is a cornerstone of a learning society, yet millions of people do not possess basic literacy skills and thus cannot be true partners in learning. Inadequate critical thinking skills are a further problem. This problem is difficult to measure, but it can be approached with several questions. To what extent can people distinguish truth from lies? Are sufficient numbers of people able to analyze arguments carefully and examine various points of view on an issue and reach their own conclusions? Many people in our society lack these skills.

Given the seriousness of the problem, a learning society must devote resources to remedial literacy programs. But a learning society must also focus on the root problems of illiteracy: poverty, less-than-supportive family life for children, excessive television watching, and formal schooling that has allowed individuals with low levels of literacy to pass through the system without remedial work.

Changing Assumptions   At another level, change in fundamental assumptions undergirding society influences all of society. Physicist Fritjof Capra (1983) says that our society is experiencing a paradigm shift, "a profound change in the thoughts, perceptions, and values that form a particular vision of reality" (p. 30). A paradigm is a worldview, a way of understanding and explaining reality. In other words, a paradigm is a collection of assumptions. These include assumptions about the nature of human beings and their motivations, about competition and cooperation, about the place for individual achievement and its value, about whether or not progress is a set of linear building blocks, and about the power of and place for technology.

Capra (1983) suggests that our present societal paradigm

includes these assumptions: "the belief in the scientific method as the only valid approach to knowledge; the view of the universe as a mechanical system composed of elementary material building blocks; the view of life in society as a competitive struggle for existence; and the belief in unlimited material progress to be achieved through economic and technological growth" (p. 31).

Futurist Alvin Toffler (1980) also contends that our society is beginning to experience a major paradigm shift. He comments on our changing view of progress: "Today there is a fast-spreading recognition around the world that progress can no longer be measured in terms of technology or material standard of living alone—that a society that is morally, aesthetically, politically, or environmentally degraded is not an advanced society, no matter how rich or technically sophisticated it may be. In short, we are moving toward a far more comprehensive notion of progress—progress no longer automatically achieved and no longer defined by material criteria alone" (p. 280).

The learning society is thus bombarded by a series of societal forces that affect its nature and direction. These forces affect all aspects of education. They affect elementary and secondary schools as well as institutions of higher education. These societal forces also influence nonformal education conducted by business and industry and a host of other organizations. And they often subtly influence the informal education that is a part of our daily living. None of us can escape these forces. And, likewise, the learning society, as we have defined it, cannot escape. An interesting question—one posed earlier—is whether the learning society itself can become a societal force that will influence the other forces, or whether it will (as it most often has in the past) continue to be acted on rather than become a more forceful actor itself.

Summary

As Hutchins (1968) and others have suggested, this country is becoming a learning society. Lifelong learning is a cornerstone for a learning society, which of course includes educational opportunities for adults. As I have described it, a learning society is (1) a practical idea, since all of us must learn to survive in a rapidly changing society; (2) an attitude that learning may be pursued for its own sake; (3) a unifying mechanism for bringing a diverse society together; and (4) a metaphor for a new age of defining the relation of education to learning, one in which we recognize that learning potential goes well beyond those opportunities provided by educational institutions.

Many societal forces influence the learning society: population trends (the population is getting older), economic conditions (we are moving from an industrial to a service-centered, information society), international forces (we are all part of a global community), technology (this includes everything from computers to gene splicing), illiteracy (requirements for literacy are increasing), and changing assumptions (the society is examining its most fundamental beliefs).

These forces will certainly influence a learning society. But how many of the forces themselves can, should, or will be influenced by a dynamic learning society?

3

How Higher Education
Can Contribute in a
Learning Society

Where does higher education fit into a learning society? What contributions can colleges and universities make that other agencies and institutions cannot make? And perhaps more important, what contributions *should* higher education make?

Colleges and universities, not unlike other social institutions, have histories and traditions that influence what they do and how they do it. These influences include social and economic pressures. As we move toward the twenty-first century, we see educational institutions increasingly pressured to cooperate with government and the private sector to enhance economic opportunities in their communities, states, and regions. We see adults insisting that higher education provide them with more direct educational opportunities, including degree-credit programs, noncredit offerings, and the like. Adults are also seeking for programs that meet their particular needs and interests, and they are requesting that institutions offer courses in alternative ways.

A Historical Perspective

The question of how colleges and universities fit into society goes back to the early history of educational institutions in this country. As Jencks and Riesman (1977) point out, "During the seventeenth, eighteenth, and early nineteenth centuries, American colleges were conceived and operated as pillars of the locally

29

established church, political order, and social conventions. These local arrangements were relatively stable, widely accepted as legitimate, and comparatively well integrated with one another" (p. 1). These early colleges were more like today's high schools. They did not employ a faculty of scholars. They placed little emphasis on specialized subjects, and the instruction was usually at quite an elementary level. "With the wisdom of hindsight it is tempting to conclude that these colleges influenced neither the intellectual nor the social history of their era" (Jencks and Riesman, 1977, p. 1).

All of this began to change in the early 1800s. By this time the break with England had been completed. The U.S. Constitution was accepted and in place. People began moving across the Appalachian Mountains, settling new lands along the way. This was a time for entrepreneurs. If people did not like something, they did not try to change it; they established something different, something new. Those intellectuals who did not like Harvard and Yale established competitive colleges, often around special interests. "By 1900 there were special colleges for Baptists and Catholics, for men and women, for whites and blacks, for rich and not-so-rich, for North and South, for small town and big city, for adolescents and adults, for engineers and teachers" (Jencks and Riesman, 1977, pp. 2–3). The idea of a university continued cloudy and confused until well into the nineteenth century, however. Although Yale awarded the first Ph.D. in 1861, the development of the modern university, with its emphasis on teaching, research, and public service, remained many years away.

By the mid 1800s, many colleges in this country experienced hard times. Enrollments were static or declining, the prestige of graduates was dropping, and there was great confusion about the place of these institutions in society (Veysey, 1965, pp. 3–11). The criticisms that Andrew Carnegie expressed in 1889 were widespread even in earlier decades; Carnegie complained that college students were " 'trying to master languages which are dead, [and accumulating] such knowledge as seems adapted for life upon another planet than this as far as business affairs are concerned. . . . College education as it exists is fatal to success in that domain [the business world] ' " (Veysey, 1965, pp. 13-14). A noted banker is claimed to have pronounced that he would hire no college graduates for any job in his bank. Many business leaders believed a college education useless for providing the practical everyday knowledge needed in the business world. It was clear, in short, that reform was overdue.

During the period from 1865 to 1890, a more careful conception of what "university" meant began to emerge. It was during these years that a vision of a university as a place for "practical public service," "abstract research," and "teaching standards of cultivated taste" began to emerge (Veysey, 1965, p. 12). The concept of research had its roots in Germany. The idea of teaching culture came basically from Britain, but with other European influences as well. Of the three functions, practical public service as a goal was the most American in its roots, but one could also attribute some of it to European influence (Veysey, 1965, pp 12-13).

Congress passed the Morrill Act in 1862, providing land grants to states. The sale of these lands could be used for establishing state universities. These new land-grant universities were obligated to provide agricultural and engineering instruction. And radical as the idea was, the land-grant colleges and universities opened their doors to the sons and daughters of farmers and mechanics. Many leaders in higher education saw these new institutions as potentially little more than trade schools, but excellent leadership soon made them much more than that. These institutions were also challenged to meet the demands of society, however. By the late 1800s, farmers began expressing their unhappiness with what seemed to them impractical, esoteric work at their tax-supported colleges and universities. They wanted more. They wanted practical answers to everyday problems—how to increase crop yields, how to raise more productive dairy cattle, and how to improve living conditions in remote rural areas, for example. In 1878 Congress passed the Hatch Act, making available to land-grant institutions federal dollars for practical agricultural research. With the passage of this act, land-grant institutions established agricultural experiment stations for research and testing of new ideas.

By the late 1800s, agricultural professors, traveling by train, horseback, and buggy, delivered public lectures to farmers in the far reaches of every state. University leaders began seeing the political advantage of moving the university off campus. Charles Kendall Adams, an ex-farmer, became president of the University of Wisconsin in 1892. In one of his speeches he said, "The university is not a party separate from the State. It is a part of the State—as much a part . . . as the Capitol itself" (Veysey, 1965, p. 104).

In 1909, Lincoln Steffens wrote a widely read article titled "Sending a State to College." Steffens pointed out in this article that the university at Madison would "teach anybody—anything —anywhere." Steffens cited examples of model dairy farms, machine shops, and housekeepers' conferences. He pictured the university "as a kind of living reference library for the state as a whole" (Veysey, 1965, p. 107).

When Charles Van Hise, a personal choice of Governor LaFollette, became president of the University of Wisconsin in 1903, a strong commitment to taking academic knowledge and consultation to the citizens of the state began emerging. It was during this time that the slogan, "The Wisconsin Idea—The boundaries of the campus are the boundaries of the state" first appeared.

In 1914, when Congress passed the Smith–Lever Act, land-grant institutions had available federal dollars for establishing an agricultural extension service, a visionary idea in its time. The Smith–Lever Act established a cooperative partnership among counties, the states, and the federal government to provide agricultural, family living, and informal youth education (4-H) to the people of the nation. Thus within the land-grant organization we see the three primary functions of the university supported by federal legislation and enhanced by state as well as county tax contributions (as far as agricultural extension is concerned). The Morrill Act (1862) established the land-grant university, the Hatch Act (1878) set up the research leg, and the Smith–Lever act (1914) established a formal extension function.

By the early 1900s, therefore, colleges and universities in

this country began moving in a new direction. Declining enrollments in the mid 1800s plus diminished prestige meant that some changes were necessary. Visionary lawmakers saw a role for universities in advancing agriculture and engineering when many of the Western sections of the country were not yet settled and a majority of the population lived on farms. A few philanthropists, Ezra Cornell and Johns Hopkins for example, donated money to establish universities. Others followed in the late 1800s and early 1900s.

To focus on more recent history, the period from 1955 to 1974 must surely be dubbed the golden years of higher education, at least in terms of rapid growth. The years of the 1960s, however, are viewed by many as the tarnished years when students revolted, when national guard units were called out to restore peace, and when large numbers of people lost confidence in their colleges and universities. The number of students vaulted from 2.5 million in 1955 to 8.8 million in 1974. Not only did the total numbers increase dramatically, but the percentage of eighteen- to twenty-four-year-olds enrolled in college or university degree programs rose from 17.8 percent in 1955 to 33.5 percent in 1974. Black student enrollment increased eightfold, from 95,000 in 1955 to 814,000 in 1974, and the proportion of women students rose from one-third to one-half (Keller, 1983, pp. 8–9).

In response to these rapidly increasing student numbers, higher education went on a building binge. Keller (1983) points out that institutions of higher education constructed more buildings from 1955 to 1974 than during the previous 200 years (p. 9). And there were organizational changes as well. In Wisconsin, several state teachers colleges became universities with the stroke of a pen. And a few years later they were folded into what became known as the University of Wisconsin System. Structural changes occurred in other states as well; California, New York, and Michigan are examples.

The years following 1955 also saw a great increase in the number of community colleges. In 1955 there were about 400 small community colleges enrolling about 325,000 students. Twenty years later there were 973 two-year community colleges, with an enrollment of 3.4 million students (Keller, 1983, p. 9). By 1988, community colleges numbered 1,224.

The Vietnam crisis greatly influenced higher education. Student demonstrations, often resulting in injury and property damage, affected higher education in ways not yet totally assessed. For many institutions, particularly the state, tax-supported universities, much negative fallout resulted. To use the University of Wisconsin–Madison as an example, one can still travel in the upstate regions and hear people criticize the Madison campus for not controlling its students back in the late 1960s and early 1970s. To this day, some parents will not send their children to Madison because they fear they will be corrupted by the liberal influences and may become involved in marches and protests. Of course such attitudes, lingering long after the reality, continue to affect trust in higher education as well as budget support.

All in all, as Keller (1983) indicates, "The situation in which American higher education finds itself is both less dramatic and more serious than is widely believed. What makes it less dramatic is that the colleges and universities have always been pressed to scramble to find adequate funding. . . . American colleges and universities occupy a special, hazardous zone in society, between the competitive profit-making business sector and the government owned and run state agencies. They are dependent yet free; market-oriented yet outside cultural and intellectual fashions. The faculty are inventors, entrepreneurs, and retailers of knowledge, aesthetics, and sensibility yet professionals like the clergy or physicians. The institutions pay no taxes but are crucial to economic development. . . . They constitute one of the largest industries in the nation but are among the least businesslike and well-managed of all organizations" (p. 5).

Challenges to Higher Education

As we examine colleges and universities today, we can conclude that higher education is going through a dramatic transition. In fact historians may record this transitional period as one as dramatic as the changes occurring in the late 1800s, or those that occurred from the mid 1950s to the mid 1970s. But of course the situation and its influences are quite different in the late 1980s. Today, the influences on higher education include

- changes in student enrollments
- curriculum shifts
- competition among colleges and universities and with other providers
- potential for cooperation
- new ideas about teaching and learning, including the influence of technology
- financial considerations

Changes in Student Enrollments: The pool of eighteen- to twenty-four-year-olds is declining. And this decline is reflected in the overall enrollment projections in higher education. In 1985 12.2 million students were enrolled in institutions of higher education (this includes both two- and four-year and public and private institutions). This compares to 12.5 million students in 1983 (U.S. Department of Education, 1986, p. 182).

By 1992, approximately 11.8 million students will enroll in higher education, marking a decline of 0.4 million (U.S. Bureau of the Census, 1985, p. 150). Demographers predict that 49 percent of the students enrolled in institutions of higher education in 1992 will be 25 years old or older. Fifty-five percent of these older students will be women. More than 19 percent of all students in higher education will be 35 or older. And of those students 25 or older, 75 percent will study part time. Eighty-five percent of those 35 or older will study part time (U.S. Bureau of the Census, 1985, p. 150).

Not only are the proportion of older to younger students shifting and part-time student numbers increasing, but some observers believe that a value shift is also occurring, particularly for the traditional-age students (those eighteen to twenty-two): "Today's college student has quite a different view of the world from that of his or her older sibling. . . . Compared to those who were in college as recently as a decade ago, today's young people are decidedly less altruistic, more concerned about self, and more anxious about the future. There is increased interest in landing a high-paying job, gaining public recognition as an authority in one's chosen field, and being able to supervise other people. There is less interest in environmental issues, racial understanding, and public affairs in general" (Green, Levine, and Associates, 1985, p. 10).

The changes in student enrollments, particularly the growth in older student numbers, will have far-reaching effects on higher education. One effect will be an influence on higher education's curriculum.

Curriculum Shifts: With a move toward nearly equal balance between older and younger students and a growing interest in personal achievement, certain curricular developments are predictable. Derek Bok (1986), president of Harvard University, sees five trends that will have an impact on undergraduate programs: (1) an increase in remedial work, (2) a shift from liberal arts toward more vocationally oriented studies, (3) a relaxation of academic standards, (4) the addition of vocational majors, and (5) a reduction of course requirements in the liberal arts (p. 39). Bok (1986) asks the fundamental question: What is the purpose of higher education—to gain a body of knowledge or to obtain a critical education?

Increasing numbers of older students will inevitably influence the curriculum, then. For instance, in a national survey, adults were asked what adult education courses they enrolled in and where they participated in them. Almost two-thirds of the courses were taken for job-related reasons (21 percent of the courses were taken for credit). Business and engineering schools are experiencing overcapacity enrollments, and computer science has become extremely popular. Thirty-four percent of the adult education courses were taken at two- or four-year colleges and universities (U.S. Department of Education, 1986, p. 1).

There are two issues raised here. The majority of adults who participate in education do so for job-related reasons. And 66 percent go to educational providers other than institutions of higher education. Higher education therefore faces an interesting dilemma. To encourage larger enrollments of adults, given the competition of other providers, it must take a job-related curriculum seriously. Yet many leaders in higher education and elsewhere in society believe in the strength of a liberal education, one that teaches critical thought and communication skills, emphasizes values, and stresses cultural understanding. How will colleges and universities respond to this dilemma? What will the curriculum of the future look like? More specifically, how will adult students influence the curriculum, when they can vote with their feet and bypass higher education for other providers?

Competition Among Colleges and Universities and with Other Providers: Colleges and universities vigorously compete with each other for students in the traditional age pool (recent high school graduates). This is particularly true of the smaller, private colleges, which have had higher tuition costs than the state-supported universities. With decreases in federally supported student aids, many students who might have chosen a private college enroll in a state university or community college near home so they can control costs. State-supported colleges and universities also compete with each other, particularly in certain fields. For example, colleges of agriculture have experienced enrollment declines in the mid 1980s. These colleges compete vigorously with other schools and colleges, often at the same university, to maintain student enrollments and budget levels (many school and college budgets are tied to student credit hours).

Many problems result from this often intense competition. Bok (1986) observes that competition may lead to accepting fads and a jumble of programs, "patched together to pander to every taste" (p. 25). He suggests that some institutions may resort to questionable approaches to maintaining numbers, including overly aggressive marketing, a decline in quality educational offerings, the possibility of third-rate doctoral programs for some institutions, a disproportionate amount of energy devoted to writing grant proposals, and a rush to serve the public. "Faculty members can be excessively distracted by consulting or community service activities, leaving them less and less time to teach their classes, do their research, or simply indulge in sustained, uninterrupted reflection" (p. 28). I would add to Bok's list the fact that some institutions, in a rush to appear innovative, scatter electronic teaching gadgets from computers to videos helter-skelter throughout the institution. The gadgets are used for their public relations impact rather than for their educational benefits. Let me quickly add that many colleges and universities could benefit from the application of teaching-learning technology. But when such applications are made to "wow" students and their parents rather than provide learning opportunities, they become gimmicks.

Not only is there competition among colleges and universities for students, but there is also competition for faculty and for contributions from business and industry. Research institutions in particular compete intensively for both government and private research funds.

In addition, whether they are aware of it or not, colleges and universities compete with other educational providers, particularly when we consider adult students. In 1984, over twenty-three million adults participated in some form of organized adult education activity (U.S. Department of Education, 1986, p. 1). About 14 percent of the adult population in the United States was enrolled in at least one adult education course in 1984. (These figures greatly underreport adult involvement in adult education.) Higher education does not have a monopoly as a provider of educational opportunities (if it ever did). Libraries, museums, labor unions, professional organizations, community organizations, proprietary schools, the military, and business and industry provide a wealth of educational opportunities. In fact, two- and four-year colleges and universities provided only 34 percent of these educational opportunities in 1984. Of the remaining 66 percent, the distribution was as follows: business and industry (17 percent); private community organizations such as the League of Women Voters, churches, and environmental groups (9 percent); labor organizations and professional associations (6 percent); government agencies (8 percent); vocational trade, business, and other schools (13 percent); elementary and secondary schools (6 percent); and private instruction (8 percent) (U.S. Department of Education, 1986, p. 5).

Estimates of what business and industry spend on education range from $40 to $100 billion annually (Eurich, 1985, p. 6). "Even when the salaries and wages paid during training are omitted for purposes of comparison with higher education costs, it appears that private corporations may be approaching the total amount spent annually by our nation's universities and other four-year colleges, both public and private. That figure for 1981–1982 . . . was just over $60 billion" (Eurich, 1985, p. 6). And besides offering in-service training and personal development opportunities for their employees, eighteen firms offered degree programs in 1985 (Eurich, 1985, p. 87). All are either accredited or have applied for accreditation. These degree programs range from a doctor of philosophy in policy analysis offered by the Rand Graduate Institute in Santa Monica, California, to a master of science degree in administration and in management offered by the Arthur D. Little Management Education Institute of Cambridge, Massachusetts.

Eurich (1985) says that within five years, five more industrial corporations are planning nine more degree-granting programs in high-technology fields and business administration (p. 85). "With this rate of growth, it may not be too fanciful to foresee 100—if not hundreds—of corporate degree programs in the next 50 years" (Eurich, 1985, p. 85).

Business and industry's interest in providing educational opportunities has resulted in reactions from some colleges and universities. Some have become extremely consumer oriented, trying to juggle courses and programs to meet the demands of the potential adult audience. But as Boyer (1983) points out, "There is a crucial difference between thoughtfully responding to student needs, and randomly starting programs unrelated to an institution's own objectives" (p. 32).

Boyer (1983) challenges higher education to discover (or rediscover) the unique contributions it can make to an adult population. "Companies cannot and will not go to the heart of education. Industry education, with all its variety, is not likely to achieve the understanding that can result when students and teachers can come together to test ideas, reflect upon deeper meanings, and weigh alternative conclusions. Through such encounters, information is placed in a larger context and the relationship of knowledge to life's dilemmas can be thoughtfully explored. These remain the essential goals of higher education" (p. 32). To face the competition from other educational providers, therefore, colleges and universities must decide what unique contributions they can make to the adult learner.

Potential for Cooperation: One rather obvious strategy for colleges and universities is to work out cooperative relationships with other providers. Several types of cooperation exist. Keller (1983) discusses three examples: (1) cooperative education agreements with firms to help pay students' escalating college costs; (2) an increase in instruction away from campus, often on-site at a business location; and (3) contracts with corporations to provide research dollars and electronic equipment to the university (p. 21). Keller's comments focus on cooperative endeavors for providing more up-to-date research and instruction in the area of engineering and technology.

Cooperation takes many forms. The Electronic University Network is an approach for linking colleges and universities to students, who are often employed by businesses or industrial firms. Drawing heavily on computer technology (the courses are available on computer disks with electronic mailbox connection to instructors and access to an electronic computer database library), some twenty-two colleges and universities and about twenty-five companies were involved in 1987. The Electronic University Network is not an academic institution, but sees itself as a facilitator. Spokesperson Laura Malone says, "We can provide program information and we basically bring them (our students) a package that's different than the schools themselves can deliver. That package allows our students to take classes from their home computer and get fast response from their instructors" (personal communication, Feb. 9, 1987).

New Ideas About Teaching and Learning, Including the Influence of Technology: For many years higher education has relied on a relatively limited number of instructional approaches —the large lecture followed by smaller group discussions, a lecture followed by a hands-on laboratory for most science courses, seminars or small-group discussions for more advanced topics, and of course library assignments, paper writing, and examinations.

Instructional technology has added variety to these traditional approaches by providing films, overhead visual projection, television, and occasionally self-directed instruction with computers.

Newer technology, such as the microcomputer and satellite communication, provides for an even greater expansion of the process of teaching and learning. The Electronic University Network, mentioned earlier, offers college and university courses entirely on computer disks with electronic hookups with instructors. Nova University in Florida offers degree programs via courses on computer disks. Connected Education, Inc., in conjunction with New York's New School for Social Research, offers graduate and undergraduate courses via the New Jersey Institute of Technology's Electronic Information Exchange System.

Educational technology, plus other innovations in instruction, are on the verge of revolutionizing how we think about and practice teaching in higher education. Much of this research and experimentation is not coming from higher education itself, though, but instead is coming from business and industry. "Higher education has done little to learn about teaching and learning. The university's instructional mode has scarcely changed over the past 50 years. Educational innovations are few and often of only marginal impact. . . . Seldom has interest in the learning process, its difference among individuals, and the implications for classroom methods been expressed in educational halls, much less supported and rewarded" (Eurich, 1985, pp. 55–56). However, business and industry have discovered that adults can learn in ways other than attending fifty-minute lectures on Mondays, Wednesdays, and Fridays for sixteen weeks. Business has also found that adults can learn, via computer and other technological formats, in the privacy of their offices and homes.

These not very astounding revelations are causing some

officials in higher education to scratch their heads. Do we change how we teach, and attempt to mount a faculty development program to encourage faculty to try new instructional approaches? This is not to belittle the thousands of faculty members across the country who have been experimenting with new instructional approaches. Challenged are the many more thousands who believe that lecturing for fifty minutes, three times a week, for sixteen weeks is sacrosanct.

If higher education will continue to attract large numbers of adults to its programs, shifts in instructional approaches will become a necessity. It seems ironic that business and industry are taking the lead in researching instructional approaches for adults (though we might note that business has become involved with educational technology because of the enormous profit potentials). Higher education is now challenged to follow some of the business community's new directions for teaching.

Financial Considerations: We cannot discuss the forces influencing higher education without mentioning financing. In 1987, higher education systems in twenty states made budget cuts before the fiscal year ended (Mooney, 1987, p. 1). Higher education, along with other government services, has come under the budget knife. This of course makes it exceedingly difficult to maintain present programs, to say nothing of attempting something new. These cuts, ranging from 1 to 17.5 percent, come on the heels of a series of cuts to public colleges and universities during the mid 1980s.

Budgets for private institutions have also been exceedingly tight. Keller (1983) describes the fate of Wisconsin's Milton College, which was founded in 1844 and declined from 800 students in 1970 to 210 in 1981–82. In May 1982, Milton closed its main campus for good, having been in operation for 138 years (Keller, 1983, pp. 3–4).

No matter how important all of the other changes occurring in higher education may be, budgets must be given major emphasis. Of course, many of the changes institutions are making—we will discuss a number of these in succeeding chapters—have a direct influence on their budgets and on their present and future financial status.

Summary

The foundation for the present system of higher education was established in the late 1800s. The student unrest of the 1960s created a negative image of American universities at least in some circles. Still, during the golden years of the 1960s and 1970s, an enormous amount of expansion in higher education occurred.

Current influences on higher education include (1) changing student enrollments, with greater numbers of older students attending college; (2) curriculum shifts in favor of vocationally oriented programs; (3) competition among institutions of higher education and with other educational providers, such as business and industry; (4) cooperation both among colleges and universities and with other educational providers; (5) the development of new approaches to teaching and learning, particularly involving innovative educational technology; and (6) growing financial problems for many institutions.

History illustrates that institutions of higher education constantly react to societal forces. They seldom gleefully respond and make changes, though. Indeed, colleges and universities have often changed reluctantly, preferring to do business as usual rather than make adjustments.

4

Planning for Change:
An Institutional Approach

Recently, I asked a university administrator how colleges and universities were adjusting to societal pressures. "Well," he replied, after thinking for a moment, "most of them circle the wagons. And then," he said with the hint of a smile, "they shoot toward the inside." What he meant was that they cut programs and faculty, and then they retreat to some core activity they believe they can live with and survive.

During times of cutbacks, many educational institutions do little in-depth planning, yet making a positive response to the demands of a learning society requires that they take planning seriously. Such planning, in most instances, means much more than "fine tuning" existing programs, adding a program here and dropping a program there. It may be necessary to operate on a smaller budget while at the same time responding to society's demands in new ways.

Daloz (1983) says that colleges and universities often drop new programs in times of retrenchment and readjustment: "The tragedy is that many of those programs aimed at bringing about a more equitable and just society have been eliminated or lobotomized, not because the conditions that bred them no longer exist but because the very marginality—institutional as well as philosophical—that made such programs sensitive to a changing environment also made them vulnerable to attack from those that chose not to change" (p. 34).

Present-day colleges and universities must program with limited resources. But the demands of a learning society may require new or modified programs. Thus many institutions face a dilemma. They can choose to ignore the forces requiring change. They can attempt to find new budget sources to fund new programs. Or they can choose to cut back or eliminate some programs, and modify or develop new programs to answer the learning society's challenges.

Planning can help those institutions that have chosen the latter alternative. In this chapter I discuss several common approaches to planning and their advantages and disadvantages. I also share a planning approach that is particularly slanted toward examining how a college or university should respond to a learning society. I call this a *transformation process;* it can be a subsection of an ongoing planning effort or can be the focus of a planning process alone.

Planning for Change

How do colleges and universities respond to the demands of older students who have strong career and professional motives for returning to college study? What changes ought to be made in curriculum, teaching approaches, student services, and admissions policies? How does an institution maintain a strong and rigorous set of programs, and at the same time introduce flexibility and alternative approaches that enable students to reach their goals? How does an institution develop a faculty mind-set that noncredit programming offered in the community can be as important as on-campus, degree-related teaching? What must be done to convince people that courses taught via computer or videodisk and/or satellite, and received in one's home or workplace, can have the same quality and rigor as those taught in large lecture halls? What steps will be necessary for a college or university to establish a link with a business or industrial firm and not believe that it will be "tainted" by the profit-making motive of the company?

Perhaps the most important question college and university leaders can ask is, How do we go about answering these questions—what process or processes are available, and how do we put them in place?

Planning in Higher Education: Some Approaches   There is an extensive literature on planning in higher education. For example, Chin and Benne (1976) describe three strategies for planned change, the empirical-rational, normative-reeducative, and power-coercive strategies (pp. 24–45). The empirical-rational strategy assumes that people are rational and that when given the facts about a situation and how they will gain from the change, they will change. For the normative-reeducative strategy, rationality and intelligence are not denied, but "patterns of action and practice are supported by sociocultural norms and by commitments on the part of individuals to these norms. . . . [Change] will occur only as the persons involved are brought to change their normative orientations to old patterns and develop commitments to new ones" (Chin and Benne, 1976, p. 23). For the power-coercive strategy, "the influence process . . . is basically that of compliance of those with less power to the plans, directions, and leadership of those with great power" (Chin and Benne, 1976, p. 23). Havelock (1973) develops a general change model in which he combines three approaches: problem solving; social interaction; and research, development, and diffusion. Building on Havelock's work, Lindquist (1978, p. 1) describes four change strategies:

- rational planning
- social interaction
- human problem solving
- the political approaches

I will elaborate on these in the following paragraphs.

   Rational Planning: Rational planning depends on reason and evidence as "the best way to obtain alterations in attitudes and behavior. . . . If the research is correct and the development sound, the proposed change will sell itself" (Lindquist, 1978, p. 2). But as Lindquist suggests, "Recent research and theory . . .

have found the rational model inadequate in several respects as a way to go about the introduction of change in human attitudes and behaviors, the changes which are at the heart of academic innovations. In the main, criticism has focused on the isolation of R & D from its audience, the people who supposedly are going to use these new fangled ideas or behaviors" (p. 3).

Social Interaction: Social interaction planning is based on the assumption that change occurs because of informal social contacts. New ideas are thought to be communicated through social networks, as is illustrated in the innovation diffusion studies. Everett Rogers is most often associated with this approach. "Innovation diffusion researchers find that the best route into an organization or community is through *Opinion Leaders,* those persons (or institutions) to whom others turn for advice" (Lindquist, 1978, p. 5). Other factors besides convincing arguments and evidence determine whether new ideas or innovations are accepted, of course. These include whether the new idea offers a relative advantage—whether it better meets institutional objectives or contributes to reduced costs; whether it is compatible with the institution's values, structure, and style; whether it is simple to understand and carry out; and whether it is generally of low risk and low uncertainty. And, in addition, the idea or innovation is more apt to be accepted if it can be observed in action somewhere else, or else the idea can be tried on an experimental or limited basis to see how it works (Lindquist, 1978, p. 5).

Human Problem Solving: The human problem-solving approach is based on the premise that nonrational elements exist within an organization. "There is . . . a psychological dimension to change to which neither the rational nor social models do justice. Rational planning and social interaction do form part of the equation, but . . . underlying interests, habits, fears, and prejudices compose the bulk of the iceberg" (Lindquist, 1978, p. 6). Basic to this idea of planning is dealing with human resistance to change. As Lindquist points out, the human problem-solving approach "is far more controversial in colleges and universities than R & D (rational) or social interaction, if for no other reason than that it probes sources of resistance we prefer to leave buried. Also, because it focuses at least part of its attention on our emotional needs, it conflicts with the claim that academicians are the protectors of cognitive rationality" (p. 7).

Political Approach: The political approach, as the term suggests, is based on political power. This can be utilized in important ways: "Build coalitions among influential persons and groups, then seek an authoritative decision which requires others to comply with the new idea, employ the new behavior, use the innovative product" (Lindquist, 1978, p. 7). Building power bases thus becomes a strategy for effecting change.

When Lindquist reflects on these four approaches to change, he asks, "Is it not possible to entertain the notion that humans are rational, social creatures who want to solve their hidden problems but also want to protect and enhance their vested interests? If we make such an assumption, we must combine our strategies for change. Rational research and planning is not enough. Nor is connecting innovations to opinion leaders in all the right ways. Nor is skills intervention to diagnose human needs and to reduce resistance. Nor is the most effective political maneuvering. We must do it all" (p. 9).

The idea of long-range planning in higher education is not new, but such efforts have not been very effective. Votruba (1987) says that traditional approaches to planning suffer from these shortcomings: "First, they assume a rational world in which plans can be based solely on logic. Second, they often take place in a vacuum, with little or no attention to the external forces that are likely to shape an organization's direction. Third, the planning process often becomes so lengthy and complicated that it loses much of its meaning. Fourth, planning too often takes place apart from the process of decision making. Finally, in traditional planning approaches, the process too often becomes more important than the results" (p. 195).

Others have criticized traditional planning approaches as well. Shuck (1977) claims that higher education spends too much time planning. He says that long-range planning has become a religion for higher education. "Like any viable religion, planning as formally developed today has much to commend it. It appeals both to our idealism and to our self-interest. Its precepts square with much of what we rationalize about the universe we inhabit. Its principles are relatively simple, eminently logical, and capable of great adaptability and variation. It provides doctrine, ritual, and litany to carry us through the bleak hours between our rare moments of insight, so that we may feel that we are doing something important even though not always sure how it may relate to the situation at hand. And, taken seriously, it forces us to make decisions which otherwise might be made only by default" (pp. 594–595).

David Clark (1981), professor of education at the University of Virginia, challenges the view of planning that emphasizes a rational, goal-based, sequential approach. According to him, today's accepted planning approaches include (1) setting goals, (2) developing operational plans, (3) adopting a monitoring system, and (4) establishing an evaluation system to determine the plan's achievements (p. 43). This approach to planning, he says, is based on the assumption of "an integrated view of educational organizations as goal-driven, rational systems in which operations can and should be programmed, sequenced, monitored, and evaluated in short- and long-range planning cycles" (p. 43). Clark contends that we must challenge planning based on these assumptions, because it often results in five-year plans, neatly bound and gathering dust on administrators' shelves.

Enarson (1975) argues that planners tend to make four major errors: (1) they define the problem too narrowly, failing to put it into an appropriate context, (2) they define the problem too widely with endless variables, (3) they count the countable and ignore the fact that just because one can count something, this does not mean that one should, and (4) they spend so much time counting that they fail to spend time on those matters that require judgment (p. 173).

Strategic Planning   A concept currently of great interest in higher education is strategic planning. This term was borrowed from business and industry, which in turn borrowed it from the military. The use of the word *strategic* is unfortunate, because as Peters and Waterman (1982, p. 101) point out, "Usual military metaphors severely limit our ability to think about manage-

ment sensibly." But the philosophy of strategic planning is vast-
ly superior to the more traditional long-range planning approaches. Many of those applying strategic planning have tran-
scended any difficulty that may have resulted from the military
origins of this method. (Some recent works discussing approaches
to strategic planning include Toll, 1982; Balderston, 1981;
Keller, 1983; and Simerly and Associates, 1987.)

According to Keller (1983), strategic planning is different
from long-range planning, systems analysis, and so on, in the
following ways:

1. A college or university takes an active rather than a passive
    role in deciding what will happen to it.
2. The institution looks outward, making certain that it is in
    step with the changing environment in which it exists.
3. The institution's academic strategy is competitive and rec-
    ognizes the market conditions affecting higher education.
4. Strategic planning focuses on decisions, not on documented
    plans, goals, forecasts, or analyses—the attention is on what
    should be done.
5. Strategy making blends national and economic analysis, po-
    litical perspective, and psychological influence.
6. Strategic planning focuses on the future of the institution
    above everything else (pp. 143–153).

Strategic planning "gathers the best information and forecasts;
struggles to overcome political jealousies, inertia, and sabotage;
and builds psychological awareness and commitment. Unapolo-
getically, it marries rationality and artfulness, financial facts and
politics. Good timing is essential for the sequencing of these and
for capitalizing on a sudden retirement or death, a budget crisis,
or a competitor's sharp decline in leadership or quality" (Keller,
1983, p. 149).

Keller's (1983) conceptual framework for strategic planning includes "inside" and "outside" concerns. *Inside* concerns
are (1) tradition, values, and aspirations of the institution and
its faculty, staff, and administration; (2) academic and financial
strengths and weaknesses; and (3) abilities and priorities of the

institution's leadership. *Outside* concerns include (1) environmental trends, including threats and opportunities; (2) market preferences, perceptions, and direction; and (3) the competitive situation (p. 152).

Simerly and Associates (1987) say that "strategic planning is a process that gives attention to (1) designing, (2) implementing, and (3) monitoring plans for decision making." They describe a seven-step strategic planning model:

1. Management audit—examining the institution's strengths and weaknesses, what should be changed and why, and windows of opportunity available.
2. Values clarification—identifying feelings and attitudes that the faculty, staff, and administration hold dear.
3. Mission statement—determining what the institution will contribute to society, who it will serve, how it will serve them, and social benefits that will result.
4. Clarification of aims—establishing goals and objectives (a goal is a broader, more generalized statement pointing to the future; an objective is part of a goal and includes outcomes that can be measured in time and space, is delegated to someone to carry out, and is assigned a deadline for completion).
5. Action plan—deciding how the objectives will be implemented, what the barriers to implementation are, who is in charge of implementation, what a realistic timetable is, and how success will be measured.
6. Reality test—wrestling with the question: Is it possible to attain these goals and objectives, given the resources and constraints of our situation?
7. Feedback system—knowing when goals and objectives are achieved, receiving early warnings of trouble in meeting goals and objectives, and dealing with failure (pp. 12–30).

Many academicians applaud strategic planning, but the approach also has its critics. Hunsicker (1980), writing from a business perspective, says that in attempting to follow strategic planning approaches, many planners succumb to a "paralysis of analysis." He lists three major pitfalls that such planners too often fall into: (1) too much effort spent on developing "optimal" strategies, rather than on challenging the assumptions on which these strategies are based; (2) too much time spent on evaluation of ideas rather than on generating new ideas and proposals; and (3) too much time spent looking inside the organization and not enough time examining what other organizations with similar missions are doing (p. 10).

Hunsicker is also concerned about the amount of time and money invested in strategic planning and whether the returns always warrant the costs. And again, within a business perspective, Hunsicker says that "conventional strategic planning approaches tend almost to substitute quantitative analysis for judgment and intuition . . . . I find that quantitative analyses are often most useful for providing an information base and for confirming hypotheses that have been conceived with a liberal dose of hunch, intuition, judgment, and experience" (p. 14).

A number of writers—King and Cleland (1978, pp. vi, vii) and Simerly and Associates (1987, pp. 23–29) are examples—provide guidelines for improving strategic planning:

1. *Professional planners can help in the planning process, but a college, university, department, or program must do its own planning.*

2. *Those responsible for carrying out the planning must be directly involved in the planning process.*

3. *Planning is a group activity, involving give and take from group members who are selected because they represent a variety of perspectives.*

4. *A "planning organization" must be created to organize and carry out the planning effort. Broad-based planning takes time and resources, and these must be provided for.*

5. *Strategic planning involves more than collecting and manipulating numbers.* It also includes development of mission statements, objectives, and action alternatives. Relevant databases, however, are important to planning, including both quantitative and qualitative data. Certain key administrators can often assist in collecting background data for planning groups, saving the group the time and energy for this effort. Occasionally

a planning group will spend so much time collecting data that it has little time or energy left to think about the meaning of what it has collected, to say nothing about designing new directions for the future.

6. *Administrators must be motivated to spend time on the planning process.* If administrators at various levels appear uncommitted to the planning effort, many faculty members will be far from committed. And if top-level administrators are not committed to the plans resulting from a strategic planning effort, little change will result.

7. *An assessment of environmental trends and forces plus an examination of the organization's strengths and weaknesses are important planning activities.*

8. *The planning process should include an examination of basic assumptions that people involved in the planning process hold about such things as the purpose of higher education, who should be involved in higher education programs, and how higher education programs should be carried out.* Such assumptions, if not brought to light, may often get in the way of decision making and ultimately affect change in the institution. The examination of such assumptions becomes crucial when strategic planning is concerned with an institution's response to the demands of a learning society.

9. *Future planning efforts will often depend on how well administrators and faculty members translate current planning into plans of action that are periodically monitored to make certain they are carried out, changed, or consciously abandoned.*

Planning for a Learning Society: A Review   As mentioned earlier, for higher education to contribute successfully to a learning society, it must consider the following challenges:

1. Provide curriculum, teaching approaches, student services, admissions processes, and so on that will meet the needs and interests of older students returning to colleges and universities for degree programs.
2. Provide learning opportunities that can lead to degrees by using electronic media, "at work" classes, and the like.

3. Provide noncredit learning opportunities on and off campus
    in the way of courses, workshops, conferences, and public
    lectures.
4. Meet the public service demands from the community, state,
    region, and often beyond. This includes being of service to
    government at various levels, to business and industry, and
    to other private sector organizations and community groups
    and organizations.
5. For research institutions, meet the demands of those who
    have particular problems and questions for which research
    can provide answers. Sometimes this may mean working co-
    operatively with a business or industry in developing new
    products.

A carefully developed strategic planning process can help
to meet these challenges. The success of such a planning effort
often requires a change in an institution's assumptions, including a critical examination of its traditions, however.

The Transformation Process

The transformation process is an approach institutions can follow when attempting to become more responsive to a learning
society. Though as we will see, this process can form part of a
strategic planning effort, on a deeper level it is a mind-set, a way
of thinking. The transformation mind-set includes a way of
looking at situations, at questions, at problems, at solutions that
does not stop with the obvious. We constantly ask questions
such as the following: What are the assumptions and values
underlying a particular statement? Are there additional alternatives we can consider? Is there another way of doing things, perhaps a way that does not immediately come to mind? Are we
asking the right questions?

We all are influenced by dominant worldviews or para-
digms, the prevailing assumptions of our society. We hold assumptions about such things as the value of technology, the
nature of progress, and the importance of success. We hold assumptions about our economic system, about competition and

winning, about values and ethics. We do not often talk about these assumptions. But they are a part of all of us, how we think and act. When we face a challenge—for instance, responding to the demands of a learning society—our worldview influences our thinking, our planning, our questions, and our actions. When we begin talking about future roles for higher education, a plethora of hidden assumptions guide our thinking. Sometimes we are quite aware of these assumptions, but often we are not. In many cases, these assumptions are so much a part of us that we are not even aware of alternatives to them.

For in-depth strategic planning to take place, an analysis of basic assumptions becomes critical. This is particularly so if the institutional response to a situation requires changes in curriculum, teaching-learning approaches, student services, and administrative structures. Such changes may require a transformation or a paradigm shift—a change in one's basic assumptions. Ferguson (1980) explains how to work toward paradigm shifts: "We do this by asking questions in a new way—by challenging our old assumptions . . . . Most problems cannot be solved at the level at which they are asked. They must be reframed, put into a larger context. And unwarranted assumptions must be dropped" (p. 28).

Some years ago I developed a transformation process that educators could use in examining basic assumptions about their work (Apps, 1973). Over the years I have applied this process in a variety of adult/continuing education and higher education settings. Most recently I have used it to help in improving practice in continuing education (Apps, 1985).

I base the concept of transformation process on the premise that *what we assume about something or someone influences our perceptions and in turn our actions toward that something or someone.* We do not need to be aware of our assumptions for them to influence our perceptions and actions. We can have—most of us do have—a collection of assumptions about various aspects of reality that we have never examined. This holds just as much for those of us working in higher education as for everyone else. We each hold firm assumptions about such aspects of education as its purpose, its future, who should participate in its programs, and the roles and responsibilities of instructors and administrators. Although these may be unexamined assumptions, they still shape our perceptions of higher education and how we act out our perceptions. For example, we may feel uncomfortable with older learners in our classes. One of the root causes of our discomfort may be an unexamined assumption about who should enroll in higher education degree programs. Many of us assume that these programs are primarily for young people who are continuing their formal education after high school. Until we examine these assumptions, our unease is likely to continue. If we happen to become involved in a planning effort to examine ways of providing higher education opportunities to adults, we will likely be troubled and perhaps even negative toward the idea. Of course other forces may also influence our decision making. But our assumptions are powerful sources of influence and can often inhibit change. Hidden assumptions—those that we make but are not aware of—are even more powerful because they influence our actions in ways that even we do not always recognize.

The important point is that we knit the transformation process into whatever planning effort we are involved in—whether it is an intensive strategic planning effort, or the development of a new course, or a new teaching strategy. We can apply the transformation process at a departmental level, at a college or school level, or at an institutional level. We can also apply the process when a new idea is being considered, say a weekend degree program or a satellite videotaped course offering. In any case, if our focus is on higher education's contributions to a learning society, our assumptions with respect to four groups or phenomena need to be considered: students, academic aims, teaching and learning approaches, and curricula.

Taking the first point first, when a planning group is considering how to provide opportunities for adult learners, members may want to examine what their assumptions are about adults as learners. Questions such as the following can be explored: Why do adults, after a number of years away from formal education, return for degree-credit work? How are adult learners different from younger, more traditional students? Are there fundamental differences between older and younger learners in terms of ability to learn and the efficiency of learning? What happens to intelligence levels during the aging process? How do adults' life experiences influence how they learn, and how do they influence their expectations for instructors?

On a more fundamental level, the image of humankind can be examined. An image of humankind can be defined as "a set of assumptions held about the human being's origin, nature, abilities and characteristics, relationships with others, and place in the universe" (Markley and Harman, 1982, p. 2). We can explore such basic questions as the extent to which people are first rational beings, with feelings representing subordinate or inferior segments of their being. "This empirical view relegates the speculative world of art, music, poetry, and religion to a position of lesser reality" (Markley and Harman, 1982, p. 55). We could explore the assumption that a person's individual identity and success in life are measured by material possessions and/or occupational status. We could examine the assumption that human beings are separate from nature, and that the goal of humankind is to control nature. "Humankind, so long subservient to nature, now finds itself in an increasingly powerful role as the creator of its own environmental context. However, given the highly interdependent links in the ecological chain, our capacity for manipulation of the environment must give way to an enlarged sense of symbiotic responsibility," according to Markley and Harman (1982, p. 54).

Examining aims for a program or college could include wrestling with such questions as, What is the role of our college or university in providing opportunities for adult learners? How does what we do at our college or university compare with what other institutions of higher education in the area do? How does what we plan to do compare with what other providers of adult/continuing education are doing? What are our aims with respect to providing noncredit opportunities? What do we assume about noncredit opportunities? Are they an integral part of what the institution should be offering, or are they merely "moneymakers"? What are our aims for public service, such as assisting government agencies, working with organizations in the community, and the like? How does public service activity rank among our various aims? What do we assume about the relative importance of this activity?

Examining assumptions about teaching and learning, particularly with the goal in mind of making the institution more accessible and relevant to adults as well as younger students, requires answering many questions. What do we assume about the nature of teaching, particularly teaching an adult audience? If we accept the precept that teaching should no longer merely involve presenting information, what form do we assume it should take? What are our assumptions about self-directed learning? Do we have any role in assisting people with their self-directed learning activities? What do we assume the outcome of learning should be, particularly for the adult learner? The accumulation of content? The acquisition of skills for finding information, analyzing it, and making decisions about its application to particular situations or problems? The development of new views of the world, broader and deeper perspectives? To what extent do we assume that learners should have some control over the learning situation, rather than giving complete control to the instructor or the institution? How does the new educational technology, such as videotapes, computers, and satellite transmission, affect what we assume about teaching and learning?

What do we assume about curriculum and content? Are we willing to accept an adult's prior experience at work or in a volunteer organization as valuable? More to the point, are we willing to award college credit for experience if the person can demonstrate clearly that what he or she has learned is college level and is relevant to the desired curriculum? In some instances credit for electives might be considered for college-level experience that does not relate directly to the person's curriculum goals. What do we assume about the concept of core curriculum and the need for everyone to take certain courses? Are we willing to include adult learners in curriculum planning sessions, given that most of them have a clear sense of what learning they wish to pursue and are likely to hold opinions about what should be in a curriculum? What relationship do we see between the noncredit programs and the degree-credit curricula?

Should there be a relationship between the two? What relationship do we see between the curriculum we offer and the relationship to the public service work we do? What relationship do we assume should exist between the curriculum we teach and the scholarship and research activities of our faculty? Are there elements of our curriculum that we assume should not be changed under any circumstances? Why is this so? What is our position on the role of more applied courses and of liberal arts and humanities courses? These are only some of the questions that need to be considered.

An Approach to Transformation   Having set the stage, we can now turn more specifically to the nature of the transformation process. This process includes the following phases:

- developing awareness
- exploring alternatives
- making a transition
- achieving integration
- taking action

Developing Awareness: Becoming aware means recognizing that something is wrong or different. Realizing that a relatively large number of older students are enrolled at one's college or university year after year is one example of awareness. Reflecting on the societal changes that are occurring, such as the effects of technology, the increasing amounts of information available, and the expectations of business, government, and so on for assistance from higher education, represents another example. In many cases this awareness does not result accidentally, but comes from a strategic planning effort, where administrators and faculty members sit down and examine present situations and future direction. Wilson (1983) says that an institution facing uncertainty needs two things: "a star to steer by (vision) . . . [and] a radar system (environmental analysis) to pick out rocks, reefs, headlands, and clear water ahead" (p. 4).

Much has been written on how to do environmental analysis and conduct institutional research. (For example, see Morrison, Renfro, and Boucher, 1983; Dressel, 1971, 1976; Fernberg and Lasher, 1983; Cohen and Garet, 1975; Perry, 1972; de Carbonnel and Dorrance, 1973; Saupe, 1981; Hearn and Heydinger, 1985.) To consider one particular approach, Glover and Holmes (1983) describe a process for examining the external environment. Assessing the external environment includes an exploration of the social context, institutional relationships, geographical scope, and time frame in question. Social context includes demographic and geographic trends, economic factors, environmental protection, politics and government, international affairs, national defense, law and justice, values and lifestyles, health and medicine, science and technology, employment, education and other forms of training, equality of opportunity, and culture. Institutional relationships include an examination of how the institution is influenced by its relationship with its clientele, its governing bodies, its resource suppliers, and its competitors. Geographical scope includes examination of the prestige and visibility of the institution locally, regionally, nationally, and internationally. Time frame refers to the time period that will be examined—short range (three to five years) to long range (ten to twenty years) (Glover and Homes, 1983, pp. 8–9).

It may be useful to consider a specific example of institutional analysis. Hunter College in New York City conducted systematic research in 1982 to obtain information about its student body (Davila, 1985). The study had three objectives: to provide a statistical description of Hunter College's students, to find out what the class enrollment and scheduling preferences of the students were, and to assess the quality of student life at the college. A large-scale survey, using a standardized questionnaire, was presented to a random sample of students. The survey was designed to obtain quantifiable data about the student population and its patterns of class attendance. To obtain information about student life, researchers conducted a series of focus-group sessions, where small groups of students discussed topics about student life in depth. Focus groups included beginning evening students; advanced evening students; beginning day students; graduating day students; transfer day students; high-, middle-, and low-range academic students; students who participate in extracurricular activities; and returning women students. Students in each category were randomly selected from all students in that category, and they were paid a small stipend for their time. As a result of this systematic study, Hunter College initiated a number of reforms; these included keeping the registrar's, bursar's, admissions, and evening advising offices open until 7:00 P.M.; beginning evening classes at 5:40 to allow time for travel from work to school; providing food services until the beginning of the last evening class; establishing a child-care center for both day and evening students; and extending the hours of the women's center into the evening.

Awareness of problems in higher education not only results from strategic planning, of course. It may also come from a crisis, a budget deficit, a cut in tax support, a decrease in outside research funding, or a severe drop in student enrollments. Moreover, faculty members and administrators may develop an awareness of a problem or challenge by reflecting on their institution's actions and plans. Ferguson (1980) notes that becoming aware involves anything that "shakes up the old understanding of the world, the old priorities" (p. 89). Becoming aware is often the most difficult part of the entire process of transformation. Many people, particularly those in higher education, are often content to continue as they have in the past, making small adjustments as necessary. To face the realization that something may be wrong, or that some more substantive change is necessary, is difficult for comfortable people to accept. One approach to becoming aware is making the comfortable uncomfortable.

Exploring Alternatives: Investigating alternatives means looking at what other institutions that are facing similar situations are doing. During this phase of the transformation process, planners search for alternative ways of doing things, new answers, and new ideas, and question the way things are now done. Exploring alternatives means becoming specific about possible changes. It means asking questions such as the following: Does it make sense for our institution to invest in satellite communication equipment in order to beam courses a distance from the college or university? How might we reorganize our curriculum to better meet the needs and interests of practicing nurses in our community? And so on. During this phase of the transformation process, planners generally are faced with the possibility that something of the old way will be left behind and replaced with something new. This may affect the organization's structure, an admissions policy, the scheduling of courses, or the way that the institution responds to requests from the community for assistance. This leads to the next phase, transition.

Making a Transition: We create transitions when the old is left behind, or dramatically changed, and a new approach is adopted. This process goes counter to what most of us have learned. Most of us believe that we build on existing structures, ideas, and approaches, and do not seek to replace them. The human tendency is to somehow try to improve what is already in place. Sometimes this is possible; on the other hand, the level of change necessary often requires more than fine tuning what already exists.

When an institution begins considering leaving behind old ideas and old ways of doing things and exploring new alternatives, new sets of assumptions replace old assumptions. A person's or an institution's assumptions are in many ways a compass for action and for viewing the future. Without this compass there is confusion, loss, and unease. Bridges (1980) notes perceptively that "the reality that is left behind . . . is not just a picture on the wall. It is a sense of which way is up and which way is down; it is a sense of which way is forward and which way is backward. It is, in short, a way of orienting oneself and of moving forward into the future. . . . The old sense of life as 'going somewhere' breaks down, and we feel like shipwrecked sailors on some existential atoll" (p. 102). He refers (1980) to the time between deciding to leave something behind and fully accepting a new structure, idea, or approach to doing something as a "neutral zone" (pp. 112–114).

I firmly believe that when an individual or a group has made a decision to leave an old approach behind, a grieving process is involved. The group grieves the loss of its old way of doing things. Just as when we lose a loved one and have to work through the grief that is involved, in similar fashion a group must work through its loss and the associated grief. "The more radical the changes which evolve, the more important [it is to] recognize the element of bereavement . . . in the process of major reconstruction" (Marris, 1974, p. 151).

To minimize these problems and facilitate change, Marris (1974) suggests that groups involved in planning for major changes at their institution follow three principles: "First, the process of reform must always expect and even encourage conflict. Whenever people are confronted with change, they need the opportunity to react, to articulate their ambivalent feelings and work out their own sense of it. Second, the process must respect the autonomy of different kinds of experience. . . . Third, there must be time and patience, because the conflicts involve not only the accommodation of diverse interests but the realization of an essential continuity in the structure of meaning. Each of these principles corresponds with an aspect of grief, as a crisis of reintegration which can neither be escaped, nor resolved by anyone on behalf of another, nor hurried" (p. 156).

Achieving Integration: Achieving integration means putting the pieces that evolved from the transition phase back together. It is a reformulation of something new, perhaps with some remnants from the past. But it is a new way of thinking, often based on a new set of assumptions. Achieving integration also requires becoming comfortable with the new ideas, new assumptions, and new ways of thinking that have emerged from the transition phase. Sometimes it is difficult to know when integration has occurred. At other times we know immediately. We are more comfortable with our work. We feel less stressed. And our work seems to have more importance and meaning. Often we must act on our new ideas before integration can fully take place.

Taking Action: Taking action specifically means doing something with the new ideas. It means putting into operation some new approaches for making adult learners more comfortable in college and university classrooms and in other higher education settings. It may mean new approaches to providing instruction to younger students who must attend colleges and universities part time. It means the possibility of public service involvement that we may not have seen as necessary, important, or even within the mission of the institution in the past. The action phase is the test of the transformation process. When an institution begins to act on its new assumptions, people will quickly discover whether they really understood and completely accepted the discussion in the early phases of the process. Attempts at action will often motivate a planning group to re-examine earlier phases in the transformation process. Attempting a certain activity may cause a new awareness, and thus a new involvement in transformation.

For that matter, working through any phase of the process may send the group back to an earlier phase. The transformation process, as I have outlined it, is not a linear one, but a dynamic process that moves back and forth, with the possibility that more than one of the phases of the process may be occurring at the same time. As dynamic and fluid as the process may appear, it is nevertheless crucial for a planning or decision-making group to understand it. This is particularly so if the decisions under consideration are of greater consequence than merely being a fine tuning of existing policies and procedures.

Summary

Making a response to the demands of the learning society means that higher education must take planning seriously. The literature of planning is extensive. Havelock (1973), Chin and Benne (1976), and Lindquist (1978)—to mention a few writers in this area—have developed elaborate planning models.

But planning critics such as Shuck (1977) claim that higher education spends too much time planning. Clark (1981) says that most of the existing planning approaches emphasize a rational, goal-based, sequential approach—which sounds good but often results in written documents that gather dust in administrators' offices. And Enarson (1975) lists errors planners make: defining a problem too narrowly, defining a problem too broadly, counting the countable and ignoring the rest, and spending too much time counting and not enough time on matters requiring judgment.

In recent years, much of the literature has focused on "strategic planning" as an approach higher education should use in making planning decisions. Keller (1983), an advocate of strategic planning, says that institutions should focus on both inside and outside concerns. Inside concerns include the traditions and values of the institution. Outside concerns consist of environmental trends, market preferences, and the competitive situation.

But widely accepted planning approaches may not be sufficient to help higher education make the more dramatic changes that are often necessary for an institution to respond to the demands of a learning society. An institutional transformation may be necessary.

Institutional transformation includes five phases: (1) developing awareness, (2) exploring alternatives, (3) making a transition, (4) achieving integration, and (5) taking action. To systematically examine an institution's potential contribution to a learning society, we can apply the transformation process in terms of four groups of phenomena: students, academic aims, teaching and learning approaches, and curriculum.

5

Reconsidering the Institution's Mission and Charting New Directions

Deciding how to respond to older learners and how to meet the demands for outreach and public service often requires that an institution examine its basic aims. Such an examination can have broad implications. As McDermott (1975) points out, "The adult student population represents not only new financial blood for static and dying institutions but an opportunity for the rethinking of such basic issues as the nature and purpose of education, the social and community role of educational institutions, academic isolation, and similar problems" (p. 271).

Aims for Higher Education

It is not easy to rethink an institution's aims and direction. Nor is it a task most administrators and faculty relish tackling. Yet this would seem a critical time for such an examination. As Alpert (1985) suggests, "The current period of economic retrenchment has called into sharp focus the question of the nation's commitment to its institutions of higher education and equally serious questions regarding the responsibilities of universities in society. Retrenchment has also revealed within the academy serious problems related to management and governance, on the one hand, and identity and purpose on the other" (p. 242).

Many other criticisms have been leveled against higher education as well. For example, Kirk (1978) summarizes four "principal afflictions of American higher education." The first he calls *purposelessness.* He says that colleges and universities have confused "claims and hopes: college as mere socialization and sociability . . . ; college as boring means to job-certification; college as temporary sanctuary for the aimless and the neurotic; college as a huge repository of 'facts' and specialized undertakings; . . . college as an alleged instrument for elevating the 'culturally deprived' or 'minorities'; college and university simply as an industry, employing hundreds of thousands of people at good salaries, supplying 'research' services to the state or private industry, furnishing public entertainment through quasi-professional sports and other diversions" (p. xii).

Kirk calls the second affliction *intellectual disorder.* He criticizes the "cafeteria-style" curriculum offered at many institutions, where students pick and choose courses. There is no core to the curriculum and little direction. He also criticizes the "compartmentalizing of knowledge, leading at best to the development of elites unable to communicate one with another" (p. xi).

Kirk's third concern is the *size* of many institutions. For him, large size is a problem: "The effect of this inhumane scale upon professors and instructors, souring their tempers and frustrating their intellects, has been as disagreeable as its effect upon the rising generation and perhaps more ominous" (p. xi).

The fourth problem concerns the *inadequate preparation* of many college freshmen. Kirk lambastes primary and secondary schools for poorly preparing students entering institutions of higher education.

Most of us have heard these and similar criticisms many times before. The truth, within the smoke and fire of these emotionally charged complaints, is a concern for purpose, for aim and direction, for mission. As colleges and universities wrestle with how to respond to a learning society, they must wrestle with aims. It is not difficult to find advice on what the aims of a college or university should be.

In his *Paideia Proposal* (1982), Adler writes about what he believes the aims of all education should be—and he says that education is more than schooling (elementary, secondary, college, or university): "The ultimate goal of the educational process is to help human beings become educated persons" (p. 9). For Adler, an educated person is one who has acquired organized knowledge, developed intellectual skills, and has an enlargement of understanding, insight, and aesthetic appreciation.

In his classic work *The Idea of a University* ([1852] 1959), John Henry Cardinal Newman says this about a university's aims: "I believe, as a matter of history, the business of a university is to make this intellectual culture its direct scope, or to employ itself in the education of the intellect . . ." (p. 149). For Newman, intellectual culture means thinking about knowledge in a particular way: "When I speak of knowledge, I mean something intellectual, something which grasps what it perceives through the senses; something which takes a view of things; which sees more than the senses convey; which reasons upon what it sees, and while it sees; which invests it with an idea" (p. 138).

Rhodes (1978) believes that Newman has much to say to us today: "He confronts us today, provoking us to a more profound inquiry into the ultimate nature of our humanity, urging us to embrace knowledge, not as an abstraction to be savored in isolation, but as a guide to and a servant of a life of openness, of freedom and of high purpose, both for the individual and for society. . . . The university . . . should regard its primary mission neither as career training nor as character development but rather as the training of the mind. Such a mission . . . has both value in itself and also value in furtherance of the overarching goals of society" (p. 40).

Dennehy (1982) argues that the purpose of education should be "the opportunity of each person to develop his or her intellectual, moral, aesthetic, and spiritual capacities" (p. 185).

Friedrich (1982) asks fundamental questions such as these: What is it essential to know and why? And what is the role of education in providing the answers? He offers five responses to his questions:

1. Education means careers—education should enable students to obtain better jobs than they would otherwise be able to find.

2. Education transmits civilization—knowing the foundations of one's country, literature, and the arts, what it is that makes people human.
3. Education teaches how to think—the key is not what a person knows, but how he or she evaluates each fact or argument.
4. Education liberates the individual—it encourages the person to develop the potentialities of the self, with the realization that everyone's self is different.
5. Education teaches morals—concern for the moral outcomes of one's actions (pp. 66-72).

Unique Aims

As I pointed out earlier, higher education is not by any means the sole provider of educational opportunities for adults. Libraries, vocational schools, museums, community organizations, and business and industry all sponsor educational opportunities for older learners. The kinds of questions faculty and administrators in higher education must face are the following: What unique contributions can higher education make, given the existence of many other educational providers? What can higher education do better than anyone else? What can higher education provide that others will not?

To examine these questions, it is helpful to assess what has influenced the aims of colleges and universities in the past. Kerr (1982) traces the forces that have molded the modern university. He argues that there are two primary forces: the land-grant movement, which resulted from the Morrill Act of 1862, and federal support of scientific research, support that began during World War II (p. 46). The land-grant movement was a response to rapid industrial and agricultural development occurring during the last half of the nineteenth century and to criticism that colleges and universities were elitist. Kerr believes that federal funding may have had more influence on American universities than the land-grant movement. As a result of large amounts of federal research dollars funneled into major research universities, we began to see federal influence on research agendas and on degree programs and outreach efforts. With individual faculty researchers seeking research funds with little or no attempts at institutional coordination of this funding, universities, according to Kerr, began to lose control of their own destinies. He suggests that other changes included an improvement in graduate teaching at research institutions, but at the same time a subtle discounting of undergraduate education; increased rifts between scientists and humanists (partly because the scientists obtained far more research money than the humanists); and a concentration of federal resources at relatively few institutions (pp. 57–67).

Few universities turned down the federal dollars or set guidelines on what the limits to their research might be. The practice of supporting university research with federal dollars continues to greatly influence the aims of these institutions. Colleges and universities are clearly looked to as major actors in the so-called knowledge industry. And there is a clear trend for knowledge-producing universities to develop ties with business and industry, which are the major users of the research results. Thus industry, by virtue of what it will or will not fund in the way of research, helps to set the mission of a college or university. Funding from foundations has a similar influence on institutional aims. If an institution wants to be considered for funding from a foundation, it must march to the foundation's tune for funding priorities.

For tax-supported institutions, we must also not overlook the influence of the states on college and university aims. In fact, in some states, the responsibility for determining mission, role, and scope for colleges and universities rests with the state and is exercised through its legislature, the state higher education board, and so on. In other states, where more authority for mission is given to university governing bodies, such as boards of regents, the aims are nonetheless influenced by state funding dictates and overall state goals—attention to economic development, for example, with an expectation that all state agencies and institutions (including colleges and universities) will make a contribution.

These trends at least implicitly influence the aims of many colleges and universities in this country. But what about

broader needs? What about the thousands of adults
ther education? What about the community organi
institutions that could benefit from the research re
will these individuals and groups be served? Few fede
dollars support these types of programs. Some founuaa.....,
notably the Kellogg Foundation, have provided funds for colleges and universities interested in expanding their research and
teaching in the area of adult/continuing education, and have
assisted some institutions in strengthening their continuing education activities. Such foundation encouragement influences
colleges and universities in making responses to the demands of
a learning society.

Higher education faces many problems as it looks ahead.
Yet it knows that for its survival, it must respond to those who
are willing to provide financial assistance, such as the federal
and state government. A fundamental question remains: To
what extent do colleges and universities follow the priorities of
granting agencies and foundations, or to what extent do they
determine their own aims for the future? To what extent can
these institutions identify their own aims and yet accommodate
outside resource requirements such as those imposed by granting agencies?

Higher Education Goals for a Learning Society

What are examples of higher education aims that reflect an interest in meeting the needs of a learning society? As we might
guess, there is no unanimity of thought. Some believe a major
focus of programs for adults should be a focus on the liberal
arts. Along these lines, Zwerling (1984) writes that "usually,
when we speak about the re-education of adults, we are in fact
speaking about retraining (for some career) . . . . Much less frequently do we speak about re-education in the liberal arts . . . .
There are literally millions of Americans who completed their
undergraduate education since the Second World War who
could profit from a re-immersion in the liberal arts—either because they were 'too young' to reap the benefits of a liberal
education when they went to college or because they attended

a college at a time when the curriculum was in disarray, a time when the idea of comprehensive general education was in disrepute and graduates came away with little to help them integrate either human history or their own personal histories" (p. 80). Some colleges and universities have developed special liberal arts degree programs for adults—Duke University is an example.

Other institutions have focused on providing continuing education opportunities for the professions, with a heavy emphasis on engineering and medicine. Still others have attended to special needs of the adult population, particularly assisting women with returning to the job market or making career changes—the College of St. Catherine in St. Paul, Minnesota, and Alverno College in Milwaukee are examples.

Land-grant institutions and their cooperative extension services have a long tradition of working with adults and communities. Cooperative extension organizations are searching for new direction and new aims for the future. A recent national publication, *Revitalizing Rural America*, focused on the contributions of cooperative extension programs in improving the economy of rural America. Their aims have included "1. Providing a perspective on local development issues, 2. increasing the knowledge base for individual and community decisions, 3. developing the skills necessary to achieve individual and community goals, and 4. helping to shape the decision-making environment" (U.S. Department of Agriculture, 1986, p. 23).

Deciding on Aims

Faculty and administrators often view working out a mission statement as having considerably lower priority than their many other responsibilities. Recently I worked with a college involved in a long-range planning effort, and I asked the dean for the mission statement. His reply was, "We've got one around here somewhere; in fact we've got a file with several of them."

For many, a mission statement is a public relations tool handed to those asking about an institution's program. As Martin (1985) writes, mission statements are "deep yet lofty, broad yet complex, important yet ignored" (p. 40). He continues that broader needs? What about the thousands of adults seeking further education? What about the community organizations and institutions that could benefit from the research results? How will these individuals and groups be served? Few federal research dollars support these types of programs. Some foundations, notably the Kellogg Foundation, have provided funds for colleges and universities interested in expanding their research and teaching in the area of adult/continuing education, and have assisted some institutions in strengthening their continuing education activities. Such foundation encouragement influences colleges and universities in making responses to the demands of a learning society.

Higher education faces many problems as it looks ahead. Yet it knows that for its survival, it must respond to those who are willing to provide financial assistance, such as the federal and state government. A fundamental question remains: To what extent do colleges and universities follow the priorities of granting agencies and foundations, or to what extent do they determine their own aims for the future? To what extent can these institutions identify their own aims and yet accommodate outside resource requirements such as those imposed by granting agencies?

Higher Education Goals for a Learning Society

What are examples of higher education aims that reflect an interest in meeting the needs of a learning society? As we might guess, there is no unanimity of thought. Some believe a major focus of programs for adults should be a focus on the liberal arts. Along these lines, Zwerling (1984) writes that "usually, when we speak about the re-education of adults, we are in fact speaking about retraining (for some career) . . . . Much less frequently do we speak about re-education in the liberal arts . . . . There are literally millions of Americans who completed their undergraduate education since the Second World War who could profit from a re-immersion in the liberal arts—either because they were 'too young' to reap the benefits of a liberal education when they went to college or because they attended a college at a time when the curriculum was in disarray, a time when the idea of comprehensive general education was in disrepute and graduates came away with little to help them integrate either human history or their own personal histories" (p. 80). Some colleges and universities have developed special liberal arts degree programs for adults—Duke University is an example.

Other institutions have focused on providing continuing education opportunities for the professions, with a heavy emphasis on engineering and medicine. Still others have attended to special needs of the adult population, particularly assisting women with returning to the job market or making career changes—the College of St. Catherine in St. Paul, Minnesota, and Alverno College in Milwaukee are examples.

Land-grant institutions and their cooperative extension services have a long tradition of working with adults and communities. Cooperative extension organizations are searching for new direction and new aims for the future. A recent national publication, *Revitalizing Rural America*, focused on the contributions of cooperative extension programs in improving the economy of rural America. Their aims have included "1. Providing a perspective on local development issues, 2. increasing the knowledge base for individual and community decisions, 3. developing the skills necessary to achieve individual and community goals, and 4. helping to shape the decision-making environment" (U.S. Department of Agriculture, 1986, p. 23).

Deciding on Aims

Faculty and administrators often view working out a mission statement as having considerably lower priority than their many other responsibilities. Recently I worked with a college involved in a long-range planning effort, and I asked the dean for the mission statement. His reply was, "We've got one around here somewhere; in fact we've got a file with several of them."

For many, a mission statement is a public relations tool handed to those asking about an institution's program. As Martin (1985) writes, mission statements are "deep yet lofty, broad yet complex, important yet ignored" (p. 40). He continues that "the mission statement is the foundation on which the House of Intellect stands. And lofty are the utterances that express the importance of our college's mission. Indeed, they float like puffy clouds over our solidly positioned edifice. Broad is the applicability assigned these statements; so broad that they are thought to cover every contingency. Yet, narrow is the gate to understanding them, and few there be that find it. No wonder, then, given the mission statement's depth and height, breadth and density, that it is so often ignored" (p. 40).

The traditional approach to writing mission statements has been to write lofty statements of mission and then trust that goals and objectives for the institution will trickle down to the administration, faculty, and staff. But Doucette, Richardson, and Fenske (1985) offer an alternative approach for developing a mission statement: "College or university missions—descriptions of overarching institutional purposes that are primarily intended to justify the institution to external constituencies—are defined here in terms of the specific activities in which institutions actually engage. These activities, in turn, are defined in terms of the institution's services, the specific clientele for whom these services are provided, and the rationale that is commonly advanced for providing them" (p. 193).

Faculty and administrators writing mission statements as a response to a learning society are challenged to reflect on what their institution can do that sets it apart from its competitors. This often means carefully assessing the unique dimensions now existing at the institution, and considering what innovations the institution is willing (and able) to invest in. How does an institution go about doing this? We will consider several examples.

At Michigan State University in 1973, President Wharton established a Task Force on Lifelong Education, which submitted a report titled *The Lifelong University: A Report to the President*. This report included the following: a definition of lifelong education, a survey of current programs and resources, a statement of university and lifelong education objectives, recommendations for needed expansion of lifelong education at the university (including desirable modifications of procedures

and programs and needed initiatives), a discussion of organizational arrangements, a review of financial considerations, and
comments on interinstitutional cooperation. The report included
twenty-two assumptions and sixty-seven specific recommendations for a model of lifelong education responsive to changing
social forces. It cited the following factors that have influenced
the demand for lifelong education programs at colleges and universities: "exponential increase in new information and techniques, technological advances, rising personal expectations, increased leisure time, growing awareness of economically and
educationally disadvantaged groups, and an emergence of new
individual and group life-styles" (Lanier, 1985, p. 1).

When the task force report was in progress, Michigan's institutions of higher education began facing severe budget problems. By 1980, Michigan State University was cutting major
units and much of the lifelong learning plan was on hold. But by
1984, with a turnaround in the budget situation, a renewed effort to implement the task force plan took place. Judith Lanier
became acting dean of the Lifelong Education Program in 1984
(she was also dean of the College of Education), and the effort
began moving forward again with vigor. In a January 1985
memo to the provost, Dean Lanier wrote, "One of LEP's [the
Lifelong Education Program's] major goals for the past year
and a half has been the development of a plan for improving
Michigan State University's outreach and continuing education
capability." In the memo she went on to mention the budget
problems that prevented the program from moving forward
more vigorously, but she also cited the reasons why the program
must continue: "Increasingly sophisticated technologies, major
shifts in demography, altered conditions in the workplace, growing interdependence among nations, new expectations for wom-
en, minorities and the aging, and numerous other such changes
pressed for institutional adaptation at a time when fewer and
fewer resources were available to support needed adaptation
and renewal" (Lanier, 1985, p. 2). In addition, she referred to
the report issued by the Michigan Governor's Commission on
the Future of Higher Education in December 1984: "The report

notes the decline in the number of college-age men and women who will be coming to Michigan's campuses for full-time study, the increasing number of adult workers who desire to improve their personal and professional lives through education, and the importance of education to social development and economic diversification in Michigan" (Lanier, 1985, p. 3). The Governor's report also recommended that Michigan's institutions of higher education clearly establish their respective roles.

Because Michigan State is a major research institution, it built on this uniqueness in responding to the demands of the learning society. The Governor's Commission affirmed this: " 'Steps [should] be taken to open wider the doors of cooperation and communication between the university research community and all sectors of the business community and between the universities, in order to maintain and enhance Michigan's reputation for excellence and assure their continued contribution to the state's well being' " (Lanier, 1985, p. 4).

As a result of the task force's report and the resultant discussions, Michigan State's mission statement began to evolve: "The university's land grant and service mission first originated in the areas of agriculture and the mechanic arts. While these emphases remain essential to the purpose of Michigan State, the land grant commitment now encompasses fields such as health, human relations, business, communication, education, and government, and extends to urban and international settings. The evolution of this mission reflects the increasing complexity and cultural diversity of society, the world's greater interdependence, changes in both state and national economy, and the explosive growth of knowledge, technology, and communications. Just as the focus on agriculture and the mechanic arts was appropriate when Michigan State University was founded, the wide range of instructional, research, and public service commitments that now characterize this university is essential today" (Lanier, 1985, p. 4).

As we have mentioned, the College of St. Catherine is a women's liberal arts college located in St. Paul, Minnesota. In 1985 its enrollment was 2,484, the largest in the college's history. The college has a long history of formal five-year plans. But much of the planning has emphasized financial projections, issues related to buildings and grounds and the like. In 1981–82, the president of the college called together a group of people to begin the next long-range planning effort. This group decided that it wanted to go well beyond previous planning efforts. Representatives of corporations were invited to speak to the group about strategic planning, what it meant, and how a college might go about doing it.

The twelve people in the planning group met for a year to develop a plan. They presented the plan to the president, but neither the president nor the group was satisfied with the results, so the group continued its work. It was expanded to about thirty or thirty-five people and began meeting at 6 A.M. for breakfast meetings because this was the only time when no one had a time conflict. At one point, the group invited in a local group-process consultant to help with the planning process.

The group soon began to focus on goals for the college and listed some twenty-four, which were grouped into three clusters: clientele, curriculum, and climate. Subcommittees were formed for each of these goal areas. The subcommittees involved others in the planning process as well. For instance, the subcommittee working on climate literally went through the campus directory and divided up everybody on campus, so that each subcommittee person called about fourteen people. It then held open campus forums and again called people on the phone and invited them to attend. These subcommittees made deliberate attempts to involve the members of the Board of Trustees, Parents' Council, President's Council, and Alumni Board in the planning effort.

By the end of the first year of planning, somewhere between fifty and seventy percent of all people on campus had attended at least one meeting or had otherwise been involved in the discussion and the creation of the long-range plan for the college. During a second year of planning, the group began taking a hard look at the social forces affecting the college and how it should respond. The climate subcommittee examined in detail questions such as how faculty and students interact with each other and what it feels like to be a member of the academic community at St. Catherine's.

The overall objective for St. Catherine's that emerged from the strategic planning efforts was for the college to become the premier women's college in the Midwest by 1990. Planners identified some 200 plus strategies to achieve specific goals in the three areas of clientele, curriculum, and climate.

The plan includes several key features. Each of the three broad goal areas includes a goal statement, a narrative statement, and a listing of specific objectives. For example, in the 1986–87 plan, within "Goal I: Educating Women—Clientele," we find the following goal statement: "To maintain a full-time equivalent enrollment of approximately 1,950 students of varying ages and backgrounds" (College of St. Catherine, 1986). The narrative statement that follows discusses St. Catherine's desire to become the Midwest's premier institution for women. This is followed by a series of specific enrollment objectives: 1,400 in the day school (both traditional-age and older students; 400 in Weekend College; 60 in graduate programs; and 100 in continuing education, certificate, and special programs. Of the 1,950 full-time equivalent students, 5 percent will be from minority groups and 7 percent of the day school enrollment will be from foreign countries (College of St. Catherine, 1986, pp. 1–2).

Similar specific objectives are presented for each goal area. The plan also includes a rating system, so that at the end of the year, each objective can be rated as to accomplishment. The five-point rating system includes the following: (1) accomplished, (2) in progress but not yet completed, (3) consciously deferred from assigned time, (4) assigned to a future time, (5) consciously rejected. These ratings become the basis for the following year's planning efforts. St. Catherine's aims are thus spelled out generally as well as specifically, and there is an emphasis on action and on the monitoring of progress toward the completion of objectives.

For its five-year planning efforts, St. Catherine's provides the following key questions for departments:

What changes have taken place in the past five years which affect our department, activities, and functions? How have you responded and how well have you responded?

What trends can be predicted for the future which will affect the department? What information can be gathered to help monitor and adapt to these trends in an ongoing fashion?

What factors have been critical in success in the past five years? What obstacles have prevented success in the past five years? What do you see as primary program strengths? Weaknesses?

For the next five years, what are your goals for the department? What do you want the department to be five years from now? Two years? Next year? How does your plan relate to the College Strategic Long Range Plan?

How can the department move toward those goals by specific strategies? What must be done to preserve program strengths? Overcome program weaknesses? Adapt to future trends?

What are the priorities among the department goals and strategies? Which are most important? Which are most feasible? How can they be ordered to provide a reasonable plan for staff activities in the coming years?

What resources will be needed to help move toward these goals? What reallocations of resources or staff can contribute to this? What additional resources would be required? What will the department be able to do if there are no additional resources? A decline in resources?

How will implementation of the plan be monitored? Revision of the plan? Evaluation of programs and activities? [College of St. Catherine, n.d., p. 16].

In a very systematic way, the College of St. Catherine is therefore developing its aims to reflect the pressures from a changing society, as well as building on the strengths and unique contributions the college can make.

Implications of Examining Aims

Wrestling with a statement of aims can help university and college planners uncover their true beliefs about an institution's purposes. Developing a statement of aims can (1) bring to light questions about traditional roles for the college or university that should continue, (2) bring out ways the institution can respond to societal change and the demands of a learning society, and (3) help form priorities for institutional aims. The process of developing a statement of aims (mission statement) can be as useful as the resulting product.

Recently, I worked with a college that conducted a year-long planning effort involving a large number of faculty and administrators. The question of mission statement did not emerge until the writing team charged with drafting the report discovered that the college's mission statement was at least twenty years old. The team wrote a revised statement. And the debate began. The college's faculty advisory group offered suggestions for revision. The college's administrative group threw out the writing team's mission statement and offered suggestions for an alternative. Then only a small minority of faculty members and administrators agreed with the alternative.

But in the process, many important questions surfaced. What unique contributions should this college make? How does what the college does relate to what is happening in other areas of higher education? What should be the relationship of the college's on- and off-campus teaching? What responsibility does the college have for older learners? What role should information technology play in the college's degree-credit teaching and in its outreach/extension efforts? What is the relationship of research programs to credit and outreach/extension programming? Which program areas should be given priority in the areas of research, teaching, and outreach/extension? At the same time that the planners were debating these questions, others emerged. What historical aims for the college should continue? What traditions

and values long held by the college should remain? After several
weeks of debate, the planners agreed on a new mission statement. Although it contained compromises, and to some people
was not totally satisfactory, it nonetheless became a mission
statement the planning group could support.

The process of developing a statement of aims (mission
statement) can thus be a vehicle for clarifying an institution's
basic philosophy. Agreement on a mission statement can set the
stage for resolving further issues such as these: Who should our
students be? What curriculum changes are necessary? What
modifications should be made in instructional methods? And
what changes in degree formats should be considered?

Summary

Deciding on what direction to take—on what response to make
to the pressures of change and the many demands confronting
a college or university—often requires an examination of basic
aims.

Colleges and universities have been and continue to be
charged with purposelessness. Yet most faculty and administrators make assumptions about the aims of their institution, although they may not always agree on what these aims are.

A further problem is for colleges and universities to focus on unique aims, those programs and activities that the particular college or university can offer more effectively than
another educational institution or another provider of adult
education opportunities such as business and industry.

Many factors have shaped the aims of higher education.
Rapid industrial and agricultural growth influenced the starting
of the land-grant college movement. Federal research dollars
have more recently influenced the aims of research universities.
Today's social changes are causing higher education to be more
responsive to older students, both on and off campus, and to
public service activities.

Michigan State University and the College of St. Catherine
are examples of institutions that have systematically examined

their aims and made changes. Hosts of other institutions are doing the same thing.

The process of examining aims and writing mission statements can itself assist an institution in considering how it should respond to social change and the demands of a learning society.

6

Meeting the Curriculum Needs
of New Learners

A learning society means new audiences seeking educational opportunities from colleges and universities. How do these new audiences influence a college or university's curriculum? Let us first be clear about the word *curriculum.* For me, curriculum includes both credit and noncredit courses, workshops, conferences, and courses offered via media, on campus and off campus. Curriculum also includes the college or university's public service activity, which may range from a team of faculty members working with a local industry to providing assistance to newly elected government officials.

New audiences have usually meant "nontraditional students" twenty-five and older who choose to return to a college or university to work on a degree. I enlarge that definition considerably. New audiences include adults returning to higher education for undergraduate and graduate degrees. But new audiences can also include

1. Professionals, who may be required to continue their education by state law and because of professional society recertification requirements.
2. The elderly, who are generally not interested in degrees but may be interested in acquiring new job skills for a new part-time career after retirement, or are interested in participating in higher education programs for the sheer joy of learning.

3. Displaced workers, who may not only have lost their jobs, but who may have had their jobs eliminated entirely. Examples include linotype operators in the printing business and spray painters in the auto industry, to cite only two of hundreds of jobs that have been replaced by technology.
4. Special groups seeking job skills and an education. Examples include the black, Native American, and Chicano population in this country plus the thousands of immigrants, particularly from the East Asian countries and from Mexico and Central America.
5. Women, particularly those who wish to enter the job market after several years away and whose children are grown or are in school.

The new student audience is large and diverse, with a variety of interests and motivations for participating in higher education programs. The explanations adults give for participating in these programs are summarized in the accompanying table.

Reasons for Participation in Adult Education

Objective	Percent
To get a new job	12
To improve or advance on a job	48
Other job-related	4
Non-job-related	35

Source: U.S. Department of Education, 1986, p. 6.

Note: The figures do not add to 100 because they have been rounded off.

Aslanian and Brickell (1980) used a broader definition of adult education to include things people might teach themselves, such as gardening or home maintenance, in addition to educational opportunities provided by agencies and institutions, including higher education. They found that 83 percent of the learners they surveyed "described some past, present, or future change in their lives as reasons to learn" (p. 49). In addition, "Moving from one status in life to another requires the learning of new knowledge, new skills, and/or new attitudes or values" (p. 34). They also found that this learning can be "acquired informally through unstructured daily experience, or through informal but self-planned study, or through formal instruction designed and conducted by others" (p. 34).

Nearly all of the transitions Aslanian and Brickell noted began with trigger events, and these triggers affected an adult's decision to learn at a particular time. Examples of triggers included having a baby, getting fired, joining the army, having a heart attack, retiring, getting divorced, and getting elected (p. 38). Within the 83 percent who were learning because of some transition in their lives, 56 percent said they were influenced because of career (p. 54).

Seventeen percent of the adult learners in the Aslanian and Brickell study "said they were learning for other reasons: for example, because they found learning to be a satisfying activity, because it kept them mentally alert, because it gave them a chance to be with other adults, because it gave them something to do with their children, because their friends had asked them to join in learning, because they admired the teacher, or simply because it filled up their time" (pp. 49–50).

The Adult Learner and Curriculum Issues

How should the diversity of adult learners and their multiple needs and interests influence a college or university's curriculum? In recent years there has been much study and criticism of college and university curricula, particularly of undergraduate programs. Boyer's 1987 book *College: The Undergraduate Experience in America* and the Association of American Colleges' 1985 report *Integrity in the College Curriculum: A Report to the Academic Community* are recent examples.

Adult learners also have concerns about curriculum. These include questions about core curriculum and liberal arts requirements, the increased attention to jobs and vocational preparation as a major emphasis of the college, and the effects of educational technology on curriculum.

The questions related to core curriculum include the following: Should a core curriculum be required of all undergraduates? What should be in it? Who should decide on it? With increasing numbers of older students with strong job-career interests, the questions are further complicated.

Trainor (1986) says that the chief problem in terms of college and university curriculum "is the idea that faculty as a whole are not responsible for the curriculum as a whole . . . . The emphasis on specialization that frequently results has a tendency to downplay the humanities, to neglect thinking and problem-solving skills, and to overlook the development of good writing and speaking skills" (p. 94).

As we have seen, Bok (1986) observes that the following trends have occurred in undergraduate education: an increase in remedial work, a shift from liberal arts toward vocationally oriented studies, relaxed academic standards, added vocational majors, and the requirement for fewer liberal arts courses (p. 39). He raises the issue of free course selection (which to many in higher education is a holdover of the "reforms" of the 1960s) versus required courses. And he underlines the issue of gaining a body of knowledge versus having a critical education: "A critical mind, free of dogma but nourished by humane values, may be the most important product of education in a changing, fragmented society" (Bok, 1986, p. 47).

How should a core curriculum be organized? At least two positions have become popular. One is that a core curriculum is organized around courses. Or it can be organized around expected outcomes. Many colleges are attempting to focus on outcomes as a way of describing their core curriculum. For example, the approach adopted by Alverno College in Milwaukee has received considerable national attention. Alverno is a liberal arts college for women with a strong focus on preparing women for professional careers. It offers its curriculum in both a weekday and a weekend format.

All Alverno students are required to pass muster in the following areas: (1) communication, (2) analysis, (3) problem solving, (4) valuing in decision making, (5) social interaction, (6) taking responsibility for the environment, (7) involvement in the contemporary world, and (8) esthetic response. Central to Alverno's curriculum is a complex student assessment process designed to measure progress in the core curriculum areas. Letter grades are not given, but students must pass course-content examinations, and they are assessed on how well they perform in each of the ability areas. "Methods of evaluating ability levels vary . . . . A student demonstrating her ability at a particular level in analysis . . . might be required to prepare a written critique of the sound and image patterns in a poem, with her English instructor and herself as the assessors. Or, at a higher level of analysis, she might participate in an off-campus project identifying patterns in labor grievances and analyzing their causes for a manufacturing concern, with the company's labor-relations director and her management instructor as assessors" (Lewis, 1984, p. 17).

To take a second example, the School for New Learning at DePaul University is an alternative college for adults. It, too, includes a core curriculum with a focus on what individuals know and can do rather than the accumulation of credit through course work. The bachelor of arts program at the School for New Learning is based on a framework of fifty competencies, grouped in five areas: (1) world of work—competencies related to the student's chosen career; (2) human community—competencies concerning understanding social groups, organizations, and society at large; (3) physical world—competencies about the natural sciences, mathematics, health, and the physical environment; (4) the arts of living—competencies concerning the fine arts, leisure, philosophy, and spiritual values; and (5) lifelong learning—competencies concerning an adult's ability to pursue education in all aspects of his or her life (School for New Learning, 1987).

The School for New Learning developed its approach mindful of the varying characteristics of adult learners. As David Justice, dean of the school, points out, "The assumptions that were made in the beginning [in the early 1970s when it was founded] were very important to the subsequent growth and development of the school . . . . If you're going to admit adults, you have to acknowledge and take into consideration the fact that they come back to school with widely varying characteristics, skills, knowledge, ability, and the like. And if you're going to be fair to them, and not make them repeat or spend time in class learning things that they already know, you have to radically individualize the programs" (personal communication, Feb. 17, 1987).

Justice describes the philosophy of the school's curriculum this way: "The idea was not a radically performance based approach as competence based teacher education in the prior decade had become, but rather an approach that tried to articulate as clearly and concisely as possible what the outcomes, what the expected characteristics of an educated adult in contemporary society ought to be. And then to work back from that through both assessment, and teaching and learning opportunities to bring each graduate up to that level" (personal communication, Feb. 17, 1987).

The School for New Learning puts heavy emphasis on individual differences. Justice explains that "the school begins for most adults with the development of evidences of prior learning and their assessment by a committee against the competence statements. Once those are assessed, the student is in a position to chart out and plan for his or her 'new learning,' hence the name for the school. We both take cognizance of, and grant credit for prior learning, and we design our curriculum to provide a variety of opportunities for adults to attain the appropriate new learning. As a result, each student's program is quite different from every other student's. . . . Since there is not a standard curriculum and there is not a standard set of majors, each student devises his or her own major with the advice and consent of an academic committee" (personal communication, Feb. 17, 1987).

Thus for both Alverno College and the School for New Learning, there is an emphasis on core curriculum, though with a considerably different slant than we ordinarily associate with the term *core curriculum.* The emphasis is not on a series of required courses that all students will take in certain areas. Rather it is on outcomes, on what the students will know and be able to do upon completion of the program. Learning opportunities are arranged into broad areas of knowledge and skills, and courses are selected based on the students' previous knowledge and experience. This is particularly the case with the School for New Learning.

A recent criticism that has challenged colleges and universities is the smorgasbord approach to curriculum. Students choose whatever courses they want. Overreaction to the smorgasbord curriculum is forcing all students to take the same courses. This is a particular problem for adult students who have varied backgrounds and knowledge, and who may have already gained much of the knowledge represented by certain required courses in a "new" core curriculum.

Another question is whether a separate curriculum should be developed for adults (or the same curriculum could be made available in alternative ways). This second issue grows out of the first. Because adults are considerably different from the younger, so-called traditional college students who come to a campus fresh out of high school, many college and university administrators argue that there should be a separate curriculum for each group. In effect, the School for New Learning just described provides an example of this approach. Metropolitan College at the University of New Orleans is another example. Metropolitan College offers both credit and noncredit continuing education and international programs with particular emphasis on adult students. Some 1,000 different programs are offered each year. And although adults may take credit courses at Metropolitan College, if they wish to earn degrees they may transfer up to 30 semester hours of undergraduate credit earned as a special student and up to 12 hours of graduate credit earned as a graduate nondegree student to degree programs at the University of New Orleans.

A number of institutions offer essentially the same curriculum to younger and older students, but for older students they offer more variety in formats—courses offered in the late afternoon or evening, off-campus courses, or courses offered on weekends. (Alverno College and the College of St. Catherine are examples, along with many other institutions.)

Still other institutions make parts of their curriculum available using a variety of media forms. The University of Wisconsin–Madison, for some of its courses, uses the educational telephone network. Students gather at network sites throughout the state and listen to an instructor. Then, via telephone, they raise questions with the instructor. Some institutions have developed television courses, videotape and audiotape courses, and computer courses. (Specific examples will follow in the chapter on teaching approaches.)

Concerns about curriculum planning are also raised. Who should be involved, how should they be involved, and what role should outside and inside environmental forces have on curriculum changes?

Much curriculum planning in higher education these days really is not curriculum planning at all. At many colleges and universities, the curriculum grows out of a department's view of its discipline area. New courses are generally developed by an individual faculty member who submits the course proposal to a departmental curriculum committee. This committee checks possible overlap with other courses. But often the committee spends little time discussing why the course is needed (as long as enrollments are ensured), or how the course might fit into some longer-term plan for curriculum change.

On many campuses, a school and/or campus curriculum committee reviews the course proposal. Once again the primary concern is for overlap with existing courses. This campus oversight committee also often considers the comprehensiveness with which the proposal is written as another criterion for acceptance or rejection. Little attention, at any level, is spent discussing where the proposed course fits into any larger picture. And thus departmental offerings, and in turn college offerings, often develop accumulations of individual course decision making, with little or no attention to any longer-term plan.

In the noncredit area, other forces come into play. A major criterion in deciding whether or not a new noncredit course will be approved is whether it will attract enough people to pay its way. Attracting sufficient students is of course an issue for credit courses, too, but student numbers are far more of an issue for noncredit courses.

Gordon Mueller, vice chancellor of Metropolitan College,

University of New Orleans, explains the money-making situation and its effect on curriculum planning this way: "Time is a real enemy to planning, because in most continuing education shops . . . we have to live like a business. We're very much in an entrepreneurial mode. When you have half of your personnel in your budget depending on your generating revenues and enrollment it gets your attention . . . . It comes down to a real craziness of trying to keep your product developed and out the door so you can get your students and your revenue in. It seems like there's more crisis management than there is good planning, at least as much planning as we would like" (personal communication, Feb. 9, 1987).

Mueller goes on to explain the particular problems that he and Metropolitan College have faced in the past several years (mid 1980s): "I think we've had a lot more than our share of dislocations in the last two or three years because of the tremendous financial crisis that our state and city has been facing. This crisis has led to massive budget cuts in higher education, and that makes it tough to fight for planning time, and it does take time to prepare for our planning retreats where we systematically spell out goals and objectives for the next 18 months or two years. People are saying that all this planning takes so much time that we could actually be getting product developed and sold. . . . But you really have to plan and fight for it, it's just difficult some times" (personal communication, Feb. 9, 1987).

Cooperative extension, a part of land-grant college continuing education activity, has a long history of careful and elaborate planning taking place at county, college, and national levels. Because cooperative extension is, in part, funded from Smith–Lever federal dollars, it is mandated to do formal planning. Presently formal, four-year plans, with yearly updates, are developed by each state cooperative extension service, including four-year and annual plans of work for each cooperative extension faculty member. One could criticize cooperative extension for spending too much time planning and not enough time carrying out programs. In fact, in recent years, cooperative extension has come under considerable pressure, particularly from the executive branch of the federal government, for not keeping up to date with its programming.

An example of a long-range cooperative extension planning effort that has gained national attention is one carried out in Georgia and called Georgia: 2000. Georgia: 2000 is an interesting case study of a university and its cooperative extension attempting to respond to societal forces.

Tal DuVall, Georgia cooperative extension director, explains the reasons behind this planning effort: "I guess the idea came from two directions. Number one, and probably most important, is the change that's occurring in Georgia. The state is now the fourth or the fifth fastest growing state in the nation. There are rural changes, economic changes, and minority population changes. And there is much pressure to deal with these changes. There is migration into the sunbelt . . . . We've had a 33 percent increase in population in the last 15 years. There is trauma in agriculture that has resulted in two Georgias, a North Georgia and a South Georgia. North Georgia is economically exploding and South Georgia is stagnating" (personal communication, Jan. 21, 1987).

DuVall explained some practical reasons for the planning effort, from the institution's perspective: "I guess we went about [the planning effort] selfishly because I saw that here was a state extension service of 1600 people and a $50 million budget . . . . How long would we be funded if the state perceived us as only agricultural? So I went out and recruited 50 Georgia leaders and asked them to look at Georgia and let the Extension Service help facilitate the process. In the process of doing [the long range planning] I felt that we could learn and gain some insight [into the state's problems] and could align ourselves with the state's leadership in making decisions" (personal communication, Jan. 21, 1987).

As we have seen, curriculum planning approaches vary considerably in higher education. This is particularly so when we include noncredit continuing education activity that must earn its own way, and cooperative extension that includes budget from federal, state, and county sources and feels pressures considerably different from those experienced by degree-credit departments on campuses.

The Commission on Higher Education and the Adult Learner, a joint project of the American Council on Education (ACE), the Council for Adult and Experiential Learning (CAEL), the National University Continuing Education Association (NUCEA), and the University of Maryland University College, has developed a helpful self-study assessment and planning guide for colleges and universities. The guide seems most useful for those colleges and universities wishing to appraise the quality of their services for adult learners, or their readiness to serve adults if they are not already doing so (Warren, 1986b). Information gathered from the assessment can provide a useful base for curriculum planning intent on providing greater opportunities for adult learners.

For example, in the section "Needs Assessment," the following are examples of performance assessment statements:

"Adult learners presently enrolled have been asked to give their opinions about programs and services now available."

"Adult learners presently enrolled have been asked for suggestions as to desirable new programs or services."

"Written needs assessment has been written or is in progress."

"Needs assessment developed in consultation with interested external institutions and agencies" (Commission on Higher Education and the Adult Learner and the American Council on Education, 1984).

Working through this self-assessment exercise can be an excellent first step in curriculum planning.

Special Programs for Special Audiences

Without trying to be inclusive, in the following pages I will discuss some examples of higher education curricular efforts focusing on particular audiences.

The Elderly   A 1984 survey of who participates in adult education indicated that 5.6 percent of those 55 and older enrolled in some type of adult education course (U.S. Department of Education, 1986). This may not seem like a large percentage, particularly when compared to 16.9 percent, which is the percentage of those aged 35–54 who enroll in educational programs. But two facts should be noted. As I have pointed out earlier, the number of older persons in this country is on the rise and will continue to rise into the next century. And, second, the formal educational level of these older Americans will continue to be at an all-time high. There is, of course, a strong correlation between level of formal education and the desire to seek further education. Thus the numbers of those enrolling in adult education activities will increase, both in terms of percentage and in terms of actual numbers.

The Institute of Lifetime Learning of the American Association of Retired Persons has summarized considerable information about older learners. It reports that 27 percent of these older learners took a course at a college or university, 24 percent at a community or senior center, 18 percent at a place of business, 7 percent at a high school, and the remainder at various community-based settings such as museums, churches, synagogues, and libraries (Institute of Lifetime Learning, 1986, pp. 7–8).

Thus a large percentage of older learners will participate in higher education programs, if a number of factors are taken into account. "Older people form a distinct subgroup in terms of educational needs and interests . . . . There is a wider gap between the learning interests of young and old than between elderly rich and poor, men and women, black and white, or rural and urban residents. Adult learners have their own agendas and want the most direct route to obtaining specific knowledge. Since regular college curriculums are oriented toward degree-seeking, career-minded younger students, their mandatory courses often hold no interest for the mature learner" (Institute of Lifetime Learning, 1986, p. 9). The Institute of Lifetime Learning reports that older persons often take courses that (1) provide a continued sense of meaning through philosophy, religion, language, literature, and arts (39 percent); and (2) provide a sense of control or coping through physical education, health care sciences, business courses, and home economics (34 percent). An increasing percentage of older learners are also taking courses for job-related reasons. Nearly one-fourth of older learners gave this reason in a 1981 study (Institute of Lifetime Learning, 1986, p. 7). A fundamental question is "how the elderly, especially those with limited or outmoded educational qualifications, will acquire the skill or competence to perform tasks that are unfamiliar to them and for which they have not been equipped by earlier experience" (Morris and Bass, 1986, p. 15).

Some would argue that the task of providing such skills falls to the vocational and technical schools. But Morris and Bass (1986) argue that colleges and universities can play an important role: "A university can provide a concentrated period of competency building which equips interested elders to perform complex significant tasks to fill new and significant service or decision-making roles in their communities . . . . A university can develop a liaison and active coalition with non-profit civic groups and public authorities to ensure that a mechanism exists for moving from competency acquisition into significant roles" (p. 16).

A number of colleges and universities across the country have developed continuing education programs designed specifically for older adults interested in educational, cultural, and social opportunities. A recent publication of the National Association of Retired Persons lists some ninety-three programs designed specifically for older learners in thirty-four states plus the District of Columbia (Institute of Lifetime Learning, 1986).

Many college and universities have policies where those past sixty-two or past sixty-five may enroll in credit courses as visitors without paying a fee. Retired people have been attracted to these opportunities and have enrolled in courses ranging from English literature to horticulture. The Elderhostel is an example of an extremely successful noncredit residential program offered by colleges and universities throughout the country, and in many other countries as well.

It is clear that merely making available the traditional degree-related courses will not satisfy this rapidly growing older population. If colleges and universities wish to include this growing student audience, many will have to look seriously at new curricular options and new curriculum planning approaches —often involving older students in the planning process. Otherwise, these older learners will turn elsewhere for their continuing learning.

Business and Professional People   During the last two decades or so, many colleges and universities have increasingly offered continuing professional education. As Stern (1983) points out, "More than fifteen million people are classified as professionals in the United States. These millions have become the crucial cadres of the work force for the survival of the society and of the economy, too. As the leaders and agents of the technological revolution of our time they have to keep learning to maintain and improve their skills and knowledge. Also, increasingly they are compelled to do so by state law and professional society recertification requirements" (p. 5).

In the executive management area alone, some $80 million dollars a year is spent by corporations determined to keep their managers informed about the newest ideas in marketing, finance, and executive development (Koberstein, 1986, p. 23). Particularly through their extension and continuing education divisions, colleges and universities have devised a wide array of learning opportunities for these professionals. Some of the most innovative programs in higher education have been developed in response to demands from business and professional people for continuing education opportunities. Examples include the National Technological University, a continuing education degree program organized by various universities and corporations to provide graduate education to engineers around the world; off-campus master's of business administration programs offered by a host of institutions; special part-time programs leading to both bachelor's and master's degrees in business administration or computer science—for example, programs offered by the University of California, Santa Barbara, at its University Center at Ventura; and a host of noncredit courses, workshops, and conferences provided by a majority of the colleges and universities.

On many campuses, the continuing professional education programs are big money-makers. But they are often not seen as mainstream activities of the professional schools on these campuses. "Professional school faculty members have in the past been generally apathetic or opposed to the provision of lifelong learning. The need to deal with full-time pre-service students, who are abundantly and often vociferously present and who have always been the center of concern of formal professional training, means that the desires and problems of adult student bodies (often unfamiliar, external, and dispersed) are not viewed as significant" (Houle, 1980, p. 176).

Thus, at many institutions, professional school degree programs and continuing professional education activities are administratively separate. The former is seen as a part of the degree-credit programs of the institution, the latter a function of the continuing education division. The faculty of the professional schools and the continuing education divisions, in some larger institutions, scarcely know each other.

If higher education is going to continue making contributions to the learning society by providing learning opportunities for business and professional people, it must do considerable housecleaning. It would seem only logical that professional school faculty and continuing education faculty combine their efforts in providing continuing professional education. It would also seem logical that some of the same faculty teaching pre-professional courses would teach continuing professional education courses as well.

Career Changers   Many adults seeking assistance from higher education are career changers. And a large percentage are women, particularly women who have been out of the job market for some time and want to return. Continuing education programs focusing on women have expanded rapidly during the

past fifteen years. "To a large extent, this expansion has resulted from the increasing numbers of women seeking employment, technological changes that have reduced housework, declining birth rates, longer life spans, rising living costs, and
encouragement and support by the women's movement" (Astin,
1976a, p. 56).

In my own department at the University of Wisconsin-
Madison, women returning for advanced degrees made up about
40 percent of our graduate students in 1975. Today they represent nearly 65 percent. These figures are quite representative of
what is happening across the country.

As Astin (1976a) explains, "Women who participate in
continuing education programs are an exceedingly diverse group
that does not fit the stereotype of the bored housewife dabbling
in a little culture. These women are serious, determined, and
very frequently pragmatic in their goals. Those women who enter continuing education with a strong career orientation differ
in many respects from the other participants: they express less
traditional views about the role of women, are more supportive
of the women's movement, and have more self-confidence"
(p. 59).

The number of career changers in society, both men and
women, is increasing. What adjustments will colleges and universities make in their programs to accommodate this group? Bok
(1986) puts his finger on the issue: "In the face of this new interest [adults seeking college and university programs], we need
to think more seriously about the proper place of continuing
education in the university . . . . When a university begins to attract nontraditional students in numbers several times the regular enrollment, it cannot go on squeezing in midcareer programs
during weekends and vacations. The moment has come to reconsider the place of nontraditional programs in the regular
work of the institution" (p. 120).

Examining what response a college or university will
make to the demands of the adult audience will of necessity
mean examining the curriculum. The assumption that the traditional curriculum will fit the wants and needs of an adult audience, with all of its diversity, must be challenged.

Summary

When considering curricular changes necessary for colleges and universities in light of a learning society, a broader definition of curriculum must be used. I define curriculum to include both credit and noncredit offerings, workshops, conferences, and courses offered via media on campus or at a distance. Curriculum also includes a college or university's public service activity, and for land-grant institutions, the programs conducted by cooperative extension.

The adult audiences seeking learning opportunities from higher education are diverse, ranging from those returning to school for undergraduate and graduate degrees, to professionals required to continue their education by state law, to the elderly, displaced workers, and women. A majority of those coming to higher education do so for job-related reasons. Some 83 percent seek out education because of some past, present, or future change in their lives.

With this diversity of adult learners and their wide-ranging needs, institutions of higher education are faced with the question of what curriculum changes should be made. Curriculum changes relate to core curriculum; does the concept of core curriculum fit the adult learner? There is much disagreement on the question of a separate curriculum for adult learners. With respect to curriculum planning approaches, how much should the marketplace influence what goes into a curriculum?

A systematic needs-assessment approach, with a focus on adult learners, may be one way to start a planning process. The elderly, business and professional people, career changers, women, and displaced workers all have special curriculum needs. The challenge for higher education curriculum planners is how to respond. A further challenge is how and when to integrate curricula designed for special audiences with the total curricula of the institution.

7

Diversifying Instructional
Methods and Approaches

At least three major factors influence the selection of instructional methods for older students: (1) the nature of adults as learners, (2) the availability of educational technology, and (3) the trend toward an information society or knowledge explosion.

The Nature of Adults As Learners

Much has been written about the adult as learner and about strategies for instructing adults (Apps, 1981, 1985; Knowles, 1980; Brookfield, 1986; Knox, 1986, 1977; Houle, 1984; Cross, 1981; Tough, 1982). Knowles (1980) was one of the first to claim that differences between younger and older learners exist. He popularized the term *andragogy*, which is widely used by those associated with adult education. For Knowles, andragogy means the art and science of helping adults learn. Although many authors (including Apps, 1985; Cross, 1981; Brookfield, 1986) have raised questions about Knowles' concept of andragogy, it continues as a basis for understanding differences between adults and children insofar as learning is concerned.

Knowles (1980) bases the idea of andragogy on four assumptions about adults as learners. He says that "as individuals mature: (1) their self-concept moves from one of being a dependent personality toward being a self-directed human being; (2) they accumulate a growing reservoir of experience that becomes an increasingly rich resource for learning; (3) their readiness to learn becomes oriented increasingly to the developmental tasks of their social roles; and (4) their time perspective changes from one of postponed application of knowledge to immediacy of application and accordingly, their orientation toward learning shifts from one of subject-centeredness to one of performance-centeredness" (pp. 44–45).

Many of those involved in adult education decline to accept all of Knowles' assumptions, however. In particular, his assumption about the self-directedness of adults has been challenged. Many authorities do not agree that educators of adults are limited to facilitating the learning environment and in effect do not teach. According to his argument, if adults are by nature self-directing, then we need only provide the proper conditions —some materials, a congenial learning environment, a properly raised question from time to time—and learning will occur. Indeed there are times when this teaching approach is the most appropriate. But there are many other times when the educator of adults must make decisions about educational content and must teach in a more traditional fashion, since self-directedness is probably less common than Knowles maintains: "We must conclude . . . that while self-directiveness is a desirable condition of human existence it is seldom found in any abundance. Its rarity, however, in no sense weakens the view that the enhancement of self-directiveness is the proper purpose of education; instead, it provides a compelling reason why education should pursue this end with unflagging zeal" (Brookfield, 1986, pp. 94–95).

Reading the adult education liteature, we find a number of themes that I believe have application in higher education. It will be worthwhile to comment on a few of the more important ones.

Active Role: The adult learner should have an active role in the learning process (this is of course true for younger learners as well). The adult learner (younger learners, too) can make positive contributions to the development of curriculum, the establishment of his or her own learning objectives, and the selection of learning methods.

Experience: In most learning situations, the adult brings an experience that can add to the learning environment. It must be noted, though, that there are other times when the adult's experiences may not contribute, and in fact may be a negative influence. I remember a class I was teaching made up entirely of older, returning students. One of the students insisted on sharing her social work experiences in reference to every topic we discussed, whether they were relevant or not. In fact, some of the experiences she wanted to share and insisted were "the way to do it" were not the way to do it according to established principles.

The Need for Practical Applications: Adults respond to learning that is problem centered and for which they can see applications in their work or their daily lives. In many situations the case-study approach works well. Internships have also become a popular learning approach for those topics where "hands-on" experience is critical to learning. In my own university department, we often place our older students in a variety of internship settings, many of them in business and industry, where they can learn such topics as adult training and development firsthand. Combined with classwork, the internship experience provides the problem-centered learning that many students often search for.

Concurrent Status: The adult learner is a concurrent student. The adult who participates in a degree program or takes part in other higher education opportunities is a part-time student, even if registered for full-time study. The adult student generally has a family, participates in community activities, and may work full or part time. Enrolling in a course or a workshop is but one of many tasks he or she attends to, and higher education is but one of many activities in the person's life.

The Process of Unlearning: For most adult learners, unlearning is an essential part of the learning process. Often an adult learner must set aside old ideas, old ways of thinking, and old skills. Unlearning must occur before the new learning can be attended to. The unlearning process for many adults can be a troublesome, painful process that takes time. In some ways, one can compare unlearning to the grieving process. The adult who is unlearning clearly grieves the loss of old ideas, attitudes, skills, and ways of doing things that are replaced with new approaches. Within the area of unlearning, great differences often exist between younger and older learners. Older learners have lived longer and have had an opportunity to learn more.

As More (1974) points out, "We have to undertake this process of unlearning frequently in our lives, particularly when we become adult students. And it is the experience of most adult students that this is very often not an easy task. It is not an easy task because it is tied up with the whole problem of attitude change. All of our behavior is an expression of what we are and what life has made us, and this includes the attitudes which we have developed. Everything we do reflects what we think and feel about people, events, objects and phenomena" (p. 19).

Problem Areas: Adults returning to higher education face various barriers. In research I conducted (Apps, 1981), the following emerged as problem areas—problems with concentration and time use, problems with study skills, problems relating to instructors in class situations, and problems with unlearning. For those adults entering higher education degree programs, the most dramatic difference between adult and younger freshmen was in mathematics skills, particularly algebra skills. In research conducted by the Wisconsin Assessment Center (1983) comparing adults enrolling in a college degree program as freshmen, and freshmen coming directly from a high school program, the following was noted: "On all math tests given to incoming freshmen, adults scored significantly lower than younger students. Without a doubt, the adult freshmen were less able to recall and apply concepts from algebra and geometry. . . . Without refresher coursework, many adults will be at a disadvantage in the area of mathematics" (p. 9).

In addition to these academically related problems, older students have other problems that often are not experienced by the younger, more traditional students who participate in higher education. These problems include unrealistic goals, poor self-image, social-familial problems, and a sometimes excessively practical orientation.

Many adult learners, particularly those who have been

away from formal education for many years, believe that they can accomplish far more in a period of time than is humanly possible. They are highly motivated when they enroll in a class, and they may and usually do accomplish a great deal. But they are often frustrated that they are not accomplishing more. For those entering degree programs, it generally takes several months before the person develops a more realistic view of what he or she can accomplish. During this adjustment time, instructors and fellow students must display considerable patience and understanding.

Negative self-image about ability to perform in higher education comes from being out of school for a period of time. Returning students worry that they will say something that their fellow students will think dumb, they fear that they will fail, they believe that their study skills are so rusty that they cannot keep up with the other students, and so on. In some cases their study skills are rusty, but a few months of study and perhaps a study skills workshop generally solve the problem. Attaining some success soon after they enroll helps bolster a shaky self-concept. Instructors should plan to give early feedback. An examination, a paper assignment, or even a verbal comment in response to a contribution in class discussion helps a returning student know where he or she stands.

A family problem or a negative comment by a friend or an employer can seriously inhibit an adult's learning. When he or she decides to participate in a degree program, a workshop, or a noncredit course, in many ways it is a decision that involves several other people. A spouse and children often create stress for the adult learner, even when they are supportive of the activity. Money is involved—for fees, baby-sitters, and transportation. And travel, class, and study time are involved, time that could otherwise have been spent with the children or with a spouse. When the spouse and/or children do not approve of the person's involvement in higher education, the stresses, as might be expected, are even worse.

It is important for instructors of older students to realize that the student's experience, intellectual ability, and learning style are but a sample of the factors influencing performance in a classroom, independent study course, workshop, or whatever activity is involved.

How does this knowledge help instructors and administrators make decisions about instructional approaches? Are the differences between younger and older students so great that instructional approaches must be different for the two groups of learners?

The differences between younger and older students, with a few exceptions, are in fact not so great that dramatic shifts in instructional approaches need be made to accommodate adult students. But it may be necessary for higher education to make some rather important shifts in its instructional approaches to accommodate all of its students, young and old alike. Many of the principles for adult learners apply equally well to younger learners. In research I conducted (Apps, 1981, pp. 112–113) to describe exemplary characteristics of instructors of adult students, I discovered the following. Outstanding instructors of adult learners are (1) more concerned about their students than about things and events, (2) know their subject matter, (3) can relate theory to practice and can relate their field to other fields, (4) are confident as instructors, (5) are open to a wide variety of teaching approaches, (6) share their whole person rather than segregating their instructional role from the rest of their lives, and (7) encourage course work that goes beyond course objectives. Many younger students tell me that they would also prefer instructors with these characteristics.

Let us come back to instructional methods for a moment. According to my research, the exemplary instructor of adult students is one who uses a variety of teaching approaches. Just as there is no one best teaching approach in teaching younger students, the same holds when teaching adults. Some educators of adults argue that small-group discussion, with ample involvement of students and little involvement of the instructor except to raise questions and keep the discussion going, is the only way to teach adults. My research and that of others (Brookfield, 1986; Freedman, 1987) simply does not support this premise.

That is not to suggest that small-group discussion should be eliminated as an instructional approach. It should not, of course. It is an excellent teaching approach, and should be used where it is important that experiences be shared and multiple viewpoints explored.

There are also times when the lecture approach is valid and is an excellent choice. It is particularly appropriate when it is necessary to provide new information, quickly, to a large group. Lecturing also can be a strong motivator for learners, encouraging them to go on to do further learning through reading. And a lecture, if done well, can illustrate how at least one person is able to wrestle with a large amount of information and integrate and make sense out of it (assuming that the instructor involved does this when lecturing).

But there are other alternatives, of course. With the availability of educational technology, and in particular with the tremendous amount of information available to most higher education students with a few keystrokes of a computer, it may not necessarily make sense for professors to spend time dispensing information in lecture halls crowded with students rapidly scratching notes.

When making decisions about instructional approaches for adult learners, three kinds of factors seem most important: (1) the students themselves, their learning styles, their formal education, their work and other life experiences, and their reasons for enrolling in a higher education program; (2) the nature of the content being considered—the extent to which it is entirely new to the students, such as certain aspects of computer science might be, or the extent to which the students may have already had some practical experience with the material, as in the case of a study of family relationships; and (3) the instructional resources available (not every institution has computer-assisted instruction or satellite communication technology readily available to all of its instructors).

This suggests that instructors of adult students are not charged with learning one instructional approach and following it without variation. As in instructing younger students, a variety of approaches may be used, including lectures, discussions, lecture-discussion, and independent study, as well as a broad range of instructional technology—computer-assisted instruction, courses on television, educational telephone, radio with call-in, satellite communication, and so on. This brings us to our next topic, the influence of the information society on instructional approaches.

The Availability of Educational Technology

Some of the most innovative instructional approaches include the use of educational technology, particularly the use of computers, videotapes, and satellite communication. As we will see, these have a wide range of applications in higher education.

A criticism of much educational technology of the past, including television, radio, and film, was its emphasis on one-way communication. A student sat and listened or listened and watched but was not otherwise involved. Computers offer the potential for much more than this. As Bork (1987) explains, "The main advantage of the computer as a way of learning is that it allows us to make learning interactive for all students. We can then pay attention to the needs of each student by individualizing the learning experience" (p. 201).

Most colleges and universities have now incorporated computers into their on-campus instructional programs in one way or another. Computers offer an interesting potential for teaching adults, because computer courses can be offered in a distance format. The adult student need not travel to a campus, or for that matter travel anywhere, because he or she can participate in the course from a home computer.

Nova University in Fort Lauderdale, Florida, has experimented for several years in offering nontraditional degree programs for adult students. Often controversial, and criticized by the more traditional colleges and universities, Nova has continued to innovate. As mentioned earlier, Nova developed a computer-based degree program that involves microcomputers, modems, and telecommunication networks. Five degree programs that use the computer as a basis for instruction are currently offered: doctor of arts in information science, doctor of arts in training and learning, doctor of education in computer education, doctor of science in computer science, and master of science in computer-based learning. Students from twenty-six different states conduct on-line classwork in conjunction with lecturers who teach the seminars. Students complete their on-line work, directly tied to Nova's main computer. They do their off-line work with their own microcomputers, using word processing software. Students can ask questions via electronic mail. In the Nova program, they spend an average of forty hours per course on-line and double that amount working with their microcomputer. Each course lasts six months and includes two weekend seminars (Friday night and all day Saturday). Five seminar sites are distributed throughout the United States.

Another example of extensive computer course offering is the Electronic University Network in San Francisco. Rather than offering its own degrees, the Electronic University Network is a consortium of instructors and accredited colleges and universities throughout the country that delivers courses and degree programs via personal computers. The network connects the personal computers of students to the personal computers of instructors via standard telephone lines.

Students may enroll in individual courses, in professional certificate programs, or complete degree programs. Degree programs offered include associate in arts, associate in science in management, bachelor of arts, bachelor of science in business administration, and master of business administration. Short-term certificates for credit are available in information management, operations management, management of human resources, marketing, finance, and accounting. A typical course includes readings in textbooks and study guides, assignments to be completed on course disks, and question-and-answer sessions via electronic mail with the instructor. The great advantage of the Electronic University Network program for adult students is their opportunity to study at home, at their own pace.

University of Wisconsin–Madison Professor Ken Lee teaches a course in nutrition that is simultaneously videotaped and presented live to remote classrooms via cable television. Lee is thus able to reach as many as 750 students at one time but in different locations, and also to make his course available to the public off campus. Though Lee's course has been well accepted,

there have also been problems: "It didn't sound at all complicated, but after I got into it, I saw that it was extremely complicated," he said. When asked if he would do it again, he replied,
"Yes, I would do it again, but it is so time consuming" (personal communication, Jan. 15, 1987). Lee believes that once he
has moved his course into a videotape format, further offerings
will be less time consuming:

> I've done the hard work of changing everything
> over to a visual format, putting everything on col-
> ored paper instead of white because the white pa-
> per is too bright. Once you do all that, then you
> can get creative. If you really did a good job with
> something in the past, and it's on video tape, you
> can take that piece of tape and show it again. No
> need to reinvent the wheel. If you had a guest lec-
> turer who subsequently took another job, which
> happened to me, I can show part of this lecture
> rather than say, "Well, we used to have a really
> great person come to us and talk, but he's no long-
> er available." So what it does—you're building a
> library, a video library, which can be used directly
> in instruction. You're eliminating the need for going
> into a filing cabinet and pulling out a yellow pad
> and notes, interpreting what you've written there
> and updating it, and then telling the students again,
> based on memory, of what you told them a year or
> a semester ago. With the video tapes you don't
> need to do that. You can just go look at the tapes,
> see how you did it, and you can make the neces-
> sary improvements and updates [personal commu-
> nication, Jan. 15, 1987].

California State University at Chico uses satellite teleconferencing to offer several of its courses to off-campus students.
Covering some 33,000 square miles of Northern California, and
with a resident population of 600,000 people, the university
faced the question of how to service such a wide area by relying
on instructors traveling to remote sites. The most distant site is

located in a high school in Yreka, 173 miles north of the campus. The easternmost site is 140 miles away, at the U.S. Sierra Army Depot at Herlong.

On-campus students attend their classes "live" with the off-campus students. The courses are taught by regular on-campus faculty, and all the students pay the same fees, no matter where they might be taking a particular course. The system currently involves one-way video and two-way audio. In using this system, sixteen new classrooms were essentially created without the need to hire additional faculty or build new buildings.

Many of the relatively new educational technologies allow learners to work alone, often in their homes, and at their own speed. There are great advantages to this approach to instruction, particularly for the busy adult who is juggling family, work, and community responsibilities. Research by Michael Moore (1986), who was formerly with the Open University in Great Britain, found that students studying at a distance expect the following:

1. *They want a solid body of knowledge that may include attention to skills and attitudes.* For most adult learners there is great interest in practical knowledge that will help them keep up to date with their professions and their personal interests.

2. *They assume that the knowledge will be presented with accompanying guides to learning.* These guides can include suggested strategies for learning the material, and, when both print and media materials are presented, should include attempts to show the relationships between the two. One of the shortcomings of many off-campus, independent study programs is maintaining the interest and motivation of the participant. Such approaches as informal exercises, reading interspersed with periods of listening to tapes, watching video, or computer work—depending on the format of the course—will help to ensure continuing motivation and interest.

3. *Learners expect to actively participate in the learning process.* This may mean writing papers or responding to an instructor with electronic mail. Such "active" learning gives the participants an opportunity to think about or in effect "try on" their new learning.

4. *Once such a learning product is created, the partici-*

pants expect a response from the instructor. They want to know if they have a clear understanding of the material, or if a particular application of the knowledge they have worked out is one that is consistent with the knowledge.

5. *When unanticipated problems arise, such as a crisis at home, an unforeseen job assignment, unexpected difficulty with the course, and a host of other such problems, the participants expect counsel on what alternatives might be followed.* Thus, advice and counseling are a necessary ingredient of independent study, learning-at-a-distance courses (Moore, 1986, pp. 5–10).

Learning-at-a-distance courses, whether computer-based, videotaped, cable television, radio, or some combination, require careful development. Dirr (1985) observes that "a common goal shared by those producing courses for television, radio and computer distribution is to combine the highest academic scholarship with the best possible production techniques to create courses that will motivate the learner, pace the learning, and be solid academic experiences . . . . Most courses are created by production teams that consist of subject matter experts, instructional design experts, production personnel, and research and evaluation personnel" (pp. 95–96). Dirr further points out that "in all respects, the courses are designed to be as rigorous as or more rigorous than comparable on-campus courses" (p. 96).

Several criticisms have been leveled against learning-at-a-distance courses that involve teams of production people in addition to the professor or other content people. The first and probably most obvious is the cost. Courses designed for computers and television cost thousands of dollars. On the other hand, such courses, once produced, are relatively inexpensive for a college or university to purchase and offer. In those instances where a college or university chooses to purchase an externally produced course (one produced by some other institution), "It requires faculty members to change from being creators of instruction to being managers of resources and students and from speaking for themselves to disseminating someone else's views" (Grossman, 1987, p. 104). Grossman (1987) points out that in those instances where the professor wishes to develop a course for electronic delivery, he or she is in for a rude awakening. "Instead of controlling the process, they find that they have to take a back seat to production and technical personnel. The financial backer or media producer takes charge, and while the faculty member's name may be on the course, he or she is usually only an adjunct to its development" (p. 104).

Grossman argues that it is possible to offer off-campus students quality instruction (he does not see the prepackaged media courses as quality instruction) by encouraging faculty members to develop their own media courses and programs. But such institutions should be "prepared to spend lavishly for the hardware, technical support, and the professors' extra work" (p. 104).

Keppel and Chickering (1981) offer suggestions that represent middle ground. They suggest (1) developing inexpensive, flexible materials locally that "capitalize on local resources and respond to particularly salient student motives and backgrounds and (2) taking advantage of major productions of commercial networks, educational television, and national public radio" (p. 627). Others have also criticized educational technology. Fleit (1987) suggests that "perhaps no higher expectations have been raised for computers than in the area of instruction. Totally electronic instruction—students without teachers, classrooms, books—has been predicted for at least 20 years, and yet several studies have shown that an electronic classroom may be no more effective for learning than the traditional, non-computerized one" (p. 96). Fleit is speaking from the perspective of on campus teaching, of course. Even in off-campus teaching, it is clear that an instructor must be involved for the course to be most effective. One of the problems experienced with television courses is the loneliness element, the student staring at the screen and receiving but having no opportunity to share. New course designs with opportunities for two-way communication either by telephone or through electronic mail or direct computer ties help to eliminate this problem.

Kay Kohl, executive director of the National University Continuing Education Association, also has reservations about educational technology. "I think one has to look at the utilization of technology in very hard economic terms. I am not persuaded that, given very scarce economic resources, educational television is the place I would put large amounts of dollars at this time. The production costs are so enormous that it's very hard to justify that kind of expenditure for the product you get, particularly at the undergraduate level. At the graduate level, where you have the possibility of attracting corporate sponsorship, such delivery systems have more promise" (personal communication, Mar. 26, 1987). Kohl mentions two other problems. Those potential participants who have not had college experience have great difficulty with a correspondence, self-directed format, while those more affluent learners who already own home computers and VCRs are quite accustomed to self-directed learning via computer and video. But as Kohl notes, "I doubt that universities will have the capacity to gear up rapidly to address the needs of this audience (the more affluent learners). I think it will be the commercial publishers in the commercial realm who will get there first" (personal communication, Mar. 26, 1987).

Even with the many problems and concerns voiced by administrators and faculty members, information technology will have a considerable influence on higher education, particularly with off-campus courses.

Bonham (1983) believes that computer mania is sweeping the country, with profound implications for educational policy decisions. "For the first time in the history of American education, a significant new force is almost exclusively controlled by profit-making corporations, with the result that much of the future shape of computer education is being determined by computer manufacturers and major textbook publishers. Profit margins and sales goals only rarely coincide with educational effectiveness" (p. 72). Thus decisions about technology, particularly computers, will be made. But who will make them, and how much will the decisions be educational decisions based on the proper use of the machinery in educational programs, and how much will they be based on the gift incentives provided by major computer manufacturers?

Although there are clearly problems with educational

technology, particularly computers, higher education cannot ignore them. As I explained earlier, adults have many educational opportunities available to them. It is clear to me that higher education can make some unique contributions to an adult's learning. But this will mean making some adjustments in the traditional ways of doing things, including how educational technology is incorporated into instructional programs both off and on campus. As Robert DeSio (1987), director of university relations for IBM, emphasizes, "Educators who make effective use of the new technologies will be the most competitive in the marketplace. There are too many university campuses that are not exploiting the use of the new technologies in the learning process. You are not only supposed to be experts in the disciplines and subject areas, but also in the process of learning and education" (p. 12).

The Trend Toward an Information Society

For a decade or more we have heard that we are moving from an industrial society to an information society. Writers such as Naisbitt (1982) and Toffler (1980) have described in some depth how they believe the vast amounts of information available these days will have a dramatic effect on nearly all aspects of our lives.

As we have seen, higher education is very much a part of the information society, since it generates new information through research and scholarship and distributes information through various instructional programs. A concern that I constantly hear from almost all instructors is how to find time to include information in their courses that they believe should be included. Institutions are also constantly wrestling with curriculum development concerns, trying to integrate new information with their offerings, adding new courses, combining courses, and ultimately debating whether the length of study for degrees should be extended because there is so much to learn.

Not only does the so-called "information explosion" affect degree-credit programs at colleges and universities, but it has a dramatic affect on the continuing education programs.

For example, in 1986, in the field of engineering, the following were noted as the half-lives of engineers' skills: software engineer, 2.5 years; electrical engineer, 5 years; mechanical engineer, 7.5 years (National University Continuing Education Association, 1987, p. 19).

Not only has there been a great increase in the amount of information that exists, but the way information is stored and transmitted has changed dramatically in the last two or three years. For example, as I mentioned in Chapter Two, with the advent of the compact disk–read-only memory (CD-ROM), it is possible to store as much as 250,000 pages of information on a 4¾″ disk. With the optical digital disk it is possible to store as much as a million pages of information on one disk, including illustrative material. It is thus possible for persons to have entire libraries of material available to them on disk.

In addition, the on-line computer database service industry has grown tremendously in the last few years. In my office I have access to some 300 different computer databases with a few keystrokes. Many other people, particularly those in business and industry, have similar arrangements. No longer is it necessary to travel to the library to have access to vast amounts of information that is constantly added to and updated.

As prices come down and the accessibility to these databases becomes easier, increasing numbers of people will have these vast information sources available. This situation raises some fundamental questions for higher education and the instructional approaches it uses, no matter what the age of its students. In particular, it brings us to the most fundamental of questions that educators have raised down through the centuries: What is knowing? And in what way can someone help another person come to know something?

I believe that it is easy for those of us in higher education, as well as for everyone else involved with education for that matter, to be deluded into believing that accumulating information equals knowing. According to this argument, as the store of information increases, we must make certain that our students accumulate ever-increasing amounts of it; this will make them well educated. It is rather easy to accept this premise, perhaps even to encourage it. But it is also easy to argue that as we emphasize the accumulation of information, we are in fact preventing knowing from taking place. To clarify this, I must say something about the sense in which I am using the word *knowing*. Of course epistemology—the subject of knowing and how we come to know—has been of concern to philosophers and others for centuries. For purposes of this discussion, knowing means an integration of new information with the experience, thoughts, ideas, and values of the person receiving the information. This suggests that there is an important difference between accumulating information and knowing.

Through one means or another, we have all accumulated vast amounts of information. Often we can recite it on command and share it with others. This information resides within us almost untouched, depending of course on the accuracy with which we were able to perceive it. Knowing, on the other hand, means we have done something with the information. We have wrestled with it, thought about it, reworked it, compared it to other information, contrasted it with our personal experience, tried it out against our values and beliefs of what we accept is right and proper. This is the stuff of knowing.

Critical thought—the ability to analyze ideas, search for their inner meanings, discover and digest the metaphors that are used, and examine the assumptions underlying the information—is an important part of knowing. But knowing, as I wish to use the word, means more than this, because *to know something means to come into a personal relationship with it*—to bring the self into the discussion and not remain aloof or "objective." Palmer (1983) talks about *objectivism*, meaning placing undue emphasis on objectivity in education: "Objectivism is institutionalized in our educational practices, in the ways we teach and learn. There, through the power of the 'hidden curriculum,' objectivism is conveyed to our students; our conventional methods of teaching form students in the objectivist world-view. If you want to understand our controlling conception of knowledge, do not ask for our best epistemological theories. Instead, observe the way we teach and look for the theory of knowledge implicit in those practices. That is the epistemology our students learn—no matter what our best contemporary theorists may have to say" (p. 29). Coming to know something is a personal act. To know is to become personally involved.

Coming to know also means seeing the relationships between what is known and new ideas or information. Because human beings have conveniently categorized information into areas called disciplines, we have great difficulty in working across disciplines, in knowing in more than one field. Capra (1975), a physicist who writes about quantum theory and its relationship to Eastern thought, observes that "the most important characteristic of the Eastern world view—one could almost say the essence of it—is the awareness of the unity and mutual interrelationship of all things and events, the experience of all phenomena in the world as manifestations of a basic oneness. All things are seen as interdependent and inseparable parts of the cosmic whole: as different manifestations of the same ultimate reality" (pp. 116–117).

Through his study of modern physics, Capra (1975) concludes that "material objects are not distinct entities, but are inseparably linked to their environment . . . . Their properties can only be understood in terms of their interaction with the rest of the world" (p. 195). He further underscores the oneness of the universe: "We cannot decompose the world into independently existing smallest units. As we penetrate into matter, nature does not show us any isolated 'basic building blocks,' but rather appears as a complicated web of relations between the various parts of the whole. These relations always include the observer in an essential way. The human observer constitutes the final link in the chain of observational processes, and the properties of any atomic object can be understood only in terms of the object's interaction with the observer" (pp. 56–57).

Thus, knowing means a personal relationship with what is to be known, and it also means being aware of the relationships of information across and between disciplines. Knowing also often includes seeking the relationship of new information to organized systems of knowledge represented by such traditional disciplines as physics, biology, economics, psychology, or sociology. Also, in many cases new information must be related to indigenous knowledge—that knowledge that people have already gained from doing whatever they do. For example, an engineer, a physician, or a teacher has a vast store of knowledge coming directly from day-to-day practice.

Schön (1983) calls this "knowing in action" (p. 50). He argues that we have long followed a philosophy of "technical rationality" that suggests that intelligent practice is the application of knowledge from the appropriate discipline or disciplines. He challenges this, and suggests that practitioners often rely on their own practical knowledge, which may be informed by a particular discipline but sometimes comes into conflict with the discipline's knowledge. Knowing, then, must include a concern for practitioner knowledge. Practitioner knowledge can be subtle, in the sense that certain practitioners may know how to do something but do not know how to describe what they do. In these situations, the instructor is challenged to first accept and recognize the importance of practitioner knowledge, to assist practitioners in identifying and communicating their knowledge. Then it is the instructor's task to help practitioners build relationships of understanding between the new information that formal study has identified and the practical knowledge that they already have.

Instructional Approaches

What is the relevance of the preceding discussion to the choice of instructional approaches? For years, a popular area of research has been to compare the relative merits of various instructional forms. Are lectures better or worse than group discussions? Are films better instructional devices than slide-tape sets? Are computers better instructional devices than videotapes? Almost all of these studies use recall of information as the dependent variable for the research. And even with such an extremely narrow view of success (recall of information), study after study has shown little difference among the various instructional approaches used.

The important question then becomes, What is the goal of the instructional effort? As I have discussed in an earlier work (Apps, 1985), it is possible to describe three general educational goals. Drawing on Jürgen Habermas (1972) as a foundation, I suggested the following broad outcomes for learning:

- technical learning
- learning for meaning
- emancipatory learning

A few comments will help to clarify these concepts.

Technical Learning: Technical learning means accumulating the necessary information and skills so that one might better perform in a job or career. Such learning is often described by specific, identifiable outcomes. Some educators refer to this category of learning as "competency or performance based."

Learning for Meaning: Learning for meaning might better be described as interactive or communicative learning. Here the emphasis is not on a skill to be learned or some information to be attained so that one can better perform a particular task, but instead is on obtaining meaning from the educational experience. Such educational activities as a discussion of English literature, an examination of the Civil War, or a discussion of values and morality in elementary education would fall within this category of learning. The outcome is not a skill or competency, but rather a better understanding of something, a new perspective perhaps. Liberal arts programs for adults would fit this category of learning.

Emancipatory Learning: The final category, emancipatory learning, involves a complex and often more controversial view of learning. Emancipatory learning has as its purpose the freeing of people from the personal, institutional, or environmental forces that may prevent them from seeing new perspectives for their lives, from attaining broader and deeper goals in their lives, from gaining some control over their lives and their communities and beyond.

Emancipatory learning contains critical, integrative, and action phases. In the critical phase, the learner is assisted in questioning present situations, examining assumptions, challenging current ways of viewing the world, and analyzing what is currently known about something. For example, if the continuing education program is concerned with providing union officials with leadership training, and an emancipatory learning approach is followed, then participants would first analyze their present situation. What are current labor-management relations like? What is bargainable in labor contracts and what is not? And so on. Likewise, if a continuing education program is designed for middle management people, then questions about the responsibilities of middle managers, the decisions they are allowed to make, the way in which they are encouraged to communicate with workers and with top-level management, and so forth are examined.

The second phase of emancipatory learning, the integrative phase, seeks information from a wide array of sources to help provide a broad perspective on the questions that develop from the first, critical phase: "Emancipatory learning integrates a variety of points of view; it brings together opposing positions, it examines the past and the present, it includes knowledge from a wide sweep of disciplines, and, very importantly, it includes one's own views and feeling" (Apps, 1985, p. 152).

The third phase of emancipatory learning, the action phase, means that participants are guided in their actions about what they have learned so far in the process. The union leaders try out their new learning; the middle managers attempt to carry out what they have learned. The action phase is a test of the learning, but in addition, it is a confirming phase. Based on the results of the action taken, the participants enter into a new critical phase, and the process repeats itself. In effect, there is a constant reflection-action process taking place, as described by Freire (1970). We do not learn in isolation from practice, but rather we learn, practice, relearn, perhaps unlearn, practice again, and so on. There is a constant interaction of reflection (study) and action. They are in constant interchange with each other, each informing the other. Thus the old assumptions of technical rationality discussed by Schön (1983) are challenged. With respect to the preceding discussion of knowing, emancipatory learning is the most in depth, the most comprehensive form of knowing. Technical learning is the most superficial, the least comprehensive form of knowing, with learning for meaning falling in between.

These remarks suggest that instructors need to decide on the form of learning that they are trying to accomplish—technical, learning for meaning, or emancipatory. Then it is necessary to determine the instructional approach or approaches that will help students reach this level of learning. For example, lecturing and the one-way use of television, radio, and educational telephone are expedient ways of accomplishing technical learning. Lecture-discussion, small-group discussion, and computer instruction with provision for interaction between students and instructor and among students are ways of accomplishing learning for meaning. All of these methods may be employed as a part of emancipatory learning, provided that there is ample opportunity for learners to carry out the critical, integrative, and action phases of the learning process. The instructional method is not as important as a clear knowledge of the educational goals, from the standpoint of both the learner and the instructor. Of course, one lecture after another over a period of weeks will do little to enhance emancipatory learning. Likewise, small-group discussion week after week without information input and carefully guided questions will contribute little to emancipatory learning. Concentration on a single method because it is "the best" for adult learning is folly. Generally a combination of several methods, with a sense of what is to be accomplished, will make a difference.

One final point about learning outcomes. Earlier I discussed the issue of the unique contributions of higher education to the continuing learning of adults. I talked about the many providers of educational opportunities that operate today and the wide choices available to adult learners. It would seem to me that as higher education examines its potential contributions, it is specially qualified to carry out learning for meaning and emancipatory learning. Almost every provider of educational opportunities for adults provides technical learning. But few providers outside of higher education are uniquely qualified to provide learning for meaning and emancipatory learning opportunities.

Summary

In making decisions about the most suitable instructional methods for adult learners, it is important to understand the nature of adults as learners, to be aware of the available educational technology, and to consider the influence of the learning society.

Adult learners generally expect to take an active role in the learning process, bring a background of experience that can aid or hinder learning, respond to problem centered learning, are concurrent students, and often require unlearning.

With the availability of information technology, educators are challenged as to how to supplement information that is readily accessible to students on computer databases, compact disks, and other sources.

But many problems exist with understanding and properly using technology. A major difficulty is keeping clear the difference between accumulating information and learning. College and university educators are challenged to apply instructional approaches to accomplish particular learning outcomes. Levels of learning outcomes include (1) technical learning, (2) learning for meaning, and (3) emancipatory learning.

Many providers of educational opportunities for adults provide technical learning opportunities. Higher education is uniquely qualified to provide learning for meaning and emancipatory learning opportunities.

8

Exploring Alternative
Degree Formats

Many older learners specifically seek degrees from colleges and universities. They may have completed one or more years of college-level work, but then dropped out of school to work or care for a family. Some may never have attended college. A degree opens doors to new careers, personal growth, and well-being for these older students. But because of family, work, and community responsibilities, they may not be able to participate in traditional degree programs requiring extensive on-campus daytime attendance. Increasingly, colleges and universities are changing degree formats to accommodate these older learners. These changes include adjusting present degree programs and devising special degree programs ranging from weekend offerings to those provided via satellite or computer. In addition, new institutions have been organized to serve the needs of older students seeking degrees.

Traditional Program Adjustments

Although the overall degree requirements—course requirements, number of credits, and residency—remain the same, many colleges and universities offer courses in the late afternoon or evening and once a week in a three-hour block. Some courses are offered on weekends. Older students working toward degrees often combine taking courses during "nontraditional" times with regularly scheduled courses or summer school courses in order to complete their degree requirements.

At the University of Wisconsin–Madison, for example, an extensive late afternoon and evening course offering is available. In my own department, students are able to take about three-fourths of their graduate course work during late afternoons, evenings, and weekends. This work, combined with independent study and attendance at regular day courses during the fall or spring semester or in summer school, will earn a master of science degree. A student may also work toward a doctor of philosophy degree in this manner, but at some point during the doctoral program, full-time attendance for two semesters is required. In my home department, one or two courses a semester are also taught at remote locations around the state, to allow those students who want to study part time easier access. Our students ultimately put together graduate programs that combine courses taken off campus with late afternoon, evening, weekend, and regular daytime semester offerings.

There are several advantages to modifying existing degree programs for older students. Generally, the regular daytime faculty teach all the courses, including those offered in nontraditional formats. Staffing in this fashion mollifies critics who often cry "lack of quality" when colleges and universities offer off-campus, evening, or weekend courses. Full- and part-time students and older and younger students often take courses together and gain from each other. The quality of a degree earned through taking courses in nontraditional formats is seldom challenged, because the traditional and nontraditional approaches both occur in the same degree program.

We can also identify some disadvantages to modifying existing degree programs to make them more available for older students. Students with work responsibilities often find it difficult to meet full-time study requirements that remain a part of many graduate degree programs, particularly at the doctoral level. For some, taking course work over an extended period of time, often four or five or more years, results in earlier course work becoming obsolete before final comprehensive examinations are written. Also, taking one course a semester for several years requires unflagging and continuing motivation. Some people simply cannot keep their work, family, and other responsibilities going and at the same maintain motivation for course work each term.

Nevertheless, many colleges and universities across the country offer degree course work in the pattern I have just outlined. Whether these programs will be able to continue attracting older students remains to be seen, particularly in light of the many alternative programs that have been and are currently being developed.

Special Adult-Oriented Degree Programs

Many colleges and universities have developed degree programs specifically with the older student in mind. In most instances, these degree offerings are in addition to the traditional programs designed for full-time younger students who attend daytime classes. In our research we found many examples of these special degrees.

Mentioned earlier, the College of St. Catherine in St. Paul, Minnesota, strives to serve both older and younger students. It offers a weekend and evening college program, where the average student age is thirty-three. The average age for day programs is twenty-five, higher than for many institutions. At St. Catherine's, 40 percent of the students enrolled in all college programs attend part time. The weekend college was designed specifically for women who work full time.

George Mason University, in Fairfax, Virginia, offers a bachelor of individualized study degree. According to the college's promotional brochure, this approach "offers mature students an academically sound program providing an alternative to traditionally structured baccalaureate degrees." To be eligible for the program, applicants must have at least eight years of life experience since high school graduation and must have accumulated at least thirty semester hours of college credit with satisfactory grades. Students may earn a maximum of four credits for experiential learning, demonstrated by a portfolio illustrating the learning. They may also contribute credits earned by television courses and other nontraditional modes of learning that are certified by accredited institutions of higher learning. In addition, course work taken though the military, government agencies, and private corporations may be transferred into the program, provided that such course work is evaluated as college-level work by the American Council of Education.

The degree requires 128 semester hours of course work with basic requirements in English, science or mathematics, the humanities, and the social or behavioral sciences. Working with an academic adviser, students design and complete an individualized program of courses related to their particular interests. This becomes their individualized major. They must also complete a final project related to the major. Courses do not necessarily have to be taken at George Mason University; they may also be taken at any member institution of the Northern Virginia Consortium. Besides George Mason, this consortium includes Marymount College of Virginia, Northern Virginia Community College, the University of Virginia and Virginia Polytechnic Institute and State University Northern Virginia Centers, and Strayer College.

In addition to the bachelor of individualized study program, George Mason University offers a master of arts in interdisciplinary studies, which requires thirty-six hours of graduate-level work. This program will accept up to six hours of experiential learning and up to twelve hours of transfer credit, including credit for graduate work completed outside a university setting. Moreover, George Mason has an extensive on-campus program with undergraduate liberal arts degrees and graduate (including doctoral) and professional degrees in nearly ninety fields.

California State University, Dominguez Hills (Los Angeles) offers an external master of arts in humanities degree. Available through the Division of Extended Education, the degree stresses cultural knowledge, perceptual skills, and creative production. Students enrolling must hold a bachelor's degree and meet other minimum entry requirements. The degree requires thirty semester units. Up to nine credits may be transferred into the program.

Students enroll in a series of independent study courses.

Learning materials include books, student study guides, study questions, explanations of terms and concepts, and when appropriate, cassette tapes, art reproductions, excerpts from important writers and their works, bibliographical essays, and short monographs. Grading is based on the students' written assignments. Many of the courses require active participation by the students. For example, "Humanities Encounter: Film" requires watching and analyzing movies with a special focus on the techniques and content of the medium. "Humanities Encounter: Art" requires visiting three local museums to examine their architecture and collections. "Humanities Encounter: History" involves exploring the historical roots of the students' own communities.

The State University of New York at Stony Brook offers a master of arts in liberal studies in an evening format. Courses are available on the Stony Brook campus as well as at various regional locations. A few courses are offered via radio. The degree requires thirty credit hours of study, including foundation courses in the arts and humanities, the social and behavioral sciences, and the natural and applied sciences; theme or subject courses; electives; and a master's essay. Anyone with a college degree may enroll in this program. Students include those seeking professional training as well as those studying toward the master of arts in liberal studies.

Duke University, in Durham, North Carolina, offers a master of arts in liberal studies, with several courses designed particularly for the program. According to the promotional material, the degree is intended for the "motivated adult who may have been away from academic life for several years." The program is designed for business leaders, educators, and professionals who may have specialized undergraduate degrees and have discovered the value of a liberal arts education. Catherine Johnson, staff assistant to the program, notes that "while the Master of Liberal Studies degree is certainly useful in the work place, most students are in this program simply to learn" (personal communication, Sept. 24, 1986). In 1986 seventy-five students were enrolled. Students indicate that the greatest strengths of the program are its flexible schedule and the quality faculty members involved.

Working with a personal adviser, students design their own course of study. They are required to take at least three core courses that cut across the boundaries of traditional disciplines. A core course may combine ideas from the humanities, social sciences, and sciences. For example, one of the core courses offered is "Evolution: Formulation, Impact, and Controversies." It examines the theory of evolution from a historical, philosophical, and scientific perspective. Courses are offered on the Duke campus one evening each week and are taught by the regular faculty. Students can meet the requirements for the degree by taking one course each fall, spring, and summer semester for three years (nine courses plus a synthesis project). They may of course take more than one course a semester and finish sooner.

As an aside, it is interesting to see the number of businesspeople enrolling in liberal arts degree programs at various institutions around the country. Johnston (1986) discusses liberal education for business leaders and points out two concerns that have been debated for many years, an overemphasis on liberal education and a "real-world" scorn for liberally educated people (p. xi). He concludes with the observation that "current empirical evidence bears out the testimony of a range of business executives that the skills, abilities, and habits of mind fostered by a liberal education are of practical career value. Liberally educated managers, as a group, excel in business, and their firms reap the benefits of their excellence" (pp. 189–190).

Two degree programs mentioned earlier, those of Alverno College (Milwaukee) and the School for New Learning (DePaul University, Chicago), place an emphasis on specific outcomes. Alverno, a women's college, offers degree programs to both younger, more traditional students as well as to older students. Its "weekend college," which began in 1977, follows an "ability-based" approach to learning, and is particularly well suited to the part-time student. Students attend every other weekend. The overall goal for Alverno, for both its younger and older students, is to prepare women for professional careers. The curriculum emphasizes "core abilities" deemed necessary for women in professional careers, with periodic assessment of progress.

DePaul University's School for New Learning was estab-

lished in 1972 as an alternative college for adults. Those attracted
to the school include executives, homemakers, secretaries, laborers, self-employed professionals, and managers. Students'
ages range from twenty-four to seventy, with an average age of
thirty-five. The school is particularly appealing to adults since
courses, admissions, and registration are continuous throughout
the year; credits may be awarded for work accomplishments
and other learning experiences; classes are available days, evenings, and weekends; students can work at their own pace to
allow for family and work demands; four campus sites in the
Chicago area are available.

To earn a bachelor of arts degree, students must (1) attend a "discovery workshop" where they reflect on their goals
and develop plans for achieving them; (2) attend a "foundations
for new learning" course where they develop evidence of their
past learning accomplishments to apply toward degree credits
and also make specific plans with an advisory committee for fulfilling the remaining requirements; (3) attend a major seminar,
where critical thinking and research skills are taught; (4) participate in an externship, an independent project carried out under
the guidance of the advisory committee and in a field setting;
and (5) complete a final evaluation and summit seminar, where
they evaluate their total learning experiences in the program
and establish new learning goals. According to the promotional
materials, the School for New Learning "is organized around
the knowledge, skills, and abilities that define an educated adult
in contemporary society. The process of earning a degree is
characterized by the assessment of what individuals know and
can do rather than by the acquisition of credits through coursework."

The School for New Learning also offers a master of arts
degree for working professionals. This master's program is especially designed for experienced practitioners who work full time.
The study program is individually designed with the help of a
professional adviser and an academic mentor. The professional
adviser is an established practitioner in the student's field. To
complete the degree, participants attend courses, do independent research and guided readings, complete on-the-job projects,

and demonstrate prior learning. In addition, one night a week they attend "liberal learning" seminars with other participants to discuss such topics as leadership in a democratic society and the ethical dimensions of the professions. Most students complete a master's degree in eighteen to twenty-four months.

Faculty for both the bachelor's and master's degree programs are drawn from the faculties of DePaul University and the Chicago professional community.

Through the use of educational technology, some campuses offer degree programs in remote locations. California State University at Chico, mentioned earlier, was the first university in the California State system to offer degrees at off-campus sites, beginning in 1975. Serving sixteen remote sites in Northern California with satellite communication, the university provides courses leading to bachelor's degrees in two majors as well as certificate and minor programs. In addition, via satellite, its computer science department began broadcasting graduate-level courses leading to a master's degree in computer science in 1984. The program is designed particularly for corporate employees.

Degree Program Characteristics   We can summarize the characteristics of these special degree programs for adults as follows:

1. *Nearly all of them place some emphasis on self-directedness.* That is, the adult student is expected to be an active participant in planning his or her degree program. The meaning of self-directedness and student involvement, however, is interpreted differently by the various programs examined. Some of the degree programs just discussed are considerably more open ended than others. The School for New Learning's master of arts degree seems to be one of the most flexible, with students having much to say about what they will study and even how they will learn. Study may include at-work projects, individual readings, and independent research. Much of the academic work is done outside of a university setting, thus allowing students great flexibility in designing their study times. This great flexibility is complemented by the liberal learning seminars, which meet one night a week for ten months for four hours at a time.

In Duke University's master of arts in liberal studies program, student-designed curricula mean making decisions about which nine of several courses will be taken. And students are required to take at least three designated "core" courses. They also have the freedom to participate in directed reading and tutorial courses, which are arranged when appropriate.

The bachelor of individualized study program at George Mason University allows older students (they must have been out of high school at least eight years) an opportunity to pull together courses from a variety of disciplines to meet individual needs. All of this is done, however, within a structure of program requirements. In effect, the student is designing his or her own major but not altering the overall requirements for the degree.

2. *Several of the programs offer credit for experience.* This is viewed in two ways. One possibility is that credit may be given for life experiences that are organized as a part of the degree program and are under the guidance of a faculty adviser. On the other hand, in some instances credit may be given for life experiences a person has had prior to enrolling in the degree-credit program.

DePaul University's School for New Learning follows both these approaches. In its bachelor's degree program, as we have noted, students enroll in a "foundations for new learning" course, where they develop evidence of their past learning accomplishments and apply for degree credits. Another requirement of the program is an "externship," a field-based learning experience under the direction of an advisory committee.

At George Mason University, the development and evaluation of adult student abilities is an important part of the program. At George Mason, up to four credits may be granted for experiential learning. The student demonstrates experiential learning by putting together a portfolio of evidence that must be reviewed by the student's adviser with a credit recommendation. Students may earn more than four credits if such learning can be demonstrated through examinations, such as course equivalency examinations given by departments.

In the degree programs we have reviewed that are designed

for adults but located within colleges and universities with traditional degree programs, field-based learning is a prominent form of learning. Nearly all of the programs have some form of field experience built into their degree programs. For example, California State University at Dominguez Hills has a field-experience element built into many of its courses—visiting museums, studying the history of one's own community, and attending concerts. At Alverno College, the curriculum emphasizes practical applications of what is learned in the classroom. Students are required to apply what they are learning in concrete work situations. And their performances are evaluated by fellow students, faculty, and representatives of the business and professional community based on criteria that give a clear picture of each ability that is evaluated. For instance, student speeches and performances in group leadership situations are videotaped and then shown to outside evaluators to assess strengths and weaknesses.

3. *Nearly all the programs, to a greater or lesser extent, focus on program outcomes, not merely on credit accumulation.* Alverno College and the School for New Learning lean most strongly in this direction, with carefully specified performance outcomes expected from students. But the others, too, expect students to not only gather credits but to have some specified skills and abilities as a result of enrolling in the degree program. This philosophy appeals to prospective students and also to prospective employers of those students seeking employment based on their new degree status.

To ensure some practical, specific learning outcomes, most of the programs minimally require some sort of final project to demonstrate students' ability to apply theoretical material to practical situations.

4. *The administrative arrangements for these adult-oriented degree programs vary from institution to institution.* Some are integral to the institution, as in the case of Alverno College and the College of St. Catherine, with the same administration responsible for adult-oriented degree programs and the traditional ones for younger students. In fact, at these institutions, older and younger students are often in the same classes.

In other instances the adult-oriented degree program is located within a continuing education division of the institution. At George Mason University, the degree programs for adults are in the division of continuing education; at California State University, Dominguez Hills, the adult degree program is located within the division of extended education. At Duke University, the master of arts in liberal studies program for adults is located in the graduate school. DePaul University offers yet another administrative arrangement, with a separate school organized to administer special degree programs for adult students.

There are of course advantages and disadvantages to each of these organizational schemes. Those programs that are in separate organizations such as divisions of continuing education often have more flexibility to organize and conduct programs for adults than if they were administered by a traditional college or university department offering degree programs for younger students. On the other hand, degrees earned from programs separate from the "mainstream" of the college or university are often viewed as having less quality than the traditional ones.

5. *There is considerable variation from institution to institution in who teaches the courses in these special degree programs for adults.* At several of the institutions, the entire faculty for the adult-oriented degree program is the same faculty that teaches in the more traditional degree programs. This is true, for example, at Duke, Alverno, and St. Catherine's. On the other hand, the School for New Learning represents a staffing approach where there is a mix of instructors, some from the university and some from the business and professional community.

Considerable controversy exists over how to staff degree programs designed for returning students, particularly since these programs often involve practical, applied topics. There are many advantages to employing, on an ad hoc basis, instructors from the business and professional world who have day-to-day knowledge of the topics they teach. The instructors gain from the teaching experience, the students usually enjoy working with them, and the institution earns public relations points. But what often happens is this. The full-time faculty in the more traditional programs will say, "Not only is this degree program not following a traditional pattern, but the program doesn't even include the mainline instructors." Such comments of course really mean that here is a low-quality program. Sometimes employers also equate quality with traditional approaches and full-time, on-campus instructors. Institutions with a large proportion of adjunct or ad hoc instructors from the community must face and attempt to resolve the quality issue. One way they can do this is to develop a faculty training program where they help ad hoc instructors become acquainted with the latest research in understanding adults as learners and with appropriate instructional approaches. A second way that many institutions can help allay criticism of ad hoc faculty is to develop teaching evaluation techniques for faculty that combine reactions from students with evaluations of administrators who visit classes. These techniques are often combined with a faculty approval system that involves full-time faculty reviewing ad hoc faculty credentials and course syllabi.

New Institutions Offering Degrees for Adults

In recent years, a number of new institutions have been founded with degree programs for adult students as their primary mission.

Regents College Degrees The Regents College Degree program of the State University of New York was organized in 1970. It offers a range of college degree programs for adults, from an associate in arts in liberal arts to a bachelor of science in business, nursing, and six other areas. It also offers flexibility and self-paced study. At the time of our research, some 17,000 students were enrolled, ranging from persons in private industry and hospitals to military personnel in various parts of the world. A guiding principle for the program is that what a person knows is more important than how the knowledge was acquired. Enrollment in the program is open to everyone, and there is no residency requirement. It is appropriate for adult students who have already attended several colleges or universities, accumulating course credits but not completing a degree.

A Regents College Degree is a traditional degree. The approach to acquiring the degree is nontraditional, however. In actuality, the Regents College Degree program measures and documents learning rather than providing instruction. Students enroll in the program but take their courses at other colleges and universities. Credit can also be earned by enrolling in courses sponsored by business, industry, government, or the military; by college-level proficiency examinations; and through special assessment. Students earn special assessment credits through individualized examinations that measure the college-level knowledge they have gained from experience and independent study. The undergraduate liberal arts degrees represent a combination of study in the basic academic disciplines plus the exploration of some subject areas in greater depth.

Walden University With main offices in Minneapolis, Minnesota, Walden University offers doctoral programs for adults. Walden is a private institution whose programs are recognized in Minnesota, California, Florida, Louisiana, Washington, and Quebec, Canada. It has recently completed a self-study process and has been accepted for candidacy for accreditation by the North Central Association of Colleges and Schools. According to its promotional material, some 2,000 men and women have enrolled in its degree programs since 1970. Presently, Walden offers a doctor of philosophy degree in education, administration/management, human services, and health services. It also offers a doctor of education degree. To graduate a student must complete: "(1) a professional development plan which is updated and approved each year, (2) a minimum of 200 hours of dispersed residency [faculty-student contact], (3) curriculum assessments judged adequate by two faculty readers in: (a) seven core knowledge area modules demonstrating general knowledge and skills at the doctoral level, (b) four advanced knowledge area modules demonstrating comprehension and application of knowledge in a doctoral track (administration/management, education, human services, health services); (4) a dissertation (Ph.D.) or doctoral project (Ed.D.) and a final oral presentation; (5) (doctor of education only) a supervised internship of 200 hours" (*Walden University: Institute for Advanced Studies*, 1986, p. 7).

Students can meet these requirements while remaining employed. Credit is earned in Walden's doctoral programs through self-directed study under the guidance of carefully selected faculty members located around the country. Students in the program generally range from thirty-eight to fifty-eight years of age. From time to time, through a variety of approaches—one-week summer sessions, regional sessions, an electronic computer network (in development), and so on—students are in touch with each other and with the faculty. The university has no classrooms; its face-to-face sessions are held in existing community facilities, such as conference centers and other university facilities.

Nova University Headquartered in Fort Lauderdale, Florida, Nova is another example of an alternative university. It has operated for twenty-two years and is accredited by the Commission on Colleges of the Southern Association of Colleges and Schools. Nova has depended on ad hoc instructors, generally associated with other colleges and universities, to provide its instruction at various regional centers around the country.

In recent years, Nova has developed computer-based graduate programs for adult professionals. Presently it offers four doctorates, two master's degrees, and an educational specialist degree using a computer-based format. One of its newer programs is a doctor of arts in information science. This doctoral program is designed for librarians and other information scientists, particularly those who cannot easily commute to a more traditional program or who have family and job commitments that prevent such attendance. Entrance requirements include employment in a library or information center, an earned master of library science degree or the equivalent, and satisfactory Graduate Record Examination scores. A portfolio of professional achievement is also considered for entrance. The three-year program requires the following:

1. Completion of six core courses, one each semester. Courses include digital computers, research and statistics, database management, systems analysis, and telecommunications.

2. Attendance at two on-site seminars each semester at a re-
    gional location. Current regional locations are Fort Lauder-
    dale and Jacksonville, Florida; Wilmington, Delaware; St.
    Louis, Missouri; and Los Angeles.
3. Participation in a computer conference associated with
    each course.
4. Participation in four research practicums, which are de-
    signed so that students can investigate activities within their
    own institution or organization.
5. Completion of a major field project, a capstone activity de-
    signed to apply research to the student's work setting.

Barry Centini reflects on how Nova's use of computers in
instruction has changed its operations: "There is a tremendous
difference in learning on line. . . . We try to get a 24 hour response to student assignments from faculty. Students in a nor-
mal doctoral program will wait two weeks to get a paper back,
and now they expect a response in two days. But I think that's
predictable. If things are moving at the speed of light why can't
they come back at the speed of light?" (personal communication, Feb. 4, 1987). But he points out that problems also exist:
"You get the computer phobic person and you have a problem
because they are out there isolated and the first ladder they
have to climb is hooking in with their telecommunication" (personal communication, Feb. 4, 1987). Students can use whatever
equipment they wish, so it is difficult for the Nova staff to help
them get started. "We try to help them over the phone," Centini says, "and we try to put them in touch with other students
who have the same equipment. We're also trying to develop a
database of students who have certain equipment" (personal
communication, Feb. 4, 1987). Time zone differences also offer
a challenge. Nova generally runs courses at night, but spanning
five time zones presents many difficulties. For the night courses,
for instance, an Alaskan student must leave work early to be
involved.

National Technological University   Mentioned previously, this university is a private nonprofit institution governed by

a board of trustees who are mainly industrial executives. With headquarters in Fort Collins, Colorado, National Technological University offers a wide range of instructional television courses taught by faculty members from twenty-two of the country's leading engineering universities. The university operates an instructional television network via satellite for its students. Direct phone lines from the receiving sites to the campus classroom provide for faculty-student interaction. This interaction is enhanced with electronic mail, computer teleconferencing, and telephone office hours. Regular satellite delivery began in August 1985. National Technological University also offers noncredit short courses and workshops to introduce new advanced technology to a broad range of technical professionals. The Association for Media-Based Continuing Education for Engineers, founded in 1976, shares the satellite network with the university. (This organization currently has thirty-three member universities providing short courses and other noncredit offerings that are broadcast every day from 11:00 A.M. to 5:00 P.M. Eastern time.)

A wide range of corporations participate in National Technological University's programs, including AT&T, Boeing, Eastman Kodak, General Electric, IBM, RCA, 3M, Rockwell International, and others. In 1985-86 over 1,200 technical professionals were enrolled in 81 courses. National Technological University does not offer undergraduate programs, nor does it grant doctorates. To enroll in a graduate degree program, prospective students must write a statement of purpose describing learning goals, when and why they perceive a need for a graduate degree, and what they anticipate putting into the program and getting from it. Each degree program has additional prerequisites or requirements, including an undergraduate degree in engineering or a related area, an acceptable undergraduate grade point average, and a letter of recommendation from a supervisor.

National Technological University's "campus" in Fort Collins, Colorado, has only administrative offices. Students are scattered across the country, and few of them ever set foot on a college campus. Facilities for students to gain access to the satellite-offered television courses are provided by the students' employers, usually industrial companies, research centers, or government agencies.

Electronic University Network As mentioned earlier, the Electronic University Network is an example of a new institution designed to meet the higher education needs of students who cannot easily participate in traditional on-campus programs. Where National Technological University focuses on television courses transmitted by satellite, the Electronic University Network uses home computers. Students participate in courses from their homes, offices, or wherever else they have access to computer equipment.

The Electronic University Network is not an academic institution but instead is an educational communications system that links students with other students and with instructors throughout the United States. The network itself grants neither credits nor degrees. Transcripts are issued directly by the academic institution providing the courses over the network. All colleges and universities offering credit via the Electronic University Network are fully accredited by regional commissions on higher education.

Associate and undergraduate degrees in the arts and business are available through the network and are coordinated and administrated by Thomas A. Edison State College, under the auspices of the New Jersey Department of Higher Education. Thomas A. Edison State College is accredited by the Middle States Association of Colleges and Schools; it is authorized to grant external degrees without requiring attendance on campus. To earn one of these degrees, students take classes through the Electronic University Network, attend on-campus classes at a school in their own region (as long as the courses meet degree requirements), or enroll in traditional written correspondence courses and apply these credits to the degree desired.

The Electronic University Network also offers a master of business administration (M.B.A.) program through John F. Kennedy University's external M.B.A. program. Located in the San Francisco area, this university was founded solely for adults. To meet the requirements for the M.B.A., students must complete fifty-one units of graduate-level work in core, specialization, and integrative categories. In addition to enrolling in the electronic courses via the network, students also participate in regional seminars, where they have an opportunity to interact face to face with instructors and fellow students.

Students enrolled in the Electronic University Network are assigned electronic mailboxes where they can communicate with their instructors with a single keystroke. Enrollment in the network also entitles students and their families access to the electronic library. This consists of computer access to over sixty national databases, including a multidisciplinary encyclopedia, *Books in Print*, and indexes for general-interest magazines plus five national newspapers. Students are charged for on-line connection time, but there are no sign-up fees.

Presently some twenty-two colleges and universities provide courses through the network, which attributes its success to three main factors: overcoming time, distance, and inconvenience for the students. Motivation for institutions to participate is due to new markets for their courses. Laura Malone, a representative of the network, explains it this way: "The way in which the company markets the Electronic University Network is quite outstanding. We go to major corporations with a professional sales force. The sales force calls on the training department and describes the Network, how it operates, the kinds of degrees and certificates that are available. Then we develop a brochure that is distributed to every employee in the company. So the colleges and universities are extremely motivated because being a network, we have the power of eliciting endorsement and support from corporations" (personal communication, Feb. 9, 1987).

The Electronic University Network now has working arrangements with some twenty-five corporations across the country. In most instances, the employers pay the tuition, and they often make company computers available to employees during or after work. The average age of students tends to be in the mid thirties. They are usually mid-level managers with about two years of college completed when they enroll. They either already own a computer or plan to buy one. Student response to the network has been very positive, says Malone: "Most of our glowing response letters say things like 'it's a miracle, we never dreamed that this was possible' . . . . They're not the type of student who would have been involved in the traditional paper and pencil correspondence course. They are motivated students, but I would say they needed the added motivation of the computer. There's still something tremendously exciting about coming home at night from work and knowing there is an electronic mail message for you from your instructor" (personal communication, Feb. 9, 1987).

Comments   What do these various nontraditional degree programs have in common? How do they compare with one another and with programs at more traditional institutions? Are the nontraditional programs examples of what all higher education survivors will do in the next decade or so? Or are they passing fads that will disappear—as have other efforts to provide nontraditional degree offerings? In the marketplace for degrees we continue to hear about prospective employers looking somewhat skeptically at degrees from nontraditional institutions. Negative publicity resulting from fly-by-night degree mills does not make things easy for legitimate nontraditional programs. Also, with flat budgets or worse, some colleges and universities are abandoning nontraditional approaches in favor of the tried and true. (This reflects the assumption that with tradition goes quality.)

Some institutions offering nontraditional degrees have worked out cooperative arrangements with traditional colleges and universities and often with business and industry. Further, these nontraditional programs operate as businesses, either clearly for profit as stated in their charter, or as institutions devoted to operating without benefit of any tax support. Thus they devote considerable money to marketing, including sending salespeople on the road to market their educational wares. This approach certainly flies in the face of what happens in most traditional college and university degree programming. In recent years, though, many traditional institutions have stepped up their student recruitment programs, which is certainly one important form of marketing.

What is the place of tax-supported degree programs in the midst of this flurry of entrepreneurial educational development? Will the entrepreneurs skim off the students for highly visible and needed programs, such as those in computer science, engineering, and business management, making it difficult for traditional degree programs to continue in these areas? And can traditional colleges and universities continue to lag in their development of innovative degree programs? Adult students, particularly those with full-time employment, family, and community responsibilities—and that is the vast majority of adult students—find it increasingly difficult to attend college full time, or to even attend part time on a campus when it is inconvenient to travel there. These alternative degree programs are designed to help alleviate the accessibility problem.

The question of quality remains. Are the degrees obtained from the alternative degree programs of the same quality as those received from the more traditional colleges and universities? This question evokes a variety of responses. Increasingly, one can hear rumblings that in some instances the quality of degrees from the nontraditional programs may be higher quality than those offered by the more traditional institutions. If concern for students and attempts to provide curricula that fit the students' situations is a measure of quality, adult students give many nontraditional programs high marks. If the opportunity to tie theory to practice and relate the students' experience to what they are studying in the nontraditional programs is evaluated, the alternative programs again receive high marks. If accessibility, through media and other means, is a measure of quality, these programs once more receive high marks in most instances. And if quality is measured mostly by the quality and rigor of instruction, adult students give many of the nontraditional program offerings a thumbs up. Of course the traditional colleges and universities, particularly the research institutions, challenge the nontraditional institutions to meet their own degree of rigor. Many of the nontraditional institutions have accepted the challenge.

From the perspective of the alternative institutions, the most important question is whether they will survive. Will sufficient numbers of adult students enroll in their programs to allow them to continue in operation? Huge investments are necessary for the programs that are heavy users of electronic media such as satellite communication, videotaping, and computer learning. Will the revenues received from students and from their employers be sufficient to allow the programs to continue to compete with the more traditional programs?

Will the various alliances with traditional colleges and universities and often with business and industry that are a part of some of the nontraditional degree programs set a precedent that many colleges and universities will follow? That is, are the nontraditional degree programs for adult students the harbingers of a new look for higher education in the United States? When we look at the historical development of higher education in this country, as we did in Chapter Three, we see new directions in higher education charted by new institutions—the land-grant movement and the community college movement are two examples. Are these nontraditional higher education institutions the new wave for higher education?

Business- and Industry-Sponsored Degree Programs

As mentioned previously, Eurich (1985, p. 87) found that eighteen firms offered degree programs at the time of her research. In many cases, these are firms that were established primarily for other purposes, such as Arthur D. Little. We will look in some depth at the Arthur D. Little Management Education Institute in Cambridge, Massachusetts, which offers a one-year master of science in management program that was accredited by the New England Association of Schools and Colleges in 1976. Arthur D. Little is a major international research and consulting firm with considerable expertise in its field. This practical, field expertise is brought to the classroom. Instructors for the program are largely drawn from Arthur D. Little consultants and are supplemented by faculty from neighboring universities.

The program began as part of the company's efforts in Nigeria, where it worked with the Nigerian government and other groups in both management and economic development. It is an intensive, full-time, 11-month course of study involving more than 50 credits and 700 classroom hours of instruction. The curriculum focuses on international management issues and solutions, and is promoted as being more practical than theoretical. The institute claims that the practical orientation makes this degree different from other graduate programs in management.

The course of study includes three phases, with a two-week orientation program at the beginning. Phase I focuses on management concepts and techniques (fifteen weeks). Phase II stresses functional skills of management; this phase includes eleven weeks of classes and a two-week field trip. The field trip group visits major corporations and international institutions in four major cities in the United States, including at least one on the West Coast. In 1986, for example, the field trip included visits to IBM, Citicorp, Mobil Oil, the World Bank, the U.S. Office of Personnel Management, Bechtel Financing Services, Hewlett-Packard, and Apple Computer. Phase III integrates and applies all the skills learned in Phases I and II, focusing on advanced management practices and economic planning. Phase III lasts for sixteen weeks and includes a one-week multinational management computer game and a one-week comprehensive case series.

Each class has about sixty participants, representing twenty to thirty countries. To be admitted to the program, prospective students must pass an English language examination, have satisfactorily completed an undergraduate degree, and have letters of recommendation from supervisors and university faculty members under whom they have studied. Students are experienced managers looking for new skills. They work in government ministries, international organizations, and public and private businesses. A majority of them are sponsored by their home organizations or by international funding organizations. Their average age is thirty.

What is the future direction for the Arthur D. Little Management Education Institute? Frank G. Feeley, its president, says that "I think we're going to put more emphasis on technology, strategic planning, and on international trade, including trade as it affects developing countries. Given the difficulty in funding students from some of our traditional markets, we will clearly have to try to expand participation from students from the industrialized countries such as Japan, Western Europe and the United States. We're certainly not going to move away from the developing world, but in order to have a class of reasonable size, given foreign exchange limitations and the relative decline in the amount of aid, we're going to have to expand our enrollment from some of those areas" (personal communication, Mar. 26, 1987).

Why would a for-profit company be in the degree business? Feeley notes that the company had concerns about that, particularly in the early years: "There was some concern about a for-profit company for whom this was a sideline, taking the degree program seriously. I think we have sufficiently gotten around that by showing that both the financial and professional resources of the entire company are behind it. . . . If we were just in it for the money we wouldn't be doing it, because, compared to our other lines of business, it's not terribly profitable" (personal communication, Mar. 26, 1987).

The Arthur D. Little master of science in management program is a quality, respected, and successful degree program. It integrates the resources of a large firm, providing students with instructors who have extensive practical field experience. Will other firms, as Eurich (1985) suggests, follow Arthur D. Little's example and develop degree programs with a similar philosophy—integrating field experience with classroom applications culminating in an accredited degree? Many firms certainly have the financial resources to do this. But as Feeley so candidly points out, the profits in the "education business" are limited (personal communication, Mar. 26, 1987).

Summary

Degree offerings with an emphasis on adult students are receiving considerable attention. Many colleges and universities are adjusting current degree programs to better accommodate these students. These adjustments include late afternoon, evening, and weekend class formats; the opportunity to study part time; and off-campus offerings. Other than these changes, the degree requirements (number of credits, required courses, and so on) remain the same.

Many colleges and universities have also developed new adult-oriented degree programs. In most instances, these degree programs are in addition to the more traditional programs offered by the institution. The adult-oriented degree programs generally include (1) an opportunity for self-directed study, (2) credit for experience, (3) a focus on program outcomes, (4) a variety of administrative arrangements, and (5) variation in who serves as instructors, ranging from an ad hoc situation to a full-time, on-campus staff.

Furthermore, new institutions with adult-oriented degree programs have sprung up around the country. Always controversial, particularly from the viewpoint of traditional institutions, these new programs are attracting thousands of adult learners. Some of the programs make heavy use of educational technology such as computers and satellite communication.

A number of for-profit firms have also established degree programs. These programs often relate closely to other aspects of the firms' activities. The Arthur D. Little master of science in management program is one example of a corporate-sponsored degree.

9

Strengthening the Institution's Public Service Role

Traditionally, college and university public service has meant public lectures, touring orchestras and theater groups, art and other exhibits, radio and television programming, and the like. These activities continue to be important. But the public is asking for more. For example, at a 1987 state governors' meeting, the governors agreed that state public universities should become more directly involved in promoting economic growth (Jaschik, 1987).

Community pressure has increased for a broader and deeper public service role for colleges and universities. "This pressure is accompanied by the oft-heard demand for universities to involve themselves more wholeheartedly in the economic, social and cultural problems of their environment, and has redefined the function of service and positioned it alongside the functions of teaching and research. This identification of three distinct functions—teaching, research and service—is convenient *even though service to the community, as generally understood, in fact embraces the first two.* It indicates that some kinds of interaction between the community and the university are not expressed through the traditional forms of teaching and research" (Organization for Economic Cooperation and Development, 1982, p. 35).

The demand for college and university public service, although on the increase, has led to renewed discussions about public service itself. As an international research and innovation body concludes, "higher education institutions have different views about the service function and the way it is to be performed in relation to research and teaching. . . . Whatever approach is chosen it leads sooner or later to the need for institutions, *and particularly the universities,* to define their role more effectively in the face of increasing pressure and growing demands from the community" (Organization for Economic Cooperation and Development, 1982, pp. 35–36).

Approaches to Public Service

There has always been some debate about how to exactly describe public service in higher education. Some would argue that the outreach forms of teaching and research—offering courses off campus, providing research information to users, and so on—are service. This would mean that a college or university really has only two major functions, teaching and research, with service embedded within each of the two major functions. Focusing on two main functions for colleges and universities is a reasonable approach. But some forms of public service that I will be describing may not naturally grow out of teaching and research activities. Community problem-solving approaches, social criticism, and social action are examples. I will quickly concede that all service activity has a relationship to an institution's teaching and research, or at least it ought to. But it still makes sense to discuss service as a third function within higher education, always emphasizing that all three functions—teaching, research, and service—are closely entwined.

College and university public service can include

- consultation work conducted by faculty members
- technology transfer
- staff and employee development for business employees, government officials, and nonprofit organization leaders
- community problem solving
- social criticism
- social action
- international service

I will elaborate on each of these forms of public service.

Faculty Consultation: Consultation work by faculty members is a much criticized and sometimes poorly understood college and university public service function. Faculty consultation can be defined as that activity conducted in addition to the regular teaching and research/scholarship activities where an individual faculty member attempts to meet specific requests from a wide array of agencies, institutions, or firms. Faculty consultation can take many forms. Another university, a business firm, a government agency, or a nonprofit organization may invite a faculty member to assist it with a problem. For example, a business professor may help a firm establish a new accounting system, a computer scientist may work with a firm in establishing a new computer system, or a professor of education may lead a faculty development seminar at another university.

Aside from the fact that it is a service function, faculty consulting has some obvious advantages. For instance, faculty who consult usually bring fresh ideas and practical applications back to their classrooms. When on the consulting firing line, these faculty members have their theories and research challenged and tested. These new challenges feed back into the faculty members' research and scholarship programs. And of course consulting can help add to faculty salaries. It is the money that they make consulting that is often criticized by the general public, particularly if the faculty members work at tax-supported institutions. Faculty members are also criticized for consulting on the grounds that it may take away from on-campus teaching and research responsibilities. Most colleges and universities have established guidelines to ensure that faculty meet teaching and other on-campus responsibilities, but at the same time they encourage a certain amount of consulting because of its positive features.

Technology Transfer: The idea of technology transfer is an old one among colleges and universities in the United States, particularly among the land-grant universities. Three federal acts, beginning with the Morrill Act of 1862, encouraged the practical application of knowledge generated by colleges. The Hatch Act of 1887 established agricultural experiment stations in conjunction with the land-grant colleges. The experiment stations' major goal was to discover and experiment with practical applications of agricultural knowledge to farm situations. The

Smith–Lever Act of 1914, establishing the cooperative extension service (the county agent system), ensured that knowledge from agricultural experiment stations was made available to the public. Of course when these acts were passed, agriculture was the major activity in this country, with a large proportion of the country's population living on the land. Thus technology transfer is not a new idea. It has merely been expanded to go well beyond agricultural concerns.

Technology transfer can include contract research, cooperative research, and ongoing research. Contract research, where the college or university contracts with a business, has become one way colleges and universities can respond to the needs of business and industry in a specific sense. Cooperative research, where college and university researchers team with industry researchers, is another approach. Establishing practical applications for ongoing research is yet a third way of effecting technology transfer. An example is the development of technology centers, where scientific information is tested and refined for practical applications. In some instances, a technology center will work with a firm to help it find financial resources for using a particular technology in its business. The technology center not only brings the research and the potential user of the research together, but it also assists the user in making the technology application.

Colleges and universities have been criticized for their contract and cooperative research efforts. This has been particularly true for colleges of agriculture that have accepted grants from agribusiness firms to develop new agricultural technology. Critics argue that the agricultural colleges have sold out to the big-money interests in agriculture and have forgotten the smaller family farms that often cannot afford the new technology. Agricultural colleges argue that they have a mandate from society to carry out research, wherever it may go. They point out that many great advances in agriculture around the world have resulted from new technology. They also argue that generally less than 10 percent of their research money comes directly from business and industry in contract and cooperative research arrangements.

Harvard president Derek Bok (1982) asserts that "many

forms of technology transfer not only benefit the economy but offer opportunities to the university for new sources of income. Such income could make a distinct contribution to the equality of science—by upgrading equipment and renovating facilities, by permitting a few more fellowships for talented students, by maintaining faculty compensation, by helping young investigators get started more quickly on their research, by simply providing a little unrestricted money to encourage more venturesomeness in exploring new lines of inquiry" (p. 17).

Bok (1982) and Mangan (1987) mention dangers of technology transfer, though. One of these dangers is the prospect of money from business and industry subtly and sometimes not so subtly influencing researchers' agendas. In other words, there is a concern that "researchers are having to relinquish too much control to industry, inhibiting the free and open inquiry that people in academe have traditionally enjoyed" (Mangan, 1987, p. 11). There is also the possibility of some professors drifting away from other research and teaching assignments to participate in technology transfer. (A related concern is that researchers may devote so much time to solving short-term problems for industry that they fail to develop a more basic, long-term research agenda with unknown practical applications.) A further problem is that some firms insist that research results be kept secret, in the interest of maintaining competitive advantage. Most college and university researchers have long maintained that research results must be freely published and made available to other researchers and the public without restriction.

Staff and Employee Development: Staff development can take several forms. The simplest is for firms to pay the tuition of employee groups to attend certain credit or noncredit courses a college or university already offers. A second approach is for a business to contract with a college or university to provide employee training that goes beyond or is different from the regular courses the institution offers. In the 1987 national governors' report mentioned earlier, the governors argue that higher education should emphasize worker retraining "because of the growing number of workers moving into different types of jobs" (Jaschik, 1987, p. 19). The governors also challenge colleges and universities to change existing degree programs to give more attention to communication skills, science education (in their view, far too few students are majoring in the sciences), and international education. Employee retraining has become a particularly important public service role for many community and technical colleges.

Colleges and universities are also assisting government agencies. For example, this assistance includes orientation sessions for newly elected local government officials and keeping officials up to date on the ramifications of new legislation. Often problems emerge when colleges and universities become directly involved with these agencies, however. Crosson (1983) mentions some questions that need to be considered: "What is the appropriate relationship between the educational/scientific and the political communities? What are the service responsibilities of public institutions toward the government entity—state, county, or municipal—that provides their major source of support? Can colleges and universities serve government without becoming servile? In what ways do colleges and universities differ from state and local governmental agencies, and what are their responsibilities toward them?" (p. 54).

Community Problem Solving: Cooperative extension has long been involved with community problem solving. Its local county agents team with campus specialists and work with community leaders to identify community problems. The problems identified range from the need for better health services to refurbishing a rural village's downtown area. Once the problems are identified, the extension agent brings together research information from the university along with considerable expertise in local politics and local leadership to seek a solution to the problem. Not all community problems can be solved this way, but through its community development agents and specialists, cooperative extension has an enviable record of success.

This approach to public service calls for a special type of faculty member, sometimes called a community development specialist. The community development specialist must be well trained in the process of community problem solving, know community politics, and know what resources are available to solve a particular problem. The community development specialist works across several discipline areas because few community problems fit neatly within one discipline or one college or university department. The community development specialist draws from the social, physical, and biological sciences as well as the arts and the humanities as problems are identified and solutions are sought.

Community problem solving requires the need for interdisciplinary thinking and a faculty attitude of openness to the many challenges real community problems offer. Seldom are such problems "textbook clean"; instead they involve many unknowns, many ambiguities, and much political interplay. Some faculty members are simply not comfortable in such settings. Yet providing assistance with community problem solving can be one of the most important contributions a college or university can make toward public service.

Social Criticism: The primary social critics in our society have been the churches and the colleges and universities. For a variety of reasons, the churches have lost much of their impact as social critics. And unfortunately, in recent times colleges and universities have been reluctant to assume this role. Particularly when they are attempting to forge new cooperative relationships with groups such as business and industry, these institutions often want to avoid controversy. Yet, increasingly, the public insists that institutions of higher education become forums for discussing controversial social issues.

Bok (quoted by Desruisseaux, 1987) observes that " 'we need to encourage greater faculty interest and research in the problems of welfare, unemployment, and affordable housing. After the Great Society collapsed, we quickly lost interest, so that we will begin the next war on poverty knowing much less than we need to know.' " He says further that " 'what higher education must do . . . is [to] find ways to address some of the pressing problems facing American Society, including the persistence of poverty, a decline in values, and the loss of industrial competitiveness' " (p. 13).

On my own campus, state agricultural leaders have insisted that the College of Agricultural and Life Sciences conduct programs to examine various sides of the present agricultural crisis. Such programming is attacked in some quarters. Those who favor "sustainable agriculture" criticize programs that discuss the place for high technology in agriculture. Those persons more inclined toward technology in agriculture dismiss the sustainable agriculture discussions as old fashioned and unimportant. But if it is to carry out its responsibility as a social critic, the college has to take on all positions. Its challenge is to attempt objectivity and give all sides an equal hearing. This is the most difficult aspect of the social criticism function, since one person's objectivity is viewed by another as bias. Yet colleges and universities are among the last institutions in our society that can serve as social critics.

Taking on various social issues, albeit from as objective and balanced a position as possible, can therefore be one of the most useful contributions a college or university can make in a learning society.

Social Action: The most controversial by far of all the public service roles I have outlined is the activist role. "The approach of service through social activism goes beyond service through social problem solving and involves faculty and students and even institutions themselves as direct participants in real-world controversies" (Crosson, 1983, p. 18).

Some say there is a fine line between assisting communities with community problem solving, offering social criticism, and social activism. But the differences between these three functions are great. With community problem solving and social criticism, the college or university attempts to maintain a degree of objectivity. In community problem solving it attempts to help both with the process of solving problems and finding university and other resources that may be useful. But the problems identified and the solutions selected are those of the community and its citizens. In playing the role of the social critic, the college or university identifies a social problem and then tries to provide a balanced view of it. But with social activism, the college or university takes a position on the issue and seeks action through a variety of programming means. The dichotomy between being objective and becoming an advocate seems clear and relatively easy to understand. In practice it is not so clear, however. What about those issues where the evidence seems to overwhelmingly support one position? An example might be the effects of nuclear war. When it examines the question of nuclear war, is an institution obligated to have on its panels, in its workshops, and a part of its lecture series those who advocate limited nuclear war as a reasonable alternative to conventional war in certain situations? If the institution does not have "balance" in its presentations, should it then be criticized for taking sides and becoming overly political?

Many of us clearly remember the 1960s and early 1970s, when, on most of our campuses, considerable social action in a variety of forms took place. Those of us who experienced those years firsthand have memories of the excitement that went with the Vietnam protests, workshops, seminars, community meetings, and the like. But we also lament the personal injuries and deaths and the vast property destruction that accompanied too many of the activities. We have lived with the "fallout" from our constituencies, who believed that our leadership had lost control and that "their" colleges and universities had become dens of anarchy. Institutions of higher education of course also face the legal requirement of maintaining their nonprofit status with the Internal Revenue Service, which provides policy limitations for certain kinds of social and political action.

At many institutions, social action means the possibility of individual faculty members becoming involved with activist causes, while the campus as a whole maintains its institutional objectivity on delicate social and political questions. An easy way out is for those associated with a college or university to avoid any active involvement where social issues are concerned. However, I believe that a learning society will insist that colleges and universities enter the fray and become involved with important but usually controversial social issues that include everything from nuclear disarmament to groundwater policies. Each institution must wrestle with how far it will go in providing programming, on a continuum from providing information to advocating a particular position.

International Service: Although related to the service roles previously described, international service is also quite different. Many colleges and universities contract with international organizations to provide services to agencies, institutions, and organizations around the world. These services range from assisting with community development projects in Third World countries to serving as external evaluators for a college or university program in another country.

Land-grant universities and other agricultural colleges have a long history of providing agricultural assistance to other countries. Professional school faculty members such as those in engineering have often worked with peer institutions in other countries. For example, on my own campus, the College of Agricultural and Life Sciences has been active in developing agricultural colleges in Nigeria and Brazil, besides providing consulting assistance in Indonesia, the Gambia, and several other countries. Many other universities have similar records of accomplishment in the international arena.

Newer forms of international service include making courses available via satellite communication. And another interesting wrinkle in international service is for U.S. international workers to search out indigenous information in other countries and bring it back to the United States for possible adoption. For example, a researcher may discover a way farmers in Indonesia grow a certain crop. The U.S. researcher brings this information back to this country and introduces it to a state's agricultural extension service. Thus, international service can include a two-way flow of information.

With ever-increasing concern for world markets and world competition, international service now often includes assisting state governments, business and industry, and commodity groups in establishing international trade missions and foreign market outlets. And some colleges and universities are also offering courses for businesspeople who wish to establish trading relationships with countries such as Japan and China, teaching them something about the culture, values, and social customs of these countries. As the idea of global community becomes a reality, a learning society becomes a global learning society. We must all learn to think beyond our state and national borders.

Challenges for Higher Education

Several challenges face institutions of higher education as they attempt to enhance their public service role in a learning society. These challenges include

*   a poor understanding of what public service is
*   negative attitudes toward public service
*   the need to refine public service approaches

A Poor Understanding of Public Service: Much misunderstanding exists because of the ambiguous nature of public service. Thus colleges and universities are challenged to define what they believe should be their public service role. The prevailing view of public service at many institutions is that of faculty members giving an occasional speech at a Kiwanis Club meeting or serving on the local public library board. On the other hand, as pointed out previously, many colleges and universities are being urged to take on community economic development activities. Both the community and the educational institutions must clearly understand what is and what is not appropriate involvement for these institutions.

The Organization for Economic Cooperation and Development study (1982) mentioned earlier observes that "there is general agreement on the need for fruitful, two-way cooperation between the university and society, and on the fact that the university stands neither aside from nor above society but forms an integral part of it" (p. 23). But colleges and universities often complain that society does not provide sufficient resources to carry out public service. And, in turn, society blames colleges and universities for being too aloof and for too strongly resembling an ivory tower. The Organization for Economic Cooperation and Development study (1982) underscores this dilemma by pointing out that "On the one hand universities are said to show insufficient interest in community affairs, and in the economic and social consequences of their research and their teaching. On the other hand, there is considerable concern that the university system should not lose its way by over-direct involvement in the management of day-to-day affairs . . . . The social system looks to the university to preserve the utmost independence from it, and at the same time demands that it be accountable" (p. 32).

Negative Attitudes Toward Public Service: Attitudes toward public service are related to an understanding, or a lack of understanding, of it. It is difficult for faculty members or local citizens to have a positive attitude toward something that they do not understand. The failure of faculty members to support public service activities enthusiastically has other roots as well. Many would agree that the faculty reward system applauds research and scholarship and encourages adequate classroom teaching but only gives nodding recognition to something vaguely referred to as service. The challenge for colleges and universities attempting to meet society's demands for more public service is not only to develop a clear statement of what this service will be, but also to develop a reward system that recognizes exemplary work in the service area. This is no small task, particularly for those institutions with long and proud research traditions. Those faculty members with strong traditional feelings about research often fail to see the close connection between outstanding research and outstanding public service. For most colleges and universities, a strong public service program is in fact highly dependent on a strong research and scholarship program. Thus the modification of faculty rewards criteria in most instances will not lessen the importance of research activity but will increase the importance of public service contributions.

Until rewards criteria are changed, many faculty members will continue to hear a conflicting message—become more involved in public service, but do not expect to be rewarded for your efforts. A number of attempts have been made to develop evaluation criteria that will make it possible to properly recognize their public service contributions. For example, Elman and Smock (1985) describe in some depth guidelines for establishing an equitable reward system for faculty members engaged in public service activities. (See Chapter Eleven for more discussion of approaches to faculty rewards for continuing education and public service activities.)

The Need to Refine Public Service Approaches: More than twenty years ago, Shannon and Schoenfeld (1965) pointed to a

conflict between research and public service that still exists today: "Residence scholars are increasingly occupied with theory
oriented research, rather than with the fact-finding and action
stimulating research that is grist for the extension [public ser-
vice] mill. . . . The residence scientists willing to perform research that 'makes a difference now' are more cosmopolitan
than community oriented. Local and state research to some extent has gone out of style" (pp. 75–76). The challenge for higher education today is to do research that has broad as well as
community application.

For public service activities to meet community needs,
colleges and universities must shift away from thinking about
the community as merely a place for applying and testing research models and theories. "It is increasingly felt that a university should not respond to demands from the community with
a priori models based on theoretical expectations, and consider
the community merely as a field of application; it should, rather
broaden its concept of research and constantly realign its theoretical models on current, concrete situations. This presupposes
a new definition of the environment of higher education institutions, a new balance between functions, a new type of interaction between these institutions and the community or communities that form their environment, of which the training of
students is merely the most apparent aspect, calling for the largest share of resources" (Organization for Economic Cooperation
and Development, 1982, p. 13).

A major challenge for colleges and universities is to avoid
dumping raw research information into the hands of the public
and calling it public service. "To the public-at-large, access to
vast amounts of undigested facts is of little value. Society already suffers from a glut of data, an overabundance of information, which is usually fragmentary and often inconsistent. For
knowledge to be useful, the bits and pieces of information need
to be aggregated and synthesized into more coherent ideas, with
apparent contradictions explicated. Furthermore, useful knowledge needs to bring together all the pertinent aspects of a situation and not only with one field of specialization. Issues and
activities of different kinds are becoming increasingly interdependent; for example, technical solutions increasingly need to be

considered in light of their economic, social, political, and cultural contexts" (Lynton and Elman, 1987, p. 25).

This approach to connecting public service, research, and the community implies a partnership relationship with the community. Community needs are identified, and then research is developed or modified to meet these needs. It also means that researchers are aware of society's needs when they are conducting their research. As Bok (1982) suggests, researchers are challenged to maintain basic research agendas, but with an eye to application (p. 18).

A more specific difficulty is that most community problems do not conveniently fit within disciplines or departments. As someone once said, communities have problems; colleges and universities have departments. The Organization for Economic Cooperation and Development (1982) points out that "the structures of higher education and more particularly the universities are still, for the most part, based on the growth of knowledge and mono-disciplinary practice. When the community brings up complex, and therefore multi-dimensional situations and asks for multiple action (because a real problem is never exclusively technical, social or scientific), all the university can offer is a collection of analytical strucutures . . . . So interdisciplinarity is not just a new approach to education and research but the key to the change in the missions and social status of the university" (p. 127).

Working out arrangements for multidisciplinary responses to community problems thus becomes a major challenge. Centers, institutes, and other such organizational schemes have been used especially to conduct research of a multidisciplinary nature. Now such organizational schemes are challenged to become even broader, not only sponsoring multidisciplinary research in related areas but also including a social and often a philosophical dimension. Such centers, institutes, and so on are challenged to provide multidisciplinary public service programs as well.

Many barriers prevent multidisciplinary efforts, however. As Lynton and Elman (1987) point out, "Most of the participating faculty [in multidisciplinary programming] continue to be supported totally from departmental funds, and more often than not the time they spend on the interdisciplinary activity is looked upon as time lost to their department . . . . The flow of personnel recommendations in almost all universities is structured along the same one-dimensional departmental base as is the flow of resources. Furthermore, the criteria used for advancement focus strongly on traditional, disciplinary research that leads to scholarly publication. As a result the participation of junior faculty in multidisciplinary programs places them at considerable risk with regard to their chances for reappointment, promotion, and tenure" (p. 46).

Planning for Public Service

How do colleges and universities plan for public service activities? How can they contribute more effectively to a learning society, beyond responding to periodic requests from citizens' groups, business and industry, and others? Earlier I discussed an approach organized by the University of Georgia cooperative extension to involve community leaders from throughout the state in systematically identifying problems. Here I will describe a planning approach recently tried at the University of Wisconsin.

Building on the history of the "Wisconsin Idea" (which dates from the late 1800s), Patrick Boyle, chancellor of the University of Wisconsin–Extension, organized a Wisconsin Idea Commission. The purpose of the commission was to examine the public service (extension) function of higher education. The goals of the Commission were

1. To examine the purposes, direction, and emerging roles of higher education in the U.S. and in the state of Wisconsin.
2. To provide leadership in clarifying the purpose and direction of extension, continuing education and public service work so that it is continually responsive and relevant to the changing needs of people, communities, and society beyond the year 2000.
3. To provide background for future program, resource, and policy decisions affecting extension education [public service] and societal needs.
4. To provide the basis for development of coop-

erative working relationships between public agencies and the University among providers of continuing education.

5. To improve the visibility, credibility, and support of extension [public service] as an integral function of the university among the general public, the legislature, and key leaders in both the public and private sectors [University of Wisconsin–Extension, 1983, p. 2].

Twenty-four people were appointed to the Wisconsin Idea Commission, including representatives from the University of Wisconsin–System administration, the University of Wisconsin campuses at Madison, Parkside, and River Falls; the University of Wisconsin–Extension; the University Center System; the private colleges; and the Wisconsin Board for Vocational, Technical, and Adult Education. The deputy superintendent of public instruction was also a member. This group met monthly to examine background information, the history of higher education's contribution to public service in Wisconsin, and current state problems and needs. After a year of periodic meetings and a two-day retreat, the group agreed to focus on four broad problem areas: (1) economic development, (2) environmental protection, (3) cultural enhancement, and (4) human services such as health, education, and welfare.

The commission then sponsored a conference to discuss ways of developing the Wisconsin Idea for the twenty-first century. In addition to the commission members, representatives from business, industry, agriculture, government, the arts, environmental concerns, labor, and health fields were invited. Four national educational leaders were also asked to participate. The conference was organized around the four problem areas, with a mix of university and community leaders in each discussion group. Questions these groups discussed included

1. What policies/criteria are needed to guide partnerships among government, the private sector, and the university?
    —How can the unique contributions of each

partner be maintained? Given the advent of partnerships, and the need for particular research, can the
practice of professors working as individual entrepreneurs continue? Research professors have not
been easily influenced to change research direction
based upon specific requests from the private sector. How can adjustments in research priorities be
made? Is something lost when research professors
are encouraged to work on projects that may not
be of personal interest?

    —How will conflict of interest problems be
avoided? What criteria should the University use
when deciding which firms, groups, or organizations should be given priority for partnership arrangements? Is there a limit on the number of partnerships the University should be involved with?
What criteria should be used in making this judgment? Who has control of the knowledge that
emerges as a part of a partnership arrangement?
How will the university maintain its position of
making education and information available to all
the citizens of the state when it begins developing
partnership arrangements with particular segments
of society?

    2. How will the nature of partnerships vary,
given different sets of problems and different segments of society? What contributions can the private sector make to the more traditional educational programs carried on by the University? Should
representatives of various businesses, industries, human service organizations, and government be involved more heavily in teaching credit courses at
the University for degree seeking students? What
are the problems in doing this?

    3. How can partnership arrangements be-
tween the University and the private sector be financed?

    —How can partnership arrangements avoid
enhancing the profit margins of a particular seg-

ment of society at the expense of others? In partnership arrangements, who takes the lead? Who decides what the problems are and how they shall be
solved? How does the State of Wisconsin determine
its fair contribution in the face of the reality of
interdependence? Can it wait for the federal government? How much can be accomplished through
regional arrangements? Do state government agencies have the tools and flexibility to work directly
with private industry? What do we need to know
about balancing fiscal responsibilities and control
to achieve effective cooperation within partnerships? Will the partnerships be truly collaborative
arrangements, with sharing of financing, for instance? Is a new approach to financing higher education necessary to recognize or even continue the
contributions of continuing education to the welfare of the state?

—Who will finance partnerships designed to
serve the poor, minority groups, and non-profit organizations that cannot help finance the partnership? How can accountability be maintained for
the partner that is supported by tax dollars and
must show productivity for the tax support? How
will the outcomes of partnerships be identified and
shared? Is the old assumption still valid—if you
need new job skills, once college is completed, you
pay for the education?

4. What type of partnerships between higher
education and business/industry will emerge from
the various centers and other arrangements that are
being formed throughout the University of Wisconsin System? Can higher education and the business/
industry partner develop new knowledge together
in a shared arrangement? For example, will it be
possible for the partners to begin with an idea, do
the necessary research, and apply the research findings until a product is developed, financed, and put
on the market? Business and industry need and

want applied research, often searching for new products to produce. Consumers, too, may want new, better and different products and applications. Yet, the University research and the University community have moved toward more basic research, with application a secondary consideration. How can this disparity be accommodated? Universities have largely worked on the premise that knowledge discovered on a campus is published and disseminated broadly, with few, if any, restrictions. What new arrangements must be made to accommodate the interests of a business partner who helps finance the research, testing, and development of a new product or technological innovation and then wants to disseminate the information or product for profit, without allowing access to its competition? Is it appropriate for the University to become heavily involved not only in the research that leads to new products, but also in testing new products, product feasibility, and assisting in developing capital investment resources?

5. Will an enlarged emphasis on business relationships detract from broader and more traditional concerns in the humanities and liberal arts? What contributions can the humanities and liberal arts make to partnerships between the university and business/industry? How can the arts, for instance, be brought into discussions of economic development? [Wisconsin Idea Commission, 1986, pp. 1–2].

All of these questions were certainly not answered during the two-day conference. But the questions represent the types of concerns shared by higher education and those with whom it is establishing partnerships. Developing partnerships—several examples now exist within the University of Wisconsin–System—is one way to conduct public service activity. Such partnerships recognize the role of colleges and universities as vital participants in a learning society, since they are involved directly in educational programs that lead to societal problem solving.

As colleges and universities listen to the demands for public service from the learning society, major questions become those of definition, priority, and organization. As described earlier, definition can take many forms, ranging from technology transfer to social criticism. What the public service priorities of educational institutions should be is a question that ought to be addressed during strategy planning activities, just as the nature of the organizational approaches that can best make a strong public service contribution should be addressed at this time. It is not so important *how* the questions of definition, priority, and organization are approached, as that they are addressed and answered in the first place.

Summary

Public service programs are often seen as the poor relation of colleges and universities. But to meet the demands of a learning society, public service activity must be reexamined. This activity is poorly understood both by higher education and by the general public. I have defined public service as those programs and activities conducted by colleges and universities that respond to the requests of business and industry, government agencies, nonprofit organizations, and citizens' groups for assistance. It can take various forms: (1) faculty consultation, (2) technology transfer, (3) staff and employee development, (4) community problem solving, (5) social criticism, (6) social action, and (7) international service.

Several challenges face colleges and universities as they attempt to enhance their public service activities: (1) a poor understanding of what public service is, (2) negative attitudes toward public service, and (3) the need to refine public service approaches.

Possible ways of planning for public service activities are illustrated by a University of Wisconsin case study. This describes a planning approach aimed at developing partnerships with various community institutions, organizations, and firms, but with an emphasis on partnerships with business and industry.

10

Revamping Student Services
for New Learners

Not too long ago Corning Community College in New York State asked me for some assistance. Corning is located in a region where several steel mills had closed recently, and many unemployed steel workers had enrolled at the college. They had decided that their steel mill jobs had probably disappeared forever. And their unemployment payments had also run out. They had mortgage payments to make, families to support, and pride to maintain. Returning to school was a last resort for many of them. They knew they needed new job skills to find work.

I met with a room filled with these returning students that day at the beginning of Corning's fall term. Many of them were middle-aged men who had left high school many years before to work in the mills, as their fathers and grandfathers had done. These were normally confident men, prideful men. But in their eyes and their hands I could see anxiety and fright.

These men had been away from school for years, and many of them had unhappy memories of their high school experience. Yet they were now enrolled in college. They knew they needed new skills and knowledge in order to find another job.

This group of returning students was highly visible at Corning Community College. Increasingly, older students are becoming visible at colleges and universities across the country as they return for credit and degree programs. And they are placing a demand on student services.

166

As Knox (1980) observes, "Because past adult students participated in evening and off-campus programs, mainly in noncredit activities, they have been practically invisible to student services. It was often assumed that adults did not need special services because these were provided by family and community life. However, as there are more adults of all ages in the resident instruction, external degree, and noncredit continuing professional education programs, the need for counseling and information services for adult learners is becoming apparent" (p. 7).

Not only has there been an increase in displaced workers (both men and women) enrolling in colleges and universities, but other groups of adults have become represented as well. These include women whose children have just entered school or women whose children have grown up and left home; men and women seeking a career change; men and women who need skills to maintain or advance in their careers; and retired adults seeking life enhancement experiences.

The Present Situation

One author commented in 1975 that "colleges and universities are singularly ill-equipped to serve the needs of adults. Most campuses are handicapped by attitudes which have assigned adult learners to second-class status, have relegated them to night or extension courses, to inferior degrees, to haphazard faculty, and more. On top of this, colleges have expected adults to march to the same teaching methods and institutional procedures designed for persons preparing for rather than engaged in society" (McDermott, 1975, p. 271). Colleges and universities have made many improvements in student services for adults in recent years, but problems still exist. Three misconceptions about adult students survive on many campuses: (1) that these students are interested only in academic subjects and thus are not interested in nor require student services, (2) that their home communities will provide the necessary services, and (3) that student services for traditional-age students will meet adult student needs. Given these perceptions, it is easy to see why some institutions have made few adjustments in their student services. As Thon (1983) underlines, "Instead of examining the potential for offering unique programs, the emphasis has often been on trying to help new student populations fit in or adjust to traditional programs and services" (p. 51).

Some adult student needs do overlap with those of traditional students. Traditional and adult students both want on-campus parking if they work off campus. Both groups appreciate extended office hours for registration and counseling services. Both groups benefit from student organizations, although the makeup of such groups will often be different for older students.

On the other hand, older students have many concerns about career and job counseling, midlife development including marital and child-related problems, and job and life experience problems. Prior educational experience often sets older students apart from more traditional students, too: "The prior educational experiences of these new learners [displaced workers, minorities, career changers, and so on] frequently have been unsatisfactory. High percentages were early victims of substandard or class education. So while they may have successfully met the responsibilities of family, job, and community for many years, they carry with them a memory of 'school' as a place of judgment and rejection rather than of growth and fulfillment" (McDermott, 1975, p. 269).

As learning-at-a-distance formats become more popular for both younger and older students, colleges and universities will also need to face the question of providing student services when the student seldom, if ever, comes to the campus.

Student Services Required

Categories of student services for adult students include orientation, counseling (career, academic, and personal), academic support, and administrative services. I will discuss each of these in turn.

Orientation Services   Cohen (1980) underscores the need adults returning to school have for proper orientation: "Despite some apparent emotional and situational stability, adult learners are opening themselves to other changes as well" (p. 25). These "other changes" often include shifts in family arrangements, changes in work (an adjustment from full-time to part-time work status, for example), and of course adjusting to an academic environment. As Cohen (1980) notes, "Getting settled means achieving enough physical and psychological security in the new environment to get on with the job of learning without major distraction" (p. 2).

In successful orientation programs for adult learners, the following usually occur:

1. The institution presents its programs and services as directly as possible. Successful orientation programs do not rely solely on written materials, but also involve staff in face-to-face meetings with new adult students.
2. When possible, adult students who have successfully adjusted to the college environment assist with the orientation.
3. In library orientation programs or those involving other learning resource centers, the students are escorted to the location. In this way they learn how to deal with seemingly "obvious" things—which doors to enter, how library security systems work, and the like.
4. Successful orientation programs include both the nonacademic as well as the academic features of the program. Thus individuals such as department chairpersons and potential academic advisers are a part of the orientation procedures.
5. Orientation continues throughout at least the first semester. For example, Corning Community College establishes a mentor relationship between a new student and one who has been in the program for at least a semester. This mentor student is available to help with questions the new student may feel reluctant to ask of staff and faculty. The mentor student is available to the new student to discuss whatever is troubling him or her during the first year the student is on campus.
6. Successful orientation programs help adult students recog-

nize study skill problems—listening, reading, concentration, mathematics, note taking, examination taking—and refer them to the appropriate skills workshops. Often students do not recognize these difficulties until a few weeks into the semester.

7. Successful orientation programs begin before adult students enroll in a program. Here is where the functions of orientation and counseling overlap. Prospective adult students often seek information about institutions where they are considering studying, but at the same time they are examining themselves, their motivations, their interests, and their reasons for pursuing further formal education. These prospective students are also keenly interested in career opportunities and career decision making. Institutions often perform this combination orientation-counseling off campus in shopping centers and other locations that are easily accessible to returning students.

8. An orientation program includes special materials and activities for those learners who will learn at a distance via electronic media, correspondence study, and the like and may never set foot on the campus.

Counseling Services   Research points up the need for career counseling as an essential element of any counseling effort for adult students (Nayman and Patten, 1980; Shipton and Steltenpohl, 1981; Thon, 1983; Holliday, 1985; Tittle and Denker, 1980; Geisler and Thrush, 1975). As observed earlier, a majority of adult students return to higher education for career-related reasons. Many women, with new careers in mind, return to school when their children leave home. Both men and women return to school when they are seeking a career change. Often the decision about whether or not to return to school at all is dependent on decisions made about career opportunities. In Thon's (1983) study of 1,637 four-year colleges and universities with 300 or more students, the most important student service for adult students was career counseling. Other services that ranked high were job placement, marriage counseling, individual needs assessment, and support groups (p. 204). Shipton and

Steltenpohl (1981) emphasize tying career and other counseling for adult students to adult development: "If colleges are to truly enhance individual development and prepare students to cope with succeeding stages of development, faculty and staff advisers and counselors need to be prepared to assist students of all ages in clarifying their life, career, and academic purposes. This process of clarification can be cyclical, used again and again as developmental needs demand over the life course" (p. 691). Shipton and Steltenpohl (1981, p. 693) outline a process that counselors and adult student advisers can use to assist in career counseling:

Defining the Task: What factors prompted this person to discuss career opportunities and formal study? Has there been a divorce and a need for employment by a woman formerly dependent on her husband? Is an employer insisting on improved job skills? Does this person wish to make a career change with new challenges and opportunities?

Gathering Information: The counselor or adviser assists the adult student in gathering two types of information, information about himself or herself and information about career options and opportunities. In line with a philosophy of helping adult students to help themselves, less reliance is placed on psychological and other tests. The adult student assumes more responsibility for gathering information. "This change of locus of responsibility from the professional to the individual involved has important development and educational advantages. It enables the individual to take responsibility for his or her own planning. It provides tools for self-evaluation that can be reused when needed. It enables the individual to gain a personal grasp of the information instead of taking another's word for it. And it exemplifies the kind of self-directed inquiry or investigation that all college students need to master" (Shipton and Steltenpohl, 1981, p. 695). Helping adults find their place in the adult life cycle, according to current literature on adult development, can add to the self-development dimensions of career planning. This information will help adult students realize that adult interests and needs change over the life cycle. What a person may believe is a unique feeling may in reality be shared by many others. "Locating oneself on the human development continuum, gaining an understanding of tasks already accomplished and those yet to be achieved, realizing that one's interests and preferences change over time, understanding the crises and strains of transition periods, and visualizing what is yet to come give students of all ages a broader perspective on future possibilities as well as deeper insight into present needs" (Shipton and Steltenpohl, 1981, p. 695). In addition to exploring their own interests and goals, adult students want concrete information about careers and career opportunities.

Sorting Out Values: In addition to focusing on the obvious information about what careers seem open and promising and what preparation is necessary, the process of career exploration requires an examination of values. Which is most important —money, power, security, independence, the opportunity to be creative, adventure, or service to others? Counselors and advisers can help adult students wrestle with these questions.

Making a Choice: After students gather information and consider their values or other perspectives, they must make a choice. This choice may seem firm and in place, particularly after the systematic work just described has taken place. But further shifting often occurs once the person begins taking classes and meeting other students.

Taking Action: The decision in the fourth phase is usually firm enough so that students are able to confidently take some action. For many of them, this means making a decision about returning to higher education.

Besides career counseling, adult students also require academic and personal counseling. Academic counseling includes assisting them with course selection and meeting degree requirements. The process becomes more complicated because many adult students bring a sheaf of transcripts from other institutions. A major part of any academic counseling effort is figuring out the comparability of courses from different institutions and often helping adult students gain acceptance of credits from other colleges and universities. Even when an institution readily accepts credits, the academic counselor must often assist adult students in making new course decisions based on credits already earned. No adult student wants to repeat a course. Course titles often do not convey accurate information about course content. The academic adviser faces inspecting course outlines and interviewing adult students at length to determine the content areas various transfer courses represent.

Adult students also appreciate academic advisers who are willing to come to off-campus sites to assist with academic advising. At Seward County Community College, counselors travel to off-campus locations. As President Theodore Wischropp explains, "We take a counselor out to those outreach locations. We set up a special night usually once each semester, sometimes twice a semester where we invite the part-time students to come in and discuss progress they are making toward their degree, what the degree requirements are, and how they can best meet them" (personal communication, Jan. 21, 1987).

Although there is a strong element of personal attention within career counseling programs, successful counseling programs also assist adult students with midlife crisis difficulties, marital problems, difficulties with children, and so on. Coping with the stress that adult students face in returning to school and in juggling multiple roles becomes a major challenge for the counselor. In my own research with returning students, an increase in stress upon returning to school was noted by more than 90 percent of the students we interviewed (Flannery and Apps, 1987, p. 8). Balancing multiple roles was perceived by many of the students we interviewed as particularly stressful. One student put it this way: "I won't have time till the end of the semester. I'm not sure I can get everything all done. I'm not sure I will meet my responsibilities to the people at work, and to myself for school, and to my husband. I am trying to do too much. I really don't know where or if I could eliminate anything. There's nothing I could eliminate. I couldn't drop a course because the department wouldn't let me. I couldn't cut my hours back at work. They are already cut back so far and I have to work to make some money. What really slid was home. I didn't do any cooking and I didn't do any cleaning. You just keep going. It's like that train in the movie that just slides through to no end. You must slide right up to the end of the semester and you hope that when you hit the last day or the last exam you can walk away" (Flannery and Apps, 1987, p. 8). Unfortunately, for some students, excessive stress leads to illness and they do not walk away at the end of the semester.

Everyone who counsels adult students can assist them with managing stress. In an earlier study (Apps, 1982a), I explored ways that adult students could develop time management approaches to help them cope with the problems of managing multiple roles (pp. 12–19). Otherwise, it is important to let them know that they are not alone and that almost all other students face similar stress problems. Encouraging formation of support groups among older students also helps alleviate stress problems.

In my research, where we interviewed returning students during the first semester they were in school and again one year later, stress levels did not decline as we had anticipated. During the first semester, 90 percent said that stress was a problem for them. One year later 95 percent said that stress was a problem. We had predicted that once the returning students had become more adjusted to classes and the academic routine, stress levels would decline. But other factors, including juggling multiple roles, continued to push stress levels even higher. Helping returning students manage stress thus becomes a major challenge for counselors and everyone else who works with them.

Academic Support   Many adult learners need assistance in retrieving old academic skills, or perhaps in developing skills they never had. Few adults had learned how to read for nuances of meaning and depth of understanding. Many had never developed efficient study skills. Because mathematics is usually far in the background of many adult students, it often poses particular problems for older students. And the prospect of taking examinations terrifies many adult students. In my book *Study Skills for Adults Returning to School* (Apps, 1982b), I address approaches adults can use in sharpening these skills.

Many colleges and universities sponsor writing laboratories for students of all ages who have writing problems. Many institutions also sponsor workshops to address study-skills problems.

For instance, the University of Wisconsin–Madison's Office of Continuing Education Services offers a "Campus Survival Skills Clinic for Adults." Topics covered in hour-long segments include math skills, returning to academic writing, using study time effectively, using library resources, and others. The purpose of the clinic is to introduce adult students to the resources that are available. Follow-up courses are presented throughout the year in study skills, preparing for examinations, and coping with math anxiety.

Peer assistance and support groups can also help adult students sharpen study skills. When I interviewed several hundred returning students, a large percentage told me that they had problems concentrating. This was particularly a problem when they first returned to school. It is understandable. Most of us face lives of constant interruption, by phone calls, knocks on our door, people stopping by, and so on. When the adult student, after carefully juggling schedules, faces a two-hour block of time, he or she often has problems concentrating on an academic assignment.

Peers can often help this student realize that this is a common problem, and that nearly all students have faced it when they first returned to school. Such a realization is of great help in combating the problem.

Administrative Services Administrative services take many forms; I will touch on some of the more important ones.

Library Services: Are the library hours convenient for older students? Are reserve book policies such that older students who commute from jobs have access to them? For example, it can be very difficult for commuting students to use three-hour reserve books. It is often possible for libraries to extend overnight privileges to students, provided that they return the reserve book promptly the following morning. Better still is for the library to have enough copies of reserve books so that older students can routinely check them out for at least a couple of days.

Parking: In research I conducted on a major university campus, parking, after stress, turned up as a major barrier to adult participation on that campus (Flannery and Apps, 1987, p. 9). Because many adult students are commuters and attend part time, parking space on or near campus, days, evenings, and weekends, is essential. It is also essential that parking areas and walkways to classrooms be well lighted. In the absence of well-lighted parking areas, instructors should make arrangements to escort female students to their cars following evening classes.

Child-Care Services: Following counseling, child care was the most often expressed need in a study of returning adult women conducted by Geisler and Thrush (1975). At some institutions, the college or university itself provides day-care services. At other institutions, students are referred to private day-care centers in the area.

Financial Aid Services: Financial aid services were third in importance for returning women students in the Geisler and Thrush (1975) study. The guidelines provided to colleges and universities by the Commission on Higher Education and the Adult Learner and the American Council on Education (1984) recommend that "institution-controlled programs of student financial aid [be] available to all adult learners on a basis that reflects their levels of needs" and that "at least some institution-controlled programs of student financial aid [be] specifically earmarked for assistance to adult learners" (p. 27). Many colleges and universities require full-time study before financial aid is granted. However, a majority of older students are part time and thus ineligible. During the last few years, though, many of these rules have been relaxed, opening up financial aid opportunities.

When I returned to school at age thirty-two with a wife and three children, I met with the financial aid officer at the campus where I was to study. After several general questions about my financial status and responsibilities, she inquired as to why my parents were not helping support my additional education. When I informed her that my parents were retired, she sat back in her chair and sniffed, "Aren't you a little old to be going to school, anyway?" Thankfully, most people like this have retired or have been replaced. Today's financial officers are much better informed about older students and their financial needs.

Placement Services: Because a majority of returning students are in school for career-related needs, placement services are extremely important. But to meet older student needs, placement services must recognize their unique situation. The placement needs of older students require attention to career change, building on previous volunteer experience and community work, concern for adult development tasks, and attention to particular career restraints because of family responsibilities. Returning students completing degrees also have a specific need for developing résumés and sharpening interview skills.

Registration Procedures, Bursar, and General Information and Referral Services: These miscellaneous services are extremely important for adult students. Many changes have been made in recent years to accommodate the needs of part-time and older students. Increasingly, colleges and universities have developed computer registration services so students can register by telephone and need not drive onto campus. On-campus registration services have expanded to include evening and weekend opportunities, especially to accommodate older, working students. And mail registration is accepted at many institutions.

Challenges

Providing student services to adult students presents many challenges. Here are a few recommendations:

1. Recognize the differences among the student service needs of various groups of older students. For example, large numbers of returning students are women. As Holliday (1985) says, "The re-entry woman today is no longer just the middle class, middle-income, middle-aged woman with time on her hands for enrichment courses. Re-entry women are represented more and more by minority, lower-income women who are single parents and heads of households and single women interested in career advancement. These women are serious, determined, enthusiastic, highly motivated, eager to learn and academically successful" (p. 62).

Returning women students—especially part-time ones—have particular needs. Holliday (1985) points out that "some of the institutional factors that have excluded women are sex and age quotas, financial aid, admission policies, stringent curriculum planning and course scheduling, inadequate support services such as childcare, and faculty and staff attitudes. . . . A more serious barrier is the discrimination against part-time re-entry women. Institutions still prefer full-time students, even though the need for students has lessened the stricture on part-time enrollment. However, many institutions have regulations concerning full-time course loads and degree completion periods that particularly hinder low-income women or women with children" (p. 65).

On the other hand, students who are enrolling in non-degree programs cite adult development programs such as time management, life-planning, and communication skills as high-priority student service needs. Senior citizens indicate adult development programs as the highest priority for their student service needs (Thon, 1983, p. 206).

2. Seek to coordinate the various administrative and student service functions. Most colleges and universities have segmented student services. That is, the library system is autonomous. Registration is a separate operation. Student counseling has its own niche, and so on. An example of coordination: A career counselor works off campus with older students, but is prepared to answer questions about registration, child care, and library hours. Older students do not appreciate being bounced from one office to another (neither do younger students). And older students will not accept a "runaround." Some will march directly to the president's office and complain about their treatment, pointing out that they are paying their fees and expect service in return. Thus colleges and universities are challenged to better coordinate student and administrative services. Older students appreciate one-stop service to handle such administrative tasks as registration and transcripts, to obtain answers to questions about parking and day care, and to gain information about study skills workshops.

3. Help instructors of older students become at least minimally proficient in such areas as career counseling (particularly in their own areas of expertise) and with general student

service opportunities. Because many older students are part-time students and are either full-time or part-time workers, and because many of them commute to campus or to an off-campus site, their most consistent contact is with their instructor. Questions for their instructor will range from those related to career opportunities to registration procedures. Even though many instructors would rather not be bothered with these questions, they go with the territory. Older students see their instructor as a first source of information. Institutions are challenged to provide "survival kits" to their instructors with addresses and phone numbers of various student service offices on campus. If the instructor does not know the answer, he or she can give the student a phone number or address for further contact.

Because of the consistent contact over a semester, older students will also develop a respect for their instructors. This respect leads to many counseling situations that can become very uncomfortable for the instructor. I know that in my own teaching, which for the past decade or so has been exclusively with older students, I often hear the gory details about divorces, problems with support payments, and difficulties with children. I hear about problems at work and problems these older students face with their friends once they have returned to school. I try to listen politely. Often listening to an older student's concerns is all that is necessary. But I also listen carefully for signs of troubles where trained counselors can help, and I quickly refer them when I detect these problems. Of course, knowing when or when not to refer them is always difficult.

All in all, colleges and universities must alert their instructors to the extra time it takes when working with older students. Some instructors state flat out that they are not prepared to answer questions that go beyond the course material. I believe that this is a mistake. Older students expect more from their instructors.

4. Provide student services staff and faculty with adult development research findings and their application for older students. Knox (1980) explains why this is important: "Traditionally teaching, social work, clergy, and health professions focused attention on human development during childhood and

adolescence, and adulthood was considered a period of stability. However, in recent decades, rapid social change, pluralistic and egalitarian values, and an aging population have shifted attention to the processes by which adult life unfolds. It has been seen that adulthood is composed of much outward adaptation and internal change in combination with interests and activities that are stable over the years" (p. 6).

Because the age span for adults returning to higher education is so great (from the late twenties on into the late retirement years), they tend to have very different development needs. Not only do these needs contrast with those of younger, more traditional students, but the differences within the adult student population are also very large. For these reasons, a knowledge of adult development theory can be extremely useful: "The most fundamental way in which student services practitioners can assist adult students is by broadening their perspective on adult development. As adults better understand the orderly and sequential changes in characteristics and attitudes that have happened to them and to others in the past, they will become more able to predict and understand their subsequent behavior. A developmental perspective can enable adults to grasp essential current and unfolding features of their own lives and to recognize similarities and differences between their own lives and those of others" (Knox, 1980, p. 19). In my judgment, not only should student services and other administrative personnel become acquainted with adult development theory and application, but faculty members teaching adults could also benefit from this knowledge.

Summary

As adult students have become more visible in higher education, their need for adequate student services has also become more visible.

Three inaccurate assumptions have influenced student services for older students on many campuses: (1) that older students are not interested in student services—their studies consume all of their time, (2) that communities will provide the ser-

services adult students need, and (3) that student services for traditional-age students will meet the needs of older students equally well.

Adult students require student services in the following broad areas: (1) orientation; (2) career, academic, and personal counseling; (3) academic support; and (4) administrative services.

Challenges to colleges and universities include (1) recognizing that needs for student services vary among the various adult student groups, (2) providing integrated student services, (3) assisting instructors of older students who are often asked to perform many student service functions, and (4) helping student service staff and faculty teaching older students become familiar with adult development research and practice.

11

Changing Roles
for Faculty

As higher education responds to the demands of the learning society, faculty members, too, will face many challenges.

Categories of Faculty Members

Presently, faculty members at many colleges and universities fall into two broad categories: (1) campus faculty, including full-time instructors and assistant, associate, and full professors, who teach in degree programs, do scholarly work, and participate in limited public service; (2) continuing education faculty, represented by several groups—full-time on-campus faculty, who often perform both administrative roles as programmers as well as instructional roles in continuing education programs; full-time off-campus faculty, such as cooperative extension agents at land-grant universities; and part-time instructors, such as advanced graduate students, instructors from other colleges and universities, and business or professional people in the community who have the experience and/or credentials to teach.

These two broad categories of faculty members reflect the way that many colleges and universities view their mission—consisting of an on-campus degree program and a continuing education program both on and off campus. But as discussed earlier, society is demanding that colleges and universities participate in a learning society in ways that go well beyond present approaches.

182

New Faculty Roles

The two rather distinct categories of faculty members seen on many campuses will blur as almost all professors become involved with older students. Nearly all faculty members will thus benefit from (1) understanding the characteristics and developmental needs of adult learners, including developing instructional approaches that recognize the learning styles of adults; (2) becoming comfortable with a broad range of instructional formats as well as both on- and off-campus courses, assisting students with self-directed learning projects, and developing and teaching courses that can be presented at a distance using such media as videotape, computers, and satellite communication; (3) developing connections with business and industry and other "users" of information; (4) learning how to respond to requests from government, business and industry, and community organizations for assistance ranging from specific information needs to help with problem solving and decision making; and (5) learning how to work with faculty members representing disciplines other than one's own, so that interdisciplinary contributions can be made to many problems.

As Lynton and Elman (1987) point out, higher education needs "to expand faculty roles and activities by giving as much emphasis to the synthesis, interpretation, and transmission of advanced knowledge as to its generation" (p. 146). They further suggest that "the quality of the academic environment will be enhanced through close reciprocal relationships between strong teaching, traditional scholarship, and externally oriented professional activities, with the whole being greater than the sum of the parts" (pp. 148–149).

Many faculty members in higher education are already performing many of these tasks, but many are not, particularly those who are involved in traditional on-campus degree programs. The learning society is demanding that the entire faculty assume responsibility for some if not all of the five tasks outlined above. Few faculty members will be isolated from older students. Many of them will be asked to provide information to potential users and make their services available beyond the confines of the campus. There are of course many forces influencing this broader view of the role of faculty members.

Forces Inhibiting Faculty Change

Traditional on-campus faculty members have often resisted involvement with continuing education and other learning society activities because of a number of factors, including their attitudes and autonomy, the reward system, identity problems, a critical perspective, and poor administration-faculty relationships. These points deserve additional comment.

Faculty Attitudes and Autonomy   On many campuses, particularly those of the larger research institutions, extremely negative attitudes toward adult and continuing education efforts exist. Harrington (1977) reports on a faculty survey in the 1960s where "a cross section of faculty members put adult education thirty-seventh in importance among forty-seven college and university activities, far behind faculty rights, research, and undergraduate teaching. These experts added that in the future it should be thirty-eighth" (p. 5). Harrington traces faculty attitudes toward adult and continuing education to the early 1900s and reports on the attitudes of such notables as Thorstein Veblen and Abraham Flexner: "Back in 1918 Veblen called all extension lectures and home study courses worthless. A decade later Flexner passed the same judgment. 'Scandalous,' he cried, after a hasty look at a few correspondence operations. . . . Along with professional training for undergraduates, which he also deplored, this activity threatened to turn the American university into a 'service station' " (p. 6).

Harrington cites similar negative attitudes toward adult and continuing education among higher education administrators. " 'You can't be serious, you must be joking,' was one West Coast dean's reaction when I suggested to him in 1961 that colleges and universities should include the education of adults among their major responsibilities. 'Adult education!' he snorted, 'Extension! That means second-rate courses taught by second-rate teachers to second-rate students' " (p. 7). Another administrator polled in 1973 said, " 'We worry about standards, with adults wanting lots of admission credit for their life experience, and for what they claimed they learned in the armed services and at unaccredited and inferior institutions. And we wonder if they learn much, living off-campus, and taking one course at a time along with their full-time jobs. Besides, few of them have a genuine intellectual interest. They want a degree for career advancement, or come because they are bored. Every reason except to get educated. When bachelors and bachelor girls write to the lonesome columns, the Aid-to-the-Lovelorn twins say 'If you're looking for company or for a mate, join a church or take an adult education course' " (Harrington, 1977, p. 7).

Unfortunately, twenty years later, negative attitudes toward adult education activities persist. Many campus faculty members see adult education as clearly extraneous to the "main activity" of the campus. When pressed, many will argue that colleges and universities are for able young people directly out of high school, not for adults wishing to start over, make career changes, and the like. As Freedman (1987) points out, some campus faculty members are "vociferously hostile" toward adult continuing education activity: "These critics direct a number of charges at continuing education. Thus: It is driven not by academic but by market considerations. It is mostly practical, applied—training rather than education, eschewing the theoretical base without which study can only be superficial. Much of it is substantially different from what is offered in the regular degree curricula and therefore does not belong in the university. The students are not interested in or equipped for serious learning" (p. 13).

Although most faculty members would argue that they are progressive in their thinking and like to be viewed as liberals, their attitudes toward their own institutions tend to be extremely conservative. As Mayhew (1980) notes, faculty members "have long been socialized concerning academic and educational content, processes, and techniques. Disciplines represent the keystone, the integrity of which is safeguarded by academic departments. Courses are taught in lectures, seminars, and laboratories and represent the major way faculty members express their scholarship and expertise. The disciplinary department and traditional procedures are carefully guarded, and suggested changes are typically perceived as threats to them—as indeed they are. Consider the frequently suggested reforms of interdisciplinary courses, using educational technology, team teaching, or independent study. All challenge the traditional role of a faculty member as one who knows and will tell but only under his or her own conditions" (pp. 47–48).

At most colleges and universities, campus faculty members also have considerable autonomy in deciding what they do and how they do it: "Faculty members probably have more personal and professional autonomy than any other group of professionals employed in structured organizations. They are usually free to decide what they will teach, how they will teach it, what they will study, how they will study it, and how they will spend their time. Indeed, beyond meeting classes, holding office hours, and attending departmental and committee meetings, faculty members have few set obligations as to where they will be at what time" (Astin, 1985, p. 197).

Combine a negative attitude toward adult education with a generally conservative stance toward innovation and change, and spice that with the freedom to avoid change because of autonomy, and it becomes clear what formidable problems colleges and universities face as they attempt to excite their campus faculty about contributing to a learning society.

The Reward System   At many colleges and universities, particularly the larger research institutions, rewards to faculty come from research and scholarly productivity first, campus teaching second, and public service a distant third. An assistant professor working toward tenure gets the message early—do research and write or seek other employment. By the time the assistant professor has earned tenure, he or she has been socialized into a way of working that it is difficult to change. Of course the change is particularly difficult if a professor's institution bases its salary increases in large measure on research productivity. What incentive, if any, does a professor have for participating in adult continuing education activities? In fact, it is difficult to get that professor to think very much about new teaching approaches, using technology, or trying to understand the learning needs of older adults who enroll in his or her classes.

Some institutions are making conscious efforts to examine their reward and recognition criteria, to make certain that faculty member involvement in continuing education and public service is properly recognized. For example, at the University of Illinois at Urbana-Champaign, the Office of Continuing Education and Public Service has prepared a *Faculty Guide for Relating Continuing Education and Public Service to the Promotion and Tenure Review Process* (Office of Continuing Education and Public Service, n.d.). The report states that "outstanding teaching and research by faculty members in continuing education and public service activities should be considered as equivalent to comparable performance in resident instruction and other research activities for purposes of promotion and tenure decisions" (p. 1). Those preparing the report recognized that comparability of continuing education and public service with research activities and resident instruction "is most firmly established when the evidence used to demonstrate outstanding continuing education and public service efforts is understood and accepted by those involved in the promotion and tenure review process" (p. 1).

The National Association of State Universities and Land Grant Colleges has also published a monograph, written by Elman and Smock (1985), that describes approaches for recognizing faculty service and continuing education activities. Elman and Smock argue that professional service can be described within five general categories: "applied research, consultation and technical assistance, instruction, products, and clinical work/performance" (p. 20). They also contend that "the structural mechanisms for evaluating the level of quality must be the same as, or at the very least, compatible with the mechanisms for evaluating teaching and research" (p. 22). They go on in the monograph to illustrate approaches for measurement of quality, including (1) documentation—providing information to describe what the person did, (2) evaluation—deciding who evaluates the person's performance and what criteria are used, and (3) assessment of merit—weighting the relative importance of the specific professional service activities.

Extension and outreach units often attract campus professors by paying them on an overload basis. But these payments are generally quite modest and are not equivalent to their campus salaries. Younger professors particularly welcome this extra money, but soon discover they can earn much more through consulting efforts than through extension teaching or that they can earn more writing a textbook in their off-hours. Besides, a textbook will generally earn them more points at merit review time than their extension teaching activity.

Identity Problems   Faculty members are recruited because of their training in a tightly defined discipline area, then they are rewarded for their contributions to this discipline. It should be no surprise that their first loyalty will be to their discipline, and then to the department that nurtures the discipline. Astin (1985) effectively characterizes the identity problem that this situation creates for many faculty members, particularly at the larger research institutions: "Most faculty members identify primarily with their disciplines and their departments . . . and departments tend to be highly competitive with each other. Under these conditions, few faculty members feel any identity with the institution as a whole or any motivation to cooperate with colleagues in other disciplines. The single-minded emphasis on research and scholarly performance exacerbates these problems by pitting individual faculty members and departments against each other in an environment where one person's success may come to symbolize failure for others" (p. 187).

But as noted earlier, the demands of the learning society often require interdisciplinary efforts—faculty members working together to examine issues and solve problems. There is also need for administrators and faculty members to examine overall institutional policy and direction. This examination, to be effective, must go beyond the situation where each member of the faculty protects his or her discipline whenever new institutional directions are discussed or new programs considered. Irving Buchen (1987), president of Westfield State College, argues that "faculty members must cultivate relationships with members of disciplines other than their own. One of the most lamentable records of higher education has been the failure of many multidisciplinary relationships. The political power base of single departments has traditionally been so strong and their hold on faculty evaluation and rewards so tenacious that they have rendered many multidisciplinary efforts feeble and vulnerable. Indeed, the mortality rate of such programs is often matched only by the mortality rate of the faculty who participate in them" (Buchen, p. 25).

It would seem possible that faculty members could, at the same time, feel loyal to their discipline, have concern for their institution, and be committed to making major contributions to the learning society.

A Critical Perspective   A theme running through graduate programs is how to be critical, how to find flaws in ideas and in thinking, how to analyze research evidence to find an error or an omission, or how to challenge a conclusion reached based on another view of the evidence. Such is the stuff of strong research graduate programs. And such is the background of almost all faculty members teaching in campus programs. As we might expect, this critical attitude carries over into other faculty endeavors. When a new proposal is offered by an administrator, a faculty committee, or an individual faculty member, no matter what the subject of the proposal, the first reaction by most faculty members is to go for the jugular. It is commonly believed that stronger proposals will result from this approach. But there is the danger that after a few such drubbings by a critical faculty, creative faculty members will stop coming up with new ideas.

In the case of institutional change, perhaps a moratorium on criticism should be agreed on by all concerned until the new thinking has had a chance to build beyond its embryonic form. Encouragement, or at least hands off for a time, might generate more ideas with promise. To take a specific example, conceivably a review panel could first consider the strengths of a new proposal, or at least balance its strengths with its weaknesses, before summarily dismissing a controversial idea. Such early dismissal is often the fate of proposals intended to meet the needs of new audiences, such as adult students. That is not to suggest that ideas should not be subjected to critical review, of course. But let us not kill an idea before it is scarcely born. Academia is filled with critics. People with new and creative ideas are scarce.

Poor Administration–Faculty Relationships   As Astin (1985) says, "Faculty members are inclined to view administrators with a curious mixture of fear, suspicion, and contempt: fear because of the potential threat to their autonomy posed by the administrator's real or imagined power, suspicion because of a traditional dislike of authority, and contempt because of a belief that administrators are failed faculty members who do not have the talent to be competent teachers and scholars or who value power and authority more than teaching and scholarship. As a consequence of these attitudes, which have been reinforced by the recent emergence of collective bargaining and unionism, faculty members tend to reject out of hand any administrative proposal for change" (p. 197). Administrators thus seldom act on anything without seeking the reaction of some faculty committee. At best this approach makes for exceedingly slow decision making. At worst nothing happens because a highly critical faculty summarily rejects most if not all administratively developed ideas.

The alternative for administration is to organize committees and give them the task of coming up with new ideas, with little or no content input from administration. At my institution, I recently chaired such a committee organized by the administration. It was a long-range planning committee appointed to develop action guidelines for the college for the next decade. The reactions from the committee membership were exceedingly varied regarding the task. Two or three of the members were concerned that the administration was not making more of a contribution to the committee's work. "What ideas does the dean's office have for the future of the college?" one of them asked. Others on the committee felt that at least the dean's office could have supplied the committee with background data that would have speeded up committee deliberations considerably. Still others were rather passive about the entire activity. Their attitude could be summed up by the comments of a committee member who said, "I've been through all this before. We meet for hours, talk to each other and past each other, and even argue from time to time, but when all is said and done, more is said than done, in fact almost nothing is done. Thus I can't get very excited about what we are doing."

These observations suggest that responding to the demands of a learning society will require institutional change. After all, adult learners, business and industry, community leaders, government agencies, and a host of others who expect to have certain needs met by colleges and universities are not concerned about the institutions' decision-making structures. They are interested in results.

Why Faculty Members Participate in Continuing Education Activities

As we have just seen, many factors prevent the widespread participation of college and university faculty members in continuing education, outreach, and public service programs. But many do participate. Why?

"I enjoy the excitement of working with an adult audience, and the kinds of questions and challenges they give me," one faculty member told me. She continued, "When you're working with a group of people, and they are sitting on the edge of their chairs, and they, at a moment's notice, want to applaud you or lambast you, well that's teaching at its best, that's the electricity that I enjoy in working with adults."

Testing ideas and theories in practical situations is another reason some faculty members give for participating in continuing education programs. Discovering new research questions is a factor for some faculty members, and others say they pick up practical examples that they then introduce into their degree-credit teaching. Some suggest that the reason they enjoy working with continuing education programs is the opportunity

to see their ideas put into practice. Many of those who participate in such programs go home to almost immediately try the
new ideas they have gained. And, in some instances, faculty
members teaching in continuing education programs tell me
that they have developed contacts with people in business and
industry that have led to research grants and consulting opportunities.

Influencing Change

What strategies can colleges and universities follow that will lead
to institutional change, particularly on the part of the faculty,
who play a key role in any institutional decision-making process?

Administrative Leadership   Keller (1983) believes that
to begin solving the problems higher education faces, stronger
administrative leadership is required: "There is now a stalemate
in the exercise of power on the American campus. University
management is in shackles" (p. 27). Keller says that there is a
"persistence of biases and naivete about organizational necessi-
ties. . . . [This] makes planning, organizational behavior, good
financial practices, and modern management difficult in higher
education. Many colleges and nearly all universities are fairly
complex organizations, but one-half of the ruling group behaves
as if they were not. And the other half—the presidents and their
staffs—often refuse to introduce the operating styles and procedures from the best organization theory and practice, management, and planning, partly out of fear of faculty criticism but
partly because they usually share the biases and naivete of the
faculties, despite the need to make their complex enterprises
function better" (p. 34).

According to Keller, strong leadership is needed at the
head of each college and university. But beyond strong leaders
at the helm, colleges and universities need strong and insightful
leaders at every level, from presidents through deans, department chairs, and faculty committees to effect the changes that
we are discussing.

Institutional Planning   As I discussed in Chapter Four, a transformation process should be built into whatever planning approach is followed. The transformation process requires that those involved in planning examine their assumptions and beliefs about students in higher education, the purposes of the institution, teaching and learning, and curriculum, and attempt to reconcile any contradictions that emerge in their attitudes. For example, in a discussion of the aims of higher education, if faculty members agree that the sole instructional purpose of a college or university is to serve young people fresh out of high school programs, and they also believe that they must be a part of a learning society in order to survive, then they must resolve the obvious inconsistency. After all, an institution cannot at the same time respond to a learning society and have as its sole instructional purpose the education of young people coming directly out of high school.

We saw earlier that the transformation process involves (1) developing awareness—learning about the present situation at our institution; learning about the demands of the learning society; discovering how other institutions, agencies, and organizations are contributing to the learning society; (2) exploring alternatives—considering the contributions that our institution could make to the learning society; (3) making a transition—moving from our old views to a new view we wish to develop; (4) achieving integration—putting back together the pieces that evolved from transition; and (5) taking action—setting our new ideas in motion, beginning to make the changes that are required.

As a part of a planning effort, a transformation process can be fundamental to an institution's commitment to a learning society. Without a basic change in beliefs, changes in higher education will come slowly if at all at some institutions. This approach could also be built into a faculty development program, where the same model could be followed. Lindquist (1981) suggests something similar as content for a faculty development effort. He proposes that a faculty development program should include (1) study of human development theory and research; (2) study of alternative curriculum, teaching, and evaluation practices; (3) study of students, institutional mission, curricular and teaching practices, and organizational supports for staff and students; (4) study of "the ways we do work, and might work as an organization to regularly assess and improve our efforts" (p. 734). Other approaches to faculty development may also be followed.

Faculty Development Programs   Faculty development programs have become so popular that "there has evolved something that might be called the 'faculty development movement' and a new professional subspecialty has arisen of what might be called 'faculty developers.' These include directors of centers for the improvement of instruction, assistant deans for faculty affairs, and directors of learning resources centers" (Mayhew, 1980, p. 233).

Faculty development takes many forms. The most pervasive are those programs attempting to improve instructional approaches, particularly the use of educational technology in the classroom. Hoyle and Johnson (1987) argue that instructors will need to know a broader range of teaching approaches. "Twenty-first-century professors will need a larger repertoire of instructional strategies. Today's professors should have more knowledge about technology—the use of microcomputer programs, organized audiotape and color-slide presentations—and they should use games, simulations, and other modes of instruction that are in line with the objectives for the courses they will teach" (p. 26).

At Pennsylvania State University, faculty instructional improvement is carried out under the auspices of the Instructional Development Program Office. The focus of the program is on improving instruction. The office prepares an assortment of materials for faculty. As Maryellen Gleason Weimer, head of the program, says, "We find that [the faculty] likes very pragmatic materials and that the materials must be written in clear discursive prose. We also try to make them a bit catchy, realizing that faculty are very busy and frequently do not have either a lot of time or motivation to read materials about teaching" (personal communication, Dec. 12, 1986).

Materials include an "Instructor Survival Kit" offering suggestions for those who teach large classes. It contains recommendations to (1) involve students, (2) use small groups, (3) develop a comfortable presentation style, (4) personalize evaluation, (5) get input from students, and (6) check with colleagues to find out what works for them. For each suggestion the author presents how-to ideas and a list of resources for further information.

Other reference materials the Instructional Development Program at Pennsylvania State University has produced include "Questions Faculty Most Often Ask About Student Evaluation and the Research Responses," "Essential Sources: Our Ten Best on Teaching—An Annotated Bibliography," "Essential Sources: Our Ten Best On Learning—An Annotated Bibliography," and "Instructional Improvement: Strategies For Implementing the Changes." A newsletter entitled *ID: An Instructional Development Newsletter* is produced each month and is available to faculty members who request it on a subscription basis.

The University of Georgia's Office of Instructional Development offers

1. A weekly noon seminar where personal and professional concerns of faculty and staff are discussed and such topics as test construction and managing stress are presented.
2. Instructional improvement grants providing faculty seed money for developing new teaching approaches.
3. Media support for teaching.
4. Awards for teaching excellence.
5. A quarterly newsletter highlighting important instructional issues.
6. Computer support services including institutes on academic computing.
7. Universitywide conferences that focus on a major instructional or faculty development issue over two days.
8. New-faculty orientation.
9. Consultations with individual faculty members, department heads, and colleges and schools on matters relating to instruction (Jackson and Simpson, 1984, p. 14).

At Texas A&M University, a Center for Teaching Excellence was established to assist faculty, administrators, and teaching assistants. According to Hoyle and Johnson (1987), "The functions of the Center include encouraging innovative teaching and assisting faculty members through workshops on teaching and through individual evaluation based on classroom observation or an analysis of a videotaped lesson. The Center also assists administrators and faculty members in the evaluation of curricula and informs faculty members of current issues affecting teaching in higher education" (p. 27).

The Pennsylvania State University, University of Georgia, and Texas A&M examples are representative of the efforts many colleges and universities across the country are making toward improving instruction. However, many of these efforts do not focus on the special needs of adult learners, including the often nontraditional instructional formats that are necessary, such as once-a-week classes, off-campus classes, classes taught at a distance using electronic media, and so on.

At the University of California–Los Angeles Extension, the instructional development program focuses on improving the teaching ability of the many nonacademic professionals employed in their extension program. The program has two components: a "New Instructor Orientation," which is a three-hour program presented a week to ten days before the quarter begins for all new extension instructors, and "The Instructor Development Series," which is a group of one-day, Saturday workshops led by outstanding extension instructors, who are called Master Teachers. The Instructor Development Series is available to all extension instructors free of charge. The series includes such topics as "platform skills," "use of audiovisual materials," "testing and grading," "planning the total course," and "designing the one-day or weekend program."

At the University of Maryland's University College, the faculty development program includes (1) orientation meetings for new faculty; (2) classroom observation by experienced instructors; (3) faculty development workshops on such topics as effective presentation skills, fine tuning discussion leadership skills, and active teaching in small groups; (4) individual consultations with faculty members about new teaching approaches, resolving conflicts with students, interpreting student evaluation results, or using technology in a particular course; (5) general faculty meetings held once a semester, generally on a Saturday morning; (6) confidential rating of instructors by students; (7) a newsletter highlighting current events in higher education; and (8) excellence-in-teaching awards. The majority of the instructors involved are part-time instructors, which is similar to the situation at UCLA.

It is always difficult to assess the value of instructional improvement programs. Michael Siegel, coordinator of faculty development for University College, offered this example of a success story: "I could tell you a very elaborate story about a certain chemistry instructor we have whom we worked with and who was having very serious difficulties with the classroom. He's now gotten to the point where he's so serious about teaching and the [faculty development] program that he literally comes to every workshop he can and he is doing all kinds of things he never dreamed about doing. He is probably, as my colleague says, our greatest success story" (personal communication, Jan. 14, 1987).

Several interesting points can be made about these four examples, all viewed as quite outstanding examples of faculty development programs. The first two, at Pennsylvania State University and the University of Georgia, focus on improving the instructional approaches of full-time faculty. Some attention may be given to work with older students in nontraditional settings, but that is not a major goal. On the other hand, UCLA and the University of Maryland's University College focus on part-time instructors who work primarily with older students. Many of these instructors are business and professional people who teach classes as an additional activity in their lives.

These two kinds of faculty development programs in many ways reflect the faculty situation at many colleges and universities. The faculty who teach traditional classes and for the most part work with younger, more traditional students are treated one way, and the faculty who teach older students are instructed in another. If colleges and universities are going to make important contributions to the learning society, it would seem that some commingling of faculty members must take place. Doesn't it make sense that part-time faculty from the business and professional world who now work almost exclusively with older students might teach younger students in traditional settings from time to time? And doesn't it make sense that the more traditional faculty have an opportunity to learn about adult students and nontraditional teaching approaches, including involvement with noncredit programs, from time to time?

Mayhew (1980) argues that college and university faculty development programs are often too narrow, since they tend to focus almost exclusively on the improvement of instruction. He suggests (1980) that a faculty development program should include (1) intellectual stimulation, made possible in part by funds for summer travel, study time; (2) curriculum and instruction, assisted by funds for improving courses and improving instruction; (3) an emphasis on improving scholarship; and (4) a mental health component, with a focus on discussing such issues as resolving conflicts between teaching and research roles (pp. 234–244).

Lindquist (1981) offers the following challenges for faculty development in the future: "Postsecondary education is moving with the population curve toward a lifelong learning model. However, it is not there yet. Most college offerings are still one-shot degree programs, whether one takes that shot at 18 or 48. But there are signs all around that 'the learning society' can become a reality and that colleges can play an important role" (p. 740). According to him, faculty will "need to learn how to assess learning derived from extensive adult experience, then design educational programs to build on that learning. Faculty will need to learn how to relate to students at all stages of the life cycle. They will need to learn how to facilitate individualized learning projects. . . . Professors will need to learn how to tap community resources rather than relying exclusively on campus resources, which many adult learners will find intimidating and inaccessible. They will need to learn how to help adults plan learning projects, and they will need to learn how to act as educational brokers between learners and learning resources. . . . Perhaps most important, professors will need to develop a new appreciation of lifelong learning and learners" (p. 740).

Faculty Preparation One final approach toward assisting faculty in meeting the demands of a learning society is to build a discussion of such issues into graduate training programs, which are the source of new faculty. Unfortunately, almost no attention is presently given in these programs to any kind of college teaching, whether it be for younger or older students. The assumption has been and continues to be at almost every graduate institution that once you know your discipline area, the teaching will take care of itself. (Some graduate students will have had teaching assistant experience, where they had an opportunity to work under the tutelage of their major professor or another instructor. If he or she was a good teacher, they will have had a good role model. Unfortunately, such positive role models do not always exist.) Sometimes the system works adequately; some people seem to have a natural inclination toward teaching and quickly learn by trial and error to become excellent teachers. But often it is apparent that some teachers' training would have been useful.

Summary

As colleges and universities face the challenges of the learning society, faculty, too, will be challenged, particularly the full-time campus faculty. Many of these individuals were hired during the boom years of the 1960s and are ten to fifteen years away from retirement. "One-third of the American professors will be replaced in the next 15 years. There will be 70,000 to 130,000 new full-time faculty added between 1990 and 2010. These new professors will live the bulk of their professional lives in the twenty-first century—and they won't begin retiring until the middle of that century" (Buchen, 1987, p. 22).

The learning society will demand that new professors attend to older students, understand their learning needs, and become acquainted with the teaching approaches that can best accommodate their particular life situations—many have families and are working in addition to attending college. The learning society will challenge faculty members to become more cognizant of community resources and build them into campus programs, it will encourage the use of part-time instructors from time to time, and it will insist on faculty involvement in noncredit and other types of informal learning.

A number of forces make it difficult for faculty members to make the changes required to meet the demands of a learning society: (1) an often negative attitude toward adult education, coupled with the autonomy to carry out their own program interests; (2) a reward system that overlooks adult education; (3) identification with a discipline or department rather than with a college or university as a whole; (4) a tendency to respond to new ideas with criticism; and (5) administration-faculty relationships that are often negative.

There is great irony involved in examining the faculty at most colleges and universities. On the one hand, most faculty members pride themselves on being liberal and open-minded and constantly searching for new ideas and new approaches, particularly when they are related to their disciplinary interests. But on the other hand, when it comes to their own teaching, their departmental structure, and their view of educational aims, they are extremely conservative. They generally see no need to change and resist change at every turn.

For change to occur, strong administrative and faculty leadership is necessary. Institutional planning that involves an analysis and discussion of adults as learners, an examination of teaching approaches for adults, the development of a curriculum that will apply to a diversity of learners, and an examination of aims can help move an institution forward. Faculty development programs and graduate training programs that give attention to the concerns of the learning society will also contribute, as will increased attention to faculty awards and other forms of recognition for faculty members who perform extensive continuing education and public service functions.

12

How Higher Education
Can Thrive in a
Learning Society

Higher education must meet both external and internal challenges if it is to become a major contributor to a learning society.

External Challenges

Public Attitude   From the late 1950s to the early 1970s, higher education was a privileged institution in our society. Tax dollars from local, state, and federal sources poured into college and university coffers. New buildings, new campuses, and new programs sprang up across the country. But as we move toward the 1990s, this is no longer the case, and higher education has to justify itself and its programs at every turn. This questioning and criticism has been accompanied by many studies of colleges and universities. Some recent ones include a "A Marshall Plan for State Colleges," known more formally as "To Secure the Blessings of Liberty." The American Association of State Colleges and Universities asked a panel of educators, business leaders, and government officials to examine state colleges and universities and make recommendations for renewal (National Commission on the Role and Future of State Colleges and Universities, 1986). From the perspective of how states could make stronger contributions to education, another report—*Time for Results: The Governors' 1991 Report on Education*—includes a number of suggestions (National Governors' Association, 1986). As a third example, the Association of American Colleges (1985) produced *Integrity in the College Curriculum: A Report to the Academic Community*. In addition, Boyer (1987) and the Carnegie Foundation for the Advancement of Teaching published *College: The Undergraduate Experience in America*, a study of 29 colleges and universities involving 5,000 faculty members, 5,000 college students, and 1,000 college-bound high school students.

In addition to the formal studies such as these, there has been considerable public debate about higher education. William J. Bennett, current U.S. Secretary of Education, has criticized higher education at every turn, making such comments as " 'there is an extraordinary gap between the rhetoric and the reality of higher education' " (quoted in Palmer, 1986, p. 11). Secretary Bennett proposed slashing federal spending for higher education. And in the summer of 1987, Bloom's book *The Closing of the American Mind: How Higher Education Has Failed Democracy and Impoverished the Souls of Today's Students* (1987) topped the *New York Times* nonfiction list. Bloom criticizes higher education for abandoning sound liberal arts teaching in the 1960s for trendy, "relevant" studies where all ideas are of equal importance.

To the critical rhetoric about higher education we must add the emergence of a substantial anti-intellectual movement. Anti-intellectualism is expressed in various ways. Proponents ask why anyone should attend college when it is possible to find a high-paying job right out of high school. (This argument has disappeared in very recent years, though, as such high-paying jobs have evaporated.) On the other hand it has also been difficult for liberal arts college graduates to find jobs. Why study for four years and then discover there is no work? Those who advocate "easy answers for complicated questions" represent another thread of the anti-intellectual movement. Why examine a question in depth when a simple yes or no will suffice? Why be bothered with "all the shades of gray" when most questions are easily divided into black and white responses? And so on.

A situation of scarce resources with increasing demands affects people's attitude toward higher education, particularly when tax dollars are concerned. In recent years, national problems demanding attention have been social security, with associated health programs; drug enforcement; national health epidemics; and defense budgets. Higher education has had to take its place among the many other demands for federal dollars. A similar situation exists at the state and local levels. In recent years, many states have wrestled with declining revenues because of sluggish economies and increasing demands for social welfare, roads, prisons, health care, and economic development incentives. Along with other tax-supported programs, higher education has had its share of problems when budget cuts were made. It has had to compete vigorously for new tax dollars, or, in many cases, to maintain the status quo.

Continuing education programs also face the objection that if you are an adult, then you must pay for your education. This attitude presents a particularly difficult problem when colleges and universities see a need to involve displaced workers, low-income persons, and minorities in their programs. Who will pay for their educational opportunities?

Social Problems   Many of the country's social problems challenge higher education, directly or indirectly. As mentioned earlier, higher education must compete for scarce resources, some of which are designated for social problems. Some social problems, such as illiteracy, challenge higher education directly, although most colleges and universities do not see combating illiteracy as a major role. Nevertheless, higher education must be concerned about this issue, since college and university programs are of little value for those who lack basic skills.

Colleges and universities are also influenced by social problems about which they can do little—national defense and illiteracy are examples. But they are also influenced by those where they can make a contribution—examples include research on national health problems, and educational programs for basic education instructors.

A challenge often facing colleges and universities is which social problems or concerns should be taken on and how? Should special programs for displaced workers be organized? Should community economic programs be staffed? What are the benefits of involvement in these programs? What are the disadvantages? And how will these programs be financed? Perhaps a question at another level would be whether a college or university has an obligation to society to offer programs such as those previously outlined, given the associated financial problems and the widespread lack of acceptance by those involved in the more traditional programs?

Competition   Today's adults have many options for educational services. A college or university is only one of many. Adults may enroll in courses, even degree programs, offered by their employer or other businesses. They may attend classes offered by labor unions, professional organizations, and community organizations such as the YMCA or YWCA and the Red Cross. They may enroll in a host of programs offered by for-profit adult education agencies such as Weight Watchers, Dale Carnegie, and a host of others. Though these agencies are clearly in the education business for a profit, their fees are often lower than comparable courses offered by a college or university. And the old myth, "unless something is offered by a college or university it lacks quality," must be forever set aside. Many of these noncollegiate providers offer credit, degrees, and educational opportunity that meet licensing requirements. And these noncollegiate providers do everything colleges and universities do and more. The quality of their programs is usually as high or higher than that offered by a college or university.

Program Quality   Evaluating quality involves both an internal and an external challenge. Internally, faculty members teaching in more traditional programs have often questioned the quality of certain continuing education programs. As Alan Knox comments, "How do you judge the quality of continuing education programs, particularly in contrast with judging the quality of research? The enormous number of activities that are occurring under the rubric of extension and continuing education, and the fleeting nature of them, makes it difficult for peers to judge the quality of performance" (personal communication, Mar. 24, 1987). In the name of quality, some critics question whether a college or university should offer certain continuing education courses, workshops, or conferences. The issue comes down to institutional purpose. I will return to this below.

Externally, the question of quality includes several dimensions. Many of those selecting college and university programs want to be assured they are receiving their money's worth. This is a most difficult question to address, but it is nevertheless raised by students, and increasingly so. It is an especially important question when particular offerings on a campus are also available from other providers, and often at a lower cost.

As Freedman (1987) points out, the traditional measures of quality have been an assessment of the preparation, motivation, and intellectual quality of students; the level and character of the curriculum; the nature of the teaching methods used; the credentials of the faculty; and the quality of the facilities and learning resources (p. 105). Another approach to measuring quality focuses on outcomes: the acquisition of knowledge and skills by the students as measured by a variety of assessment methods, including written and oral examination; observation of field projects; and performance assessment in such areas as public speaking and computer work. But Freedman (1987) says that there is growing concern that the measures of quality have not gone far enough. The ultimate criterion is "the extent to which that learning can be applied beyond the classroom and the examination room to the contexts of life and work" (p. 105). This is the criterion for quality that many adult learners use in making decisions about which courses appear to be of high quality. They attempt to judge how well their new learning can be applied. There are several problems with this approach, though, particularly when it is used to judge liberal arts courses. It is difficult to see how a course in Western history, for example, can be easily and quickly applied to a person's job or life in general. Does that mean that the course is of low quality? Most would certainly say that it does not.

Another way of thinking about quality is to consider the question of whose perspective quality is being evaluated from.

The institutions'? The learners'? The taxpayers' (for tax-supported institutions)? Other providers'—how the quality of higher education compares with, say, a technical school's quality? Our colleagues'? The disciplines'? As we think about these multiple perspectives, the answers to the question "What is quality?" will vary. Which perspectives should command more of our attention? Which less? What are the risks if we slight a perspective? What are the risks, for example, if we say we are giving more credence to quality from the perspective of the learners than from, say, our colleagues' perspective? The issue of quality will become increasingly important for all aspects of adult continuing education, including those programs associated with higher education.

Information Technology   As I have discussed in Chapters Two and Seven, all of higher education must begin understanding the meaning of the many new forms of information technology. This is particularly so with that technology that stores vast amounts of information and then makes it easily and readily available. Keller (1983) underscores the magnitude of this revolution: "The rapid growth of electronic technology in the past two decades presents universities with the first major transformation in the transmission and storage of ideas and information since the introduction of printing in fifteenth-century Italy and Germany. It is an absolutely shattering development, requiring rethinking for nearly every aspect of higher education" (p. 19).

As I argued previously, the very essence of what it means to teach is being challenged. No longer can an instructor merely give out information in the name of teaching. Students can obtain information much more easily than by listening and rapidly scrawling notes. What then does the instructor do? And how does he or she do it? Not only has technology rapidly changed how information is stored and retrieved, but the means by which teaching may be done is also in the process of transformation. It is now possible to effectively teach at a distance, using satellite, videotape, computers, and other media. This technology opens up new vistas of learning opportunities for adult students. It also means that many for-profit providers, such as publishers, will find a profitable home in the educational marketplace. By using the new technology, it is possible to place on compact computer disks not only words, but images and sounds. And of course there is the possibility for interaction as a student works with a particular problem or question, and then sees and hears the results of his or her decision played back.

The challenge for higher education, particularly with respect to older students, part-time students, and those prevented from attending on-campus classes, is deciding which information media are most appropriate. Many of us recall when television proponents suggested that television would replace teachers. It did not. Then came the argument that computer-assisted instruction would be a replacement for teachers. It was not.

But now as Keller (1983), Naisbitt (1982), and many others have argued, we are clearly moving toward an information society. The challenges for higher education are different now than during the time of primitive educational television and early computer-assisted instruction. The difference is the way in which information is stored and transmitted, plus the opportunity for learner interaction. But higher education decision makers must be cautious. Kay Kohl, executive director of the National University Continuing Education Association, urges that higher education institutions look at the economics of the new technology. She is particularly concerned about putting large amount of resources into the development of educational television programs. And she is also not so sure that the off-campus, independent study approaches will work: "Correspondence study is a tough way to go to get college, and it's not necessarily the most accessible mode for somebody who is a first generation college student and perhaps ill-prepared for the college experience" (personal communication, Mar. 26, 1987).

Kohl believes those persons who can best use the new technology, such as self-help books, videotapes, and computer-assisted instruction via home computers, are already highly educated and quite affluent. Kohl sees this audience as a potential new market for colleges and universities. But she recognizes that commercial concerns such as publishers will be in a better position to capture this market (personal communication, Mar. 26, 1987).

Internal Challenges

Internal challenges facing colleges and universities may be more difficult than the external ones. Several challenges strike at the very core of how colleges and universities are organized and operate.

The Conservatism of Colleges and Universities   Historically, almost all major changes have been forced on higher education. As Knox (1987) says, "I don't think there's anything in the quality of higher education that makes it self-initiating or responsive. It's been dragged, kicking and screaming into the 20th century. It's the most conservative institution in our society so far. Individual professors are very liberal in wanting to change the world, but very conservative in trying to keep the world from changing them or their institution in any fashion" (personal communication, Mar. 24, 1987).

At least one university official sees a dim future for higher education. "I am convinced the university as an institution cannot survive," says Herbert London (1987, p. 17), a university dean. London concludes that "unless the university is harnessed or forced to reconsider its present aims—highly implausible scenarios—it does not have a future. Reports of its imminent demise are not at all exaggerated" (p. 22).

As I have argued above, quality must be maintained if higher education is to make significant contributions in a learning society. But quality is often used as a smokescreen to avoid change. Many in higher education associate quality with one particular way of doing something. On many campuses, there is a strong belief that any credit course that deviates to any extent from two or three one-hour, face-to-face lectures per week lacks quality.

I remember a few years ago when a university department wanted to offer several of its courses in a weekend format—Friday evening and all day Saturday. The planning committee worked out the schedule so that the students would receive exactly the same instructional hours had they attended class for one hour on Monday, Wednesday, and Friday. The proposal was submitted to the institution's graduate school, where it was promptly returned with a long list of questions about such things as whether students could survive that much instruction at one time, whether there would be breaks, and the like. After six months of questions and answers, and several revised proposals, the program was given permission to proceed. But there were still serious questions that its quality would somehow be compromised because its format was not traditional.

Such thinking exists throughout higher education. With change difficult, many faculty members wanting to try something different give up after the first few attempts. Yet for higher education to make a significant contribution to a learning society, it must make adjustments in format, teaching approaches, and curriculum—the items I have discussed elsewhere in this book. So that I am not misunderstood, higher education must also concern itself with quality. The criteria for quality may need redefining. Points that I have made earlier may enter the criteria for quality formula. How do learners view the impact of this course, program, workshop, whatever format is involved? Is the content, however it is provided, up to date, accurate, appropriate, and relevant? Do learners have relatively easy access to the program—meaning alternative formats such as distance education, weekend offerings, and the like? Institutions are challenged to develop such a list of criteria for quality that fits their mission and context.

Higher education must learn how to transcend its conservative nature, and applaud quality but not hide behind it when changes are suggested.

Competition for Limited Resources Within colleges and universities there is great competition for scarce resources. At many institutions the debate includes trying to determine what proportion of resources should go toward programs for older students (both degree and nondegree programs), how much budget should be devoted to public service activities, and so on. We will say more about this below.

Structure and Leadership   The structure of higher education makes change difficult. On most college and university campuses, the department is all-powerful. At the major research universities, the basic mission of a department is the pursuit of excellence. But for many departments pursuit of excellence is narrowly defined: "The most prevalent measure of departmental quality has come to be its prestige among peer groups, that is, its comparative standing in a national ordering assembled by colleagues in the discipline. . . . The improvement of prestige has become the departmental mission itself" (Alpert, 1985, p. 247).

Departments enhance prestige by building disciplinary research programs, not by developing weekend programs for adult students or mounting public service programs to solve community problems. Departments generally do not enhance prestige by encouraging their faculty to collaborate with researchers in other departments on interdisciplinary or multidisciplinary research—which the learning society often demands. Thus departmental structure can prevent campus change. To their credit, community colleges frequently have a more flexible structure, which allows them to more quickly respond to community requests and societal change.

Coupled with departmental structure, a system of faculty governance that allows faculty members to make nearly all the decisions about the operation of their departments makes change difficult at many institutions. In some respects this horizontal management system has worked well. Extremely strong departments exist across the country. The system breaks down when cross-departmental or campus issues are concerned, however. Responding to the learning society is one such cross-departmental challenge.

As Keller (1983) argues, "There is now a stalemate in the exercise of power on the American campus. University management is in shackles. While the balance of power in our Madisonian federal government has been tilting since the 1930s toward the executive branch, presidential power in U.S. higher education has gradually diminished before the buildup of a strong faculty power, and since the 1960s, the rising power of students and outside agencies. At the very time that the need for strong leadership in higher education has reached new levels of urgency, academic management is in chains. Indeed, the whole subject of administration in higher education is befuddled and bound by rusty myths and hoary notions about authority, management, and leadership" (p. 27).

Simerly and Associates (1987) observe that the traditional models of academic leaders no longer fit: "Leaders in the future will increasingly have to give up heroic models of leadership and the assumptions underlying them. Instead they will have to become developers of people and of problem-solving teams. They will need to concentrate on coaching and counseling in order to help staff members define for themselves a concept of continual professional development and self-renewal .... Effective leaders move beyond the administrative aspects of their roles and become statespersons for the organizations they represent. In this statesperson role they create a consensus for visions that require dynamic organizational cultures. ... Such leaders are future oriented, and yet they are also oriented toward producing results today" (p. 203).

Effective leadership at all levels, from the institution's president to faculty leadership, is crucial for the development of a lifelong learning college or university. Moving toward becoming a lifelong learning college or university will not only provide extraordinary benefits to learners and the community, but will provide great benefits to the institution itself (Votruba, 1987, pp. 185–188).

As we have noted, older adults seeking degrees, communities, government agencies, and business and industry are not particularly interested in the structure of the higher education or how it makes its decisions. But they are looking for results, for action, for response to their questions and concerns. The present system of campus decision making, with so much power resting with the faculty and their departments, makes response difficult. This is particularly so when the nature of the response is one that involves or should involve more than one department.

So often these days, campus leadership from the depart-

ment chair on up to president of the institution performs mostly a management role—personnel matters, budget, facilities, and
the like. The leadership role is given to the faculty, and because
of their often narrow departmental or discipline orientation and
their zeal to enhance their own professional prestige through
research and scholarship, little campus leadership takes place.
Thus many colleges and universities have a leadership vacuum.
As Kay Kohl says, "The biggest need I see right now is in attracting to the academy . . . [leadership] talent and vision . . .
at all levels . . . including the leaders responsible for serving part-
time students who can think imaginatively about how we need
to respond to what are very, very critical needs" (personal communication, Mar. 26, 1987).

    More capable, visionary leaders are certainly necessary.
But the structure on many campuses precludes their effectiveness. Changes that some institutions have made to correct the
structural problem include developing interdisciplinary centers
with teaching, research, and outreach responsibilities, and insisting that the reward system recognize good teaching and public service activity, along with research-scholarship activity. But
many more changes are necessary before higher education can
become an important contributor to the learning society.

    What Is Our Business?   Peters and Waterman (1982)
make the strong point that a business must ask itself what it is
about. Colleges and universities must ask the same question.
What unique contribution can higher education make to a learning society?

    One important dimension of a learning society is lifelong
learning. Dave (1976) defines lifelong education as "a process of
accomplishing personal, social and professional development
throughout the life-span of individuals in order to enhance the
quality of life of both individuals and their collectives. It is a
comprehensive and unifying idea which includes formal, nonformal and informal learning for acquiring and enhancing en-
lightenment so as to attain the fullest possible development in
different stages and domains of life. It is connected with both
individual and social progress" (p. 34). If we could accept this

as a reasonable definition of lifelong education, where within that definition does higher education fit? What unique contributions can higher education make to lifelong education and the learning society that the many other providers of education for adults can make less well or not at all? This is the challenge for higher education.

Many people have suggested answers to the question. In terms of unique position, Kay Kohl (1987) says that "we live in an information society, and in an information society we have a university, which is what the bank was to an industrial society" (personal communication, Mar. 26, 1987). A central storage and distribution center for information is certainly one important characteristic of colleges and universities. But to add to Kohl's bank metaphor, I would say that the bank has alongside it a mint, making new knowledge. Of course new knowledge is not minted as money is, but the analogy is close. Thus we have an institution that develops, stores, and distributes knowledge. But is this all higher education can uniquely do?

Alan Knox (1987) mentions several other forms of uniqueness: "One of [the unique roles for higher education] is to deal with content that is of a level of complexity that requires the resources of a higher education institution. Another is the ability to draw on multiple subject matter fields. For example if you're dealing with a marketing problem [that a business has presented] you're not dealing with it just as it would be in the marketing department of a business, but you can bring people in from psychology, sociology, communications, etc. to help illuminate the marketing problem in a more complete way. A third uniqueness is that you have the expertise there within the faculty of the institution to not only plan and conduct such programs, but also to identify other able people who are outside the institution to be a sort of quality control mechanism for planning and conducting such programs" (personal communication, Mar. 24, 1987).

A problem colleges and universities often face when attempting to become more active in the community is having to respond to various types of needs analyses. Interviews, questionnaires, and a variety of other needs-assessment approaches reveal a broad spectrum of community needs and wants for educational activities. But as Freedman (1987) observes, "Program planning based entirely on student needs assessments may not be compatible with what the sponsoring institution believes to be appropriate" (pp. 39–40).

    We are back to the original question of how higher education can uniquely contribute to a learning society. The following are criteria that colleges and universities can use in considering which programs should or should not be offered. I would quickly add that each institution must look at its own situation as it makes decisions about its response to a learning society. The following are starting points:

1.   The proposed program should be in conformity with the unique capabilities of the institution, as reflected in the institution's aims and mission.
2.   The proposed program should have a scholarly-research base within the institution. Some would argue that this is not necessary, that outside, ad hoc instructors can be brought in to cover areas where the college or university does not have a research base. Ad hoc instructors can certainly help to supplement instruction, but for creditability it seems important that the institution only program in areas where it has a knowledge base.
3.   Programs should be offered at a relatively advanced level. What is advanced and what is not is always a judgment call. Advanced generally means building on skills and knowledge gained elsewhere, on the job, or from some other agency or institution.
4.   Instruction should include a theoretical dimension. This does not preclude a practical orientation for programs. However, it does mean some attention, always, to theoretical considerations. This means tying back to the research or scholarly base of what is being taught, and is consistent with point 2.
5.   Most often the program emphasis should be on mental skills —problem solving, analysis, integration of ideas, decision making, judging and valuing ideas, bridging between theory

and practice. Some programs will provide opportunities for emancipatory learning, allowing learners to critically question, examine broadly, and develop action strategies.

6. When arts and humanities programs are available they are offered at a variety of levels, from the appreciation of art, music, or literature to the examination of philosophical positions about the human condition. Putting problems into a historical perspective and examining questions from an ethical position are also examples of possible program areas that can be unique for higher education.

7. Some programs may serve a "conscience-for-society" role. They may explore controversial social issues such as the distribution of wealth in the United States, national defense policy, the humaneness of the death sentence, or the relation of groundwater pollution to health.

8. Most programs should have broader rather than specific application. Freedman (1987) suggests that "in general, Extension should concentrate on concepts and skills of broad application and leave to industry the provision of on-the-job training related to the unique character and competitive position of the individual firm. Thus, however applied the course material covered in an Extension course, the applications should always have solid grounding in the theories generated by the relevant academic disciplines; and the instructors, even where they are practitioners rather than academics, should be required to have a sufficient background in those disciplines to ensure that their teaching is not of the mundanely nuts-and-bolts variety" (p. 52).

Although this seems a reasonable list of criteria for making decisions about which programs to include and which not to, another force often intervenes. Money. Self-supporting programs, for most institutions, include all or nearly all the noncredit programs plus all or nearly all the public service work. Because so much continuing higher education is market-driven, programmers constantly wrestle with what will pay and what will not. Unfortunately, this situation is likely to continue. As a result, adhering to any set of program criteria becomes extremely difficult. Administrators of such programs cannot be blamed for trying to survive.

Planning Approaches For higher education to become an important contributor to the learning society, sensible strategic planning is required. Such planning must include examining basic assumptions about higher education and its relation to various aspects of a learning society. Such a planning process may require a reexamination of aims, curriculum, and teaching approaches, and an understanding of contemporary higher education students.

Understanding Adult Learners Another internal challenge is the adult learner. College and university administrators must assist their faculty and staff in understanding the characteristics of adult learners. This includes the adult learners' motivations for learning, the effect of their developmental phases on learning, their preferred learning styles, and the milieu in which they live, earn, and learn. Many adult learners study part time and can be called concurrent students. Concurrently with their studies they often work full or part time, care for families, and participate in community activities. (More and more traditional students, those eighteen to twenty-two, have taken on the characteristics of the group I call adult learners. Many of these younger students work full or part time, some are married and have families, and many study part time. Thus accomomodations for older students will often assist the more traditional students as well.)

The adult learners also fall within several categories: professionals who are seeking additional training, career change people, women who wish to enter the job market after several years away, the elderly, and displaced workers. Not only is higher education challenged to understand the nature of adults as learners, and the differences among the various types of adult learners, but it is also challenged to provide access.

Fred Harvey Harrington, former president of the University of Wisconsin System, is concerned about the access issue. He says, "Continuing professional education has been the most successful at the University level. Clientele, mostly middle and upper class, have money to spend. Thus continuing professional education can support itself, something the University is happy about . . . [but] the universities continue to move away from helping minorities and the poor. Quality will be the rallying cry, and a subterfuge for restricting access to the university" (personal communication, Jan. 15, 1986).

Recent research in adult education has helped programmers understand why adults do and do not participate in adult education (Apps, 1979, 1981, 1985; Aslanian and Brickell, 1980; Boshier, 1973; Cross, 1981; Darkenwald and Valentine, 1985; Fitzgerald, 1984; Houle, 1961, 1980, 1984; Johnstone and Rivera, 1965). Knox (1987) mentions several strategies that programmers in continuing education can follow when encouraging participation. Situational factors such as socioeconomic status and level of formal education together with personal factors such as influence of developmental tasks combine to influence participation. (Lower socioeconomic status plus lower levels of formal education are major barriers to participation—even if the intent to participate is high.)

The strategies for effecting participation are available, but higher education must actively work toward such participation. An institution does not merely announce that it is now open to those with lower formal educational levels, to minority groups, and to others less likely to participate in higher education programs. Too often, it seems that higher education is going in the opposite direction—raising college entrance requirements. Unfortunately, space does not permit an examination of the many issues related to access and strategies for encouraging it. The larger question is whether or not higher education wants to encourage broader access to its programs.

Cooperation   The challenge for cooperation includes several dimensions. Cooperation with other providers is one challenge. Cervero (1986) notes that the issue of collaboration-competition is an important one in continuing professional education. He notes that there is little research on the topic, but considerable interest. Cervero mentions that according to a study of accredited medical schools in the United States, approximately 70 percent of these institutions cosponsor ongoing continuing medical education programs with community hospitals (p. 5).

Not only is higher education challenged to cooperate with other providers of continuing education, but many colleges and universities are challenged to work out cooperative relationships with business and industry.

Cooperation with government agencies is another challenge. Kay Kohl says that "you have a lot of state legislators who are looking to universities as a central resource in economic development. . . . When you have institutions supported by tax dollars, then these institutions most assuredly have an obligation to meet the needs of those taxpayers who are providing them with their basic support. Once a public institution gets too far away from that thought it runs a real risk" (personal communication, Mar. 26, 1987). When working on economic development programs, colleges and universities are often asked to work shoulder to shoulder with other government agencies that have economic development responsibilities.

Cooperation also means that researchers and continuing education faculty need to work together. This is particularly important for those continuing education faculty involved in technology transfer and other public service programs.

Moving Ahead During Periods of Decline   At first glance, this sounds like a contradiction. How is it possible to move forward and backward at the same time? Yet this is the challenge that many colleges and universities face, since the threat of flat budgets and budget cuts always lurks around the next corner.

Adjusting to decline is further complicated, of course, by society encouraging, often demanding, that a particular college or university offer more and often different programs in its community.

Colleges and universities have an extremely poor record of adjusting to decline. Cameron (1983) offers three reasons for this: (1) most college administrators have only had experience with conditions of growth, (2) "the values and ideology of our culture emphasize growth and expansion as being indicative of effectiveness," and (3) most college administrators have been evaluated positively if they obtained larger budgets, expanded their units, and produced more (p. 360).

Thus conditions of forced decline, a cut in state appropriations for example, are often met with total bafflement. An immediate reaction of many administrators is to tighten down and avoid risk taking: "The stress resulting from having to face conditions of decline compels individuals to engage in conservative and self-protective behaviors" (Cameron, 1983, p. 363). Also, new programs such as those responding to the demands of a learning society are sometimes viewed as causes of an institution's decline. When the budget problems occur, such new programs are often the first to be cut (weekend programs, off-campus courses, special counseling programs for adults).

In an investigation of industries' reactions to decline, Cameron (1983) studied six tobacco companies. From 1906 to 1953, these firms showed consistent growth. But with environmental threats that begin with links between health hazards and smoking, these industries started to decline. A series of other events contributed to the decline: the Surgeon General's 1964 report, the requirement that health warnings appear on tobacco packages beginning in 1965, and the banning of cigarette advertising from all radio and television from 1969 on.

But what happened? How did the tobacco firms respond? Cameron (1983) summarizes his study of the tobacco industry as follows: "The most effective tobacco firms over the thirty-year period [1950s to late 1970s] were those that acted proactively rather than reactively to conditions of decline and those that concentrated almost entirely on enhancing organizational effectiveness rather than organizational efficiency. Effective firms also paid particular attention to adapting to and manipulating the external environment rather than focusing on internal processes and procedures. In other words, the most successful firms did almost the opposite of what many colleges and universities are doing when faced with conditions of decline. Colleges and universities are often conservative, efficiency oriented, and internally focused. Effective tobacco firms were innovative, effectiveness oriented, and externally focused" (p. 371).

Continued decline seems a reality for much of higher education, and if not decline a maintenance of the status quo. And continued pressure from a learning society also seems a reality. The challenge for higher education facing decline is to make changes that will enhance its contributions to a learning society. In this way it can make a proactive response.

Summary

Internal and external challenges face higher education as it attempts to respond to a learning society. External challenges include (1) a sometimes negative public attitude toward higher education that has resulted both in budget decline and in many studies of the effectiveness of higher education; (2) social problems that compete for scarce resources, and in the case of illiteracy, affect participation potential; (3) competition with many other providers of educational opportunity for adults; (4) an image of poor quality of some continuing education programs; and (5) information technology that has revolutionized both the way information is stored and how it is communicated.

Internal challenges include (1) the conservative nature of higher education, including its slowness to change and tendency to hide behind quality and rigor when changes are proposed; (2) competition, internally, for limited resources; (3) structure and leadership problems—the department is the primary decision-making unit for many colleges and universities, and with little attention to questions that transcend departments, leadership is often stifled; (4) confusion about which programs should or should not be offered in response to the requests and demands from a learning society; (5) the need for sensible strategic planning approaches; and (6) the need to understand adult learners—their motivations for learning, barriers and constraints, participation patterns, as well as the various types of adult learners (older adults, displaced workers, business and professional people, and so on); (7) the necessity of cooperation—with other providers, business and industry, government agencies; and (8) the desirability of moving ahead during periods of decline—taking a proactive stance toward the demands of a learning society during times of budget crisis.

References

Adler, M. J. *The Paideia Proposal.* New York: Macmillan, 1982.

Alpert, D. "Performance and Paralysis." *Journal of Higher Education,* 1985, *56* (3), 241–281.

Apps, J. W. *Toward a Working Philosophy of Adult Education.* Syracuse, N.Y.: Syracuse University Publications in Continuing Education, 1973.

Apps, J. W. *Problems in Continuing Education.* New York: McGraw-Hill, 1979.

Apps, J. W. *The Adult Learner on Campus.* Chicago: Follett, 1981.

Apps, J. W. *Improving Your Writing Skills.* Chicago: Follett, 1982a.

Apps, J. W. *Study Skills for Adults Returning to School.* (2nd ed.) New York: McGraw-Hill, 1982b.

Apps, J. W. *Improving Practice in Continuing Education: Modern Approaches for Understanding the Field and Determining Priorities.* San Francisco: Jossey-Bass, 1985.

Aslanian, C. B., and Brickell, H. M. *Americans in Transition: Life Changes As Reasons for Adult Learning.* New York: College Entrance Examination Board, 1980.

Association of American Colleges. *Integrity in the College Curriculum: A Report to the Academic Community.* Washington, D.C.: Association of American Colleges, 1985.

Astin, A. W. *Achieving Educational Excellence: A Critical Assessment of Priorities and Practices in Higher Education.* San Francisco: Jossey-Bass, 1985.

Astin, H. S. "Continuing Education and the Development of Adult Women." *The Counseling Psychologist,* 1976a, *6* (1), 55–60.

Astin, H. S. (ed.). *Some Action of Her Own: The Adult Woman and Higher Education.* Lexington, Mass.: Lexington Books, 1976b.

Balderston, F. E. "Dynamics of Planning: Strategic Approaches and Higher Education." In J. Wilson (ed.), *Management Science Applications to Academic Administration.* New Directions for Higher Education, no. 35. San Francisco: Jossey-Bass, 1981.

Bloom, A. *The Closing of the American Mind: How Higher Education Has Failed Democracy and Impoverished the Souls of Today's Students.* New York: Simon & Schuster, 1987.

Bok, D. "Balancing Responsibility and Innovation." *Change,* 1982, *14* (6), 16–25.

Bok, D. *Higher Learning.* Cambridge, Mass.: Harvard University Press, 1986.

Bonham, G. W. "Computer Mania: Academe's Inadequate Response to the Implications of the New Technology." *Chronicle of Higher Education,* Mar. 30, 1983, p. 72.

Bork, A. "The Potential for Interactive Technology." *Byte,* Feb. 1987, pp. 201–206.

Boshier, R. W. "Educational Participation and Dropout: A Theoretical Model." *Adult Education,* 1973, *23* (4), 225–282.

Boyd, R. D., and Apps, J. W. (eds.). *Redefining the Discipline of Adult Education.* San Francisco: Jossey-Bass, 1980.

Boyer, E. "Higher Education Should Do More Than Imitate Its Corporate Rivals." *Chronicle of Higher Education,* May 25, 1983, p. 32.

Boyer, E. Foreword to N. P. Eurich, *Corporate Classrooms.* Princeton, N.J.: Carnegie Foundation for the Advancement of Teaching, 1985.

Boyer, E. L. *College: The Undergraduate Experience in America.* New York: Harper & Row, 1987.

Bridges, W. *Transitions.* Reading, Mass.: Addison-Wesley, 1980.

Brookfield, S. D. *Understanding and Facilitating Adult Learning.* San Francisco: Jossey-Bass, 1986.

Buchen, I. "Faculty for the Future: Universities Have a Rare Opportunity." *The Futurist,* Nov.–Dec. 1987, pp. 22–25.

Cameron, K. "Strategic Responses to Conditions of Decline." *Journal of Higher Education,* 1983, *54* (4), 359–379.

Capra, F. *The Tao of Physics.* New York: Bantam, 1975.

Capra, F. *The Turning Point.* New York: Bantam, 1983.

Cervero, R. M. "Collaboration in Continuing Professional Education." *Newsletter of the American Association for Adult and Continuing Education and National University Continuing Education Association,* Fall 1986, pp. 1, 5.

Chickering, A. W. (ed.). *The Modern American College: Responding to the New Realities of Diverse Students and a Changing Society.* San Francisco: Jossey-Bass, 1981.

Chin, R., and Benne, K. D. "General Strategies for Effecting Changes in Human Systems." In W. G. Bennis, K. D. Benne, R. Chin, and K. E. Corey (eds.), *The Planning of Change.* New York: Holt, Rinehart & Winston, 1976.

Clark, D. L. "In Consideration of Goal-Free Planning: The Failure of Traditional Planning Systems in Education." *Educational Administration Quarterly,* 1981, *17* (3), 42–60.

Cohen, D. K., and Garet, M. S. "Reforming Educational Policy with Applied Social Research." *Harvard Educational Review,* 1975, *45* (1), 17–43.

Cohen, R. D. "Assisting the Adult Learner in 'Settling-in.' " In A. Shriberg (ed.), *Providing Services for the Adult Learner.* New Directions for Student Services, no. 11. San Francisco: Jossey-Bass, 1980.

College of St. Catherine. *Program Planning and Review Recommendations for the College of St. Catherine.* St. Paul, Minn.: College of St. Catherine, n.d.

College of St. Catherine. *Revision of the Strategic Long Range Plan, College of St. Catherine: Fall 1986.* St. Paul, Minn.: College of St. Catherine, 1986.

Commission on Higher Education and the Adult Learner and the American Council on Education. *Postsecondary Education Institutions and the Adult Learner: A Self-Study Assessment and Planning Guide.* Washington, D.C.: Commission on Higher Education and the Adult Learner and the American Council on Education, 1984.

Coombs, P. H. Quoted in P. Fordham, G. Paulton, and L. Randle, *Learning Networks in Adult Education*. London: Routledge & Kegan Paul, 1979.

Cross, K. P. *Beyond the Open Door: New Students to Higher Education*. San Francisco: Jossey-Bass, 1971.

Cross, K. P. *Accent on Learning: Improving Instruction and Reshaping the Curriculum*. San Francisco: Jossey-Bass, 1976.

Cross, K. P. *Adults As Learners: Increasing Participation and Facilitating Learning*. San Francisco: Jossey-Bass, 1981.

Cross, K. P., and Valley, J. R. (eds.). *Planning Non-Traditional Programs: An Analysis of the Issues for Postsecondary Education*. San Francisco: Jossey-Bass, 1974.

Crosson, P. H. *Public Service in Higher Education: Practices and Priorities*. Washington, D.C.: Association for the Study of Higher Education, 1983.

Daloz, L. A. "Returning to the Ways of the 1950's Isn't How to Prepare for the 1990's." *Chronicle of Higher Education*, Sept. 14, 1983, p. 34.

Darkenwald, G. G., and Valentine, T. "Factor Structures of Deterrents to Public Participation in Adult Education." *Adult Education Quarterly*, 1985, *35* (4), 177–193.

Dave, R. H. *Foundations of Lifelong Education*. New York: Pergamon Press, 1976.

Davila, E. M. *Today's Urban University Students, Part 2: A Case Study of Hunter College*. New York: College Entrance Examination Board, 1985.

de Carbonnel, F. E., and Dorrance, R. G. "Information Sources for Planning Decisions." *California Management Review*, 1973, *15* (4), 42–53.

Dennehy, R. "Education, Vocationalism and Democracy." *Thought*, 1982, *IVII* (225), 182–195.

DeSio, R. "The Corporation and the Campus: Developing New Partnerships." *Challenges for Continuing Higher Education Leadership: Corporate/Campus Collaboration*. Washington, D.C.: National University Continuing Education Association, 1987.

Desruisseaux, P. "More Than Public Relations Is Needed to Repair Higher Education's Tarnished Image, Bok Says." *Chronicle of Higher Education*, July 22, 1987, pp. 1, 13.

Dirr, P. J. "Coming Home to College." *Innovation in Higher Education*, 1985, *9* (2), 92–98.

Doucette, D. S., Richardson, R. C., Jr., and Fenske, R. H. "Defining Institutional Mission." *Journal of Higher Education*, 1985, *56* (2), 189–205.

Dressel, P. L. *Institutional Research in the University: A Handbook.* San Francisco: Jossey-Bass, 1971.

Dressel, P. L. *Handbook of Academic Evaluation: Assessing Institutional Effectiveness, Student Progress, and Professional Performance for Decision Making in Higher Education.* San Francisco: Jossey-Bass, 1976.

Economic Report of the President. Washington: U.S. Government Printing Office, 1987.

Elman, S. E., and Smock, S. M. *Professional Service and Faculty Rewards: Toward an Integrated Structure.* Washington, D.C.: National Association of State Universities and Land Grant Colleges, 1985.

Enarson, H. L. "The Art of Planning." *Educational Record*, 1975, *56*, 170–174.

Eurich, N. *Corporate Classrooms: The Learning Business.* Princeton, N.J.: Carnegie Foundation for the Advancement of Teaching, 1985.

Ferguson, M. *The Acquarian Conspiracy.* Los Angeles: Tarcher, 1980.

Fernberg, J. W., and Lasher, W. F. (eds.). *The Politics and Pragmatics of Institutional Research: New Directions for Institutional Research.* San Francisco: Jossey-Bass, 1983.

Fitzgerald, G. G. "Can the Hard-to-Research Adults Become Literate?" *Lifelong Learning: An Omnibus of Practice and Research*, 1984, *7* (5), 4, 5, 27.

Flannery, D., and Apps, J. W. *Characteristics and Problems of Older Returning Students.* Madison: Research Division, College of Agricultural and Life Sciences, University of Wisconsin–Madison, 1987.

Fleit, L. H. "Overselling Technology: Suppose You Gave a Computer Revolution and Nobody Came." *Chronicle of Higher Education*, Apr. 22, 1987, p. 96.

Freedman, L. *Quality in Continuing Education.* San Francisco: Jossey-Bass, 1987.

Freire, P. *Pedagogy of the Oppressed.* New York: Herder and Herder, 1970.

Friedrich, O. "Five Ways to Wisdom." *Time,* Sept. 27, 1982, pp. 66-72.

Geisler, M. P., and Thrush, R. W. "Counseling Experiences and Needs of Older Women Students." *Journal of the National Association of Women Deans, Administrators, and Counselors,* 1975, *39* (1), 3-8.

Glover, R. H., and Holmes, J. "Assessing the External Environment." In N. P. Uhl (ed.), *Using Research for Strategic Planning.* New Directions for Institutional Research, no. 37. San Francisco: Jossey-Bass, 1983.

Green, J. S., Levine, A., and Associates. *Opportunity in Adversity: How Colleges Can Succeed in Hard Times.* San Francisco: Jossey-Bass, 1985.

Grossman, D. M. "Electronic College Courses: The Professor Must Be in Charge." *Chronicle of Higher Education,* Feb. 11, 1987, p. 104.

Habermas, J. *Knowledge and Human Interests.* Boston: Beacon Press, 1972.

Harrington, F. H. *The Future of Adult Education: New Responsibilities of Colleges and Universities.* San Francisco: Jossey-Bass, 1977.

Havelock, R. G. *The Change Agent's Guide to Innovation in Education.* Englewood Cliffs, N.J.: Education Technology Publications, 1973.

Hearn, J. C., and Heydinger, R. B. "Scanning the University's External Environment." *Journal of Higher Education,* 1985, *56* (4), 419-445.

Hodgkinson, H. L. *Higher Education: Diversity Is Our Middle Name.* Washington, D.C.: National Institute of Independent Colleges and Universities, 1986a.

Hodgkinson, H. L. "Reform? Higher Education? Don't Be Absurd!" *Phi Delta Kappan,* 1986b, *68* (4), 271-274.

Holliday, G. "Addressing the Concerns of Returning Women Students." In N. J. Evans (ed.), *Facilitating the Development of Women.* New Directions for Student Services, no. 29. San Francisco: Jossey-Bass, 1985.

Houle, C. O. *The Inquiring Mind.* Madison: University of Wisconsin Press, 1961.

Houle, C. O. *The External Degree.* San Francisco: Jossey-Bass, 1973.

Houle, C. O. *Continuing Learning in the Professions.* San Francisco: Jossey-Bass, 1980.

Houle, C. O. *Patterns of Learning: New Perspectives on Life-Span Education.* San Francisco: Jossey-Bass, 1984.

Hoyle, J., and Johnson, G. "The 21st-Century Professor, Bailing Out of the Ivory Tower." *The Futurist,* Nov.–Dec. 1987, pp. 26–27.

Hunsicker, J. G. "The Malaise of Strategic Planning." *Management Review,* Mar. 1980, pp. 9–14.

Hutchins, R. H. *The Learning Society.* New York: New American Library, 1968.

Institute of Lifetime Learning. *College Centers for Older Learners.* Washington, D.C.: American Association of Retired Persons, 1986.

Jackson, W., and Simpson, R. "The Office of Instructional Development As a Center for Personal, Professional and Organizational Renewal." *Journal of Staff, Program, and Organization Development,* 1984, 2 (1), 12–15.

Jaschik, S. "States Should Expand Use of Universities to Help Economies, Report Says." *Chronicle of Higher Education,* July 29, 1987, p. 19.

Jencks, C., and Riesman, D. *The Academic Revolution.* Chicago: University of Chicago Press, 1977.

Johnston, J. S. "Recommendations for Business and Academic Leaders." In J. S. Johnston (ed.), *Educating Managers: Executive Effectiveness through Liberal Learning.* San Francisco: Jossey-Bass, 1986.

Johnstone, J. W. C., and Rivera, R. J. *Volunteers for Learning: A Study of the Educational Pursuits of American Adults.* Chicago: Aldine, 1965.

Keller, G. *Academic Strategy: The Management Revolution In American Higher Education.* Baltimore: Johns Hopkins University Press, 1983.

Keller, G. *The Wisconsin Idea: Yesterday and Tomorrow.* Madison: Wisconsin Idea Commission, University of Wisconsin–Extension, 1986.

Keppel, F., and Chickering, A. W. "Mediated Instruction." In A. W. Chickering (ed.), *The Modern American College: Responding to the New Realities of Diverse Students and a Changing Society.* San Francisco: Jossey-Bass, 1981.

Kerr, C. *The Uses of the University.* Cambridge, Mass.: Harvard University Press, 1982.

King, W. R., and Cleland, D. I. *Strategic Planning and Policy.* New York: Van Nostrand Reinhold, 1978.

Kirk, R. *Decadence and Renewal in the Higher Learning.* South Bend, Ind.: Gateway Editions, 1978.

Knowles, M. S. *The Modern Practice of Adult Education.* Chicago: Association Press–Follett, 1980.

Knox, A. B. *Adult Development and Learning: A Handbook on Individual Growth and Competence in the Adult Years for Education and the Helping Professions.* San Francisco: Jossey-Bass, 1977.

Knox, A. B. "Understanding the Adult Learner." In A. Shriberg (ed.), *Providing Services for the Adult Learner.* New Directions for Student Services, no. 11. San Francisco: Jossey-Bass, 1980.

Knox, A. B. *Helping Adults Learn: A Guide to Planning, Implementing, and Conducting Programs.* San Francisco: Jossey-Bass, 1986.

Knox, A. B. "Reducing Barriers to Participation in Continuing Education." *Lifelong Learning: An Omnibus of Practice and Research,* 1987, *10* (5), 7–9.

Koberstein, J. A. "Short-Term Management Courses for Busy Executives Become a Big Business on Many College Campuses." *Chronicle of Higher Education,* Aug. 13, 1986, pp. 23–24.

Kozol, J. *Illiterate America.* New York: Anchor/Doubleday, 1985.

Kuhns, E., and Martorana, S. V. (eds.). *Qualitative Methods for Institutional Research.* New Directions for Institutional Research, no. 34. San Francisco: Jossey-Bass, 1982.

Lanier, J. *Memorandum.* East Lansing: Lifelong Education Program, Michigan State University, Dec. 21, 1985.

Lewis, J. "A College Capitalizing On Student Abilities." *New York Times,* Apr. 15, 1984, sec. 12, p. 17.

Lindeman, E. C. *The Meaning of Adult Education.* Montreal: Harvest House, 1961. (Originally published 1926.)

Lindquist, J. *Strategies for Change.* Berkeley, CA: Pacific Soundings Press, 1978.

Lindquist, J. "Professional Development." In A. W. Chickering (ed.), *The Modern American College: Responding to the New Realities of Diverse Students and a Changing Society.* San Francisco: Jossey-Bass, 1981.

Lindquist, J. (ed.). *Designing Teaching Improvement Programs.* Washington, D.C.: Council for the Advancement of Small Colleges, 1979.

London, H. "Death of the University." *The Futurist,* May-June 1987, pp. 17–22.

Lynton, E. A., and Elman, S. E. *New Priorities for the University: Meeting Society's Needs for Applied Knowledge and Competent Individuals.* San Francisco: Jossey-Bass, 1987.

McDermott, J. M. "Servicing the Needs of Non-Traditional Clientele: The New Resources Approach." *Liberal Education,* 1975, *61* (2), 268–274.

Mangan, K. "Institutions and Scholars Face Ethical Dilemmas Over Pursuit of Research with Commercial Value." *Chronicle of Higher Education,* July 29, 1987, p. 11.

Markley, O. W., and Harman, W. W. (eds.). *Changing Images of Man.* Oxford: Pergamon Press, 1982.

Marris, P. *Loss and Change.* London: Routledge & Kegan Paul, 1974.

Martin, W. B. "Mission: A Statement of Identity and Direction." In J. S. Green, A. Levine, and Associates. *Opportunity in Adversity: How Colleges Can Succeed in Hard Times.* San Francisco: Jossey-Bass, 1985.

Mayhew, L. B. *Surviving the Eighties: Strategies and Procedures for Solving Fiscal and Enrollment Problems.* San Francisco: Jossey-Bass, 1980.

Mooney, C. J. "Bad News for Public Colleges: Economies Slump in Many States." *Chronicle of Higher Education,* Feb. 18, 1987, p. 1.

Moore, M. "Improving Teaching at a Distance." Keynote ad-

dress, 1986 summer conference, Department of Continuing
and Vocational Education, University of Wisconsin–Madison,
Aug. 7, 1986.

More, W. S. *Emotions and Adult Learning.* Lexington, Mass.:
Heath, 1974.

Morris, R., and Bass, S. A. "The Elderly As Surplus People: Is
There a Role for Higher Education?" *Gerontologist,* 1986,
26 (1), 12–18.

Morrison, J. L., Renfro, W. L., and Boucher, W. I. (eds.). *Applying Methods and Techniques of Futures Research.* New Directions for Institutional Research, no. 39. San Francisco: Jossey-Bass, 1983.

Naisbitt, J. *Megatrends.* New York: Warner Books, 1982.

"A Nation at Risk: The Imperative for Educational Reform."
Chronicle of Higher Education, May 4, 1983, pp. 11–16.

National Commission on the Role and Future of State Colleges
and Universities. "To Secure the Blessings of Liberty: Text of
Report on State Colleges' Role." *Chronicle of Higher Education,* Nov. 12, 1986, pp. 29–36.

National Governors' Association. *Time For Results: The Governors' 1991 Report on Education.* Washington, D.C.: National Governors' Association Publications Office, 1986.

Nayman, R. L., and Patten, W. G. "Offering Effective Student
Development Programs for the Adult Learner." In A. Shriberg (ed.), *Providing Services for the Adult Learner.* New Directions for Student Services, no. 11. San Francisco: Jossey-
Bass, 1980.

Newell, L. J. *A Catalyst and a Touchstone: Involvement in
Learning.* Washington, D.C.: National Institute of Education,
1984.

Newman, J. H. *The Idea of a University.* Garden City, NY: Image Books, 1959. (Originally published 1852.)

Niebuhr, H. N., Jr. *Revitalizing American Learning.* Belmont,
CA: Wadsworth, 1984.

Office of Continuing Education and Public Service, University
of Illinois, Urbana-Champaign. *A Faculty Guide For Relating
Continuing Education and Public Service to the Promotion
and Tenure Review Process.* Urbana: Office of Continuing

Education and Public Service, University of Illinois, Urbana-Champaign, n.d.

Organization for Economic Cooperation and Development, Centre for Educational Research and Innovation. *The University and the Community: The Problems of Changing Relationships.* Paris: Organization for Economic Cooperation and Development, 1982.

Palmer, P. J. *To Know As We Are Known.* San Francisco: Harper & Row, 1983.

Palmer, S. E. "Campus Officials Assail Bennett's Attack on Colleges; Harvard's Bok Calls Secretary's Analysis 'Superficial.'" *Chronicle of Higher Education,* Oct. 22, 1986, pp. 11, 17.

Perry, R. R. "Institutional Research: Vital Third Force in Higher Education." *Journal of Higher Education,* 1972, *43* (9), 737-753.

Peters, T. J., and Waterman, R. H., Jr. *In Search of Excellence.* New York: Harper & Row, 1982.

Rhodes, H. T. "A Continuing Vision of Truth, Faith, and Knowledge." *Chronicle of Higher Education,* Feb. 6, 1978, p. 40.

Roszak, T. *The Cult of Information.* New York: Pantheon, 1986.

Saupe, J. L. *The Functions of Institutional Research.* Tallahassee, Fla.: Association for Institutional Research, 1981.

Schön, D. A. *The Reflective Practitioner.* New York: Basic Books, 1983.

School for New Learning. *1987 Course Guide.* Chicago: School for New Learning, DePaul University, 1987.

Shannon, T. J., and Schoenfeld, C. A. *University Extension.* New York: Center for Applied Research in Education, Inc., 1965.

Shipton, J., and Steltenpohl, E. H. "Educational Advising and Career Planning: A Life-Cycle Perspective." In A. W. Chickering (ed.), *The Modern American College: Responding to the New Realities of Diverse Students and a Changing Society.* San Francisco: Jossey-Bass, 1981.

Shuck, E. C. "The New Planning and an Old Pragmatism." *Journal of Higher Education,* 1977, *48* (5), 594-602.

Simerly, R. G., and Associates. *Strategic Planning and Leader-*

ship in Continuing Education. San Francisco: Jossey-Bass, 1987.

Smith, D. K. *The Learning Society.* Madison: Wisconsin Idea Commission, University of Wisconsin–Extension, 1985.

Stedman, L. C., and Kaestle, C. F. "Literacy and Reading Performance in the United States, from 1880 to the Present." *Reading Research Quarterly,* 1987, *22* (1), 8–42.

Stern, M. *Power and Conflict in Continuing Professional Education.* Belmont, CA: Wadsworth, 1983.

Stewart, D. *Adult Learning in America: Eduard Lindeman and His Agenda for Lifelong Education.* Malabar, Fla: Krieger, 1987.

Thon, A. J. "Chief Student Personnel Administrators' Perceptions of Student Services for Older Students." Unpublished doctoral dissertation, Department of Educational Administration, University of Wisconsin–Madison, 1983.

Tittle, C. K., and Denker, E. R. *Returning Women Students in Higher Education: Defining Policy Issues.* New York: Praeger, 1980.

Toffler, A. *The Third Wave.* New York: Morrow, 1980.

Toll, J. S. "Strategic Planning: An Increasing Priority For Colleges and Universities." *Change,* May-June 1982, pp. 36–37.

Tough, A. M. *Intentional Changes.* Chicago: Follett, 1982.

Trainor, S. L. "The Link: Addressing the Problems of Higher Education Through the Core Curriculum." *Innovative Higher Education,* 1986, *10* (2), 94–101.

University of Wisconsin–Extension. *Proposal: The Wisconsin Idea in the 21st Century.* Madison: University of Wisconsin–Extension, 1983.

U.S. Bureau of the Census. *Statistical Abstracts of the United States, 1985.* Washington, D.C.: Government Printing Office, 1985.

U.S. Department of Agriculture, Extension Service, Extension Committee on Organization and Policy. *Revitalizing Rural America.* Washington, D.C.: Government Printing Office, 1986.

U.S. Department of Education, Office of Educational Research and Improvement, Center for Statistics. *Participation in Adult*

Education, May 1981. Washington, D.C.: Government Printing Office, June 1982.

U.S. Department of Education, Office of Educational Research and Improvement, Center for Statistics. *Digest of Educational Statistics, 1985–1986.* Washington, D.C.: Government Printing Office, 1986.

Veysey, L. R. *The Emergence of The American University.* Chicago: University of Chicago Press, 1965.

Votruba, J. C. "From Marginality to Mainstream: Strategies for Increasing Internal Support for Continuing Education." In R. G. Simerly and Associates, *Strategic Planning and Leadership in Continuing Education.* San Francisco: Jossey-Bass, 1987.

Walden University: Institute for Advanced Studies. Naples, Fla.: Walden University, 1986.

Warren, W. H. *Adult Learners: Impetus for Change.* Washington, D.C.: American Council on Education, Commission on Higher Education and the Adult Learner, 1986a.

Warren, W. H. *Improving Institutional Service to Adult Learners.* Washington, D.C.: American Council on Education, Commission on Higher Education and the Adult Learner, 1986b.

Wilson, I. "The Benefits of Environmental Analysis." In K. J. Albert (ed.), *The Strategic Management Handbook.* New York: McGraw-Hill, 1983.

Wisconsin Assessment Center, University of Wisconsin–Green Bay. *The Adult Student.* Green Bay: Wisconsin Assessment Center, University of Wisconsin–Green Bay, 1983.

Wisconsin Idea Commission. *Suggested Questions to Guide Small Group Sessions: Wingspread Conference.* Madison: University of Wisconsin–Extension, 1986.

Zwerling, S. L. "A New Mission for Continuing Education: Teaching the Skills of the Liberal Arts." *Chronicle of Higher Education,* Mar. 28, 1984, p. 80.

Index

235